LINCOLN CHRIS P9-CQK-910

MUQONCISTERIAN UNIVERSITY

Ｊｗ 56
v. 2

RESEARCH CENTER

VINDICATION

The name and word of the Eternal God
proven and justified by

EZEKIEL'S PROPHECY

and revealing what must speedily come
to pass upon the nations of the world.

◎

Comments by J. F. Rutherford

Author of

CREATION DELIVERANCE
RECONCILIATION GOVERNMENT
PROPHECY LIGHT
and other books

◎

BOOK TWO
First printing 1,000,000 copies

Publishers

WATCH TOWER
BIBLE AND TRACT SOCIETY
International Bible Students Association
BROOKLYN, NEW YORK, U. S. A.
Also
London, Toronto, Strathfield, Cape Town, Berne,
Magdeburg, and in other countries

TO

JEHOVAH

THE KING ETERNAL

THIS BOOK IS DEDICATED

"But the Lord is the true
God, he is the living God,
and an everlasting King:
at his wrath the earth shall
tremble, and the nations
shall not be able to abide his
indignation."—Jer. 10:10.

*"Let thy name be magni-
fied for ever."*—2 Sam.
7:26.

Copyrighted 1932
by
J. F. RUTHERFORD

Made in U. S. A.

INTRODUCTION

JEHOVAH'S holy name will be vindicated by the elimination of all unrighteousness from the universe. He has foretold as much by the mouth of his faithful prophets of old. Now he is causing such prophecy to be fulfilled and to be understood. Ezekiel's prophecy is devoted especially to the means Jehovah employs for the vindication of his name.

Vindication, Book Two, discloses the many enemies of Jehovah in and about the realms of "Christendom". It makes known the hypocritical religionists other than those who claim to be Christians and shows the destiny of such. It tells how Satan has commercialized the human race and why the commercial systems that control both the sea and the land have oppressed the people and reproached the name of Jehovah God. It shows Jehovah God will destroy oppressive commercialism and deliver the oppressed people into full light and liberty.

The prophecy of Ezekiel, as explained in this book, shows also how Satan has builded his great organization, invisible and visible to man, by which he has exploited the people and reproached God's name, and why God has permitted Satan thus to do unhindered until the

128142

present time. Herein is made known the chief
officer of Satan that will lead the fight on the
side of Satan at the battle of Armageddon and
how that wicked organization, both visible and
invisible, shall be completely destroyed. It tells
of the complete downfall and destruction of Satan himself following the destruction of his organization and how the world will be cleaned up,
and how the restoration of the people will proceed in righteousness. Above all, it shows the
vindication of Jehovah's holy name.

VINDICATION

BOOK TWO

VINDICATION

CHAPTER VI

ENEMIES

JEHOVAH by his Word makes known his purpose to uncover Satan and his organization, fully expose that wicked one to the eyes of all who earnestly desire righteousness, and to destroy Satan and his entire organization, that all creation may know that Jehovah is the only true and almighty God. It is necessary to know God and his King in order to live; hence the great act of vindication of Jehovah's word and name results beneficially to those who seek life everlasting in happiness and in peace.

At all times Satan has endeavored to keep the people in ignorance concerning Jehovah God and his Christ and his kingdom. For this reason it is written concerning Satan, the invisible god of this world, that he "hath blinded the minds of them which believe not, lest the light of the glorious gospel of Christ, who is the image of God, should shine unto them". (2 Cor. 4:4) For many centuries, unhindered in his wicked course Satan has kept the people in ignorance of the truth; but he must reach the end of his way, because God has so decreed. Long ago Jehovah placed his Word before mankind, and he has magnified his

Word above his name; but now, having reached the end of Satan's world, and the time for Jehovah to act, he will magnify both his Word and his name. He now makes it possible for men to have an understanding of his Word and the meaning of his name. A knowledge of Jehovah, his King and his kingdom, is vitally necessary to those who love righteousness and who would live, and therefore the prayer of such is: "Teach me good judgment and knowledge: for I have believed thy commandments."—Ps. 119: 66.

To his covenant people the Jews God gave his Word, and had they gladly obtained a knowledge thereof and walked in the way of his Word that people would have been preserved and greatly blessed by the Lord God and would have been his chosen people above all others on the earth. The Jews were both ungrateful and unfaithful, and they failed as a nation.

Christ Jesus came to earth clothed with a full knowledge of the Scriptures and he taught the Jews the truth, but only a few gave heed to his teachings. He told them that they erred because they did not know the Word of God, nor his power.—Matt. 22: 29.

The peoples of "Christendom", whom Jerusalem specifically foreshadowed, have been furnished with the Word of God and given an opportunity to know it and they have erred and gone in the wrong way because they know not God and his power. "Christendom" has not feared God; but the people thereof, and particularly the leaders, have walked on in ignorance and in darkness, being willingly ignorant of the things that God has given them the opportunity to know. (Ps. 82: 5) Both Jerusalem and "Christendom" are described as having less wisdom than the ox or the ass. "The ox knoweth his owner, and the ass his master's crib, but Israel doth not know, my people doth not consider. Ah sinful nation, a people laden with iniquity, a seed of evil doers, children that are corrupters! they have forsaken the Lord, they have provoked the Holy One of Israel unto anger, they are gone away backward."—Isa. 1: 3, 4.

In this day a knowledge of Jehovah, of his King and of his kingdom is of greatest necessity for the peoples of good will. There are many people within the borders of "Christendom" and outside thereof who may now seek to know and to understand the Word of God and greatly profit thereby. To aid such truth-seekers attention is here called to the divinely appointed way of obtaining a knowledge and understanding of the Lord. "The fear of the Lord is the beginning of knowledge; but fools despise wisdom and instruction." (Prov. 1: 7) It is the fool that hates knowledge and refuses to receive it and profit thereby.

The peoples of the world are now in great distress and perplexity and are ignorant of the reason therefor and they know not what can bring them relief. God's Word contains all and complete information concerning the same. The man who fears God and desires to do his will, and who then diligently seeks to know and to understand, will have his faith and his work rewarded. "Yea, if thou criest after knowledge, and liftest up thy voice for understanding; if thou seekest her as silver, and searchest for her as for hid treasures; then shalt thou understand the fear of the Lord, and find the knowledge of God. For the Lord giveth wisdom: out of his mouth cometh knowl-

edge and understanding. He layeth up sound wisdom
for the righteous: he is a buckler to them that walk
uprightly. He keepeth the paths of judgment, and
preserveth the way of his saints." (Prov. 2:3-8)
"Receive my instruction, and not silver; and knowledge rather than choice gold. For wisdom is better
than rubies; and all the things that may be desired
are not to be compared to it." (Prov. 8:10, 11) "The
heart of the prudent getteth knowledge; and the ear
of the wise seeketh knowledge."—Prov. 18:15.

The great issue is now between Jehovah God and
Satan the wicked one, and the final determination of
that question at issue is near at hand. One purpose
in publishing the truth is to disclose to the people
Satan and his wicked organization, but the chief reason for the publication of the truth is that the people
might learn of the goodness of Jehovah God and of
his complete remedy for the ills that afflict humankind.
Let the people now learn and understand that no human power can lift the world out of its degradation,
suffering and distress, but that Jehovah God, by and
through his kingdom, will destroy that which oppresses mankind and will bring peace, prosperity and life
and happiness to those who love him and who obey
his righteous laws. His kingdom on the earth, now
beginning, will first dash to pieces the wicked, oppressive organization of Satan, and the Lord will then
speak peace and prosperity to the people. The reason
for the woes that now afflict the people on earth is,
as stated in God's Word, to wit: "Woe to the inhab-
iters of the earth, and of the sea! for the devil is
come down unto you, having great wrath, because he
knoweth that he hath but a short time." (Rev. 12:12)

The "short time" here mentioned means that in the very near future the great question at issue between Jehovah and the Devil will be finally settled at the battle of Armageddon, and which must take place before lasting blessings can come to the peoples of the earth. Those who now get a knowledge and understanding of the reasons for that battle, and what will be the result, and what will follow after, and who then apply that knowledge in a wise manner, will be greatly blessed.

The chief ambition of Satan has ever been to have man worship and serve him, even as some have worshiped and do worship and serve Jehovah God. It was that selfish ambition that led him to rebel against God and caused him to dispute the supremacy of Jehovah God and to challenge God to put men on the earth whom Satan could not take away from God and cause to curse Jehovah. This challenge of Satan to Jehovah put at issue Jehovah's word and his name and the supremacy of the Almighty God. Since men are by nature born to look to a higher power, religion has been the chief means by which Satan has deceived and led men into his trap. By this means he has induced some to worship him directly, while others he has induced to worship various objects and things and thus to worship Satan indirectly; and this he has done that he might turn the people away from the true God.

Satan first organized the people on the plains of Shinar and started them in the way of the practice of the Devil religion. In the course of time all the peoples and nations of the earth, with the exception of the Israelites, practiced the Devil religion in some form.

When God selected for himself the descendants of faithful Abraham and called them Israelites, and later Jews, he gave to that people his law commanding that they should have no other God aside from Jehovah. "I am the Lord thy God, which have brought thee out of the land of Egypt, out of the house of bondage. Thou shalt have no other gods before me. Thou shalt not make unto thee any graven image, or any likeness of any thing that is in heaven above, or that is in the earth beneath, or that is in the water under the earth."—Ex. 20: 2-4.

Manifestly God gave the Israelites that law to protect them from the subtle and wicked influence of the Devil and to afford them an opportunity to maintain their integrity toward Jehovah. A few of that people, who are designated in the Scriptures as "the remnant of Israel", did remain true and faithful to God and did maintain their integrity toward him; but the nation as a whole fell away to the Devil and indulged in Baal or Devil worship, and for that reason God destroyed Jerusalem.

The Jews, or Judeans, of Jerusalem, being the covenant people of God whom he used to make pictures foreshadowing greater things to come, specifically typified or foreshadowed "Christendom"; that is to say, the people and nations that practice the so-called "Christian religion", and that claim to serve and worship Jehovah God and his Christ. The true worshipers of Jehovah God on earth were organized into a company by Christ Jesus and his apostles, and these who faithfully followed Christ Jesus have been called Christians, although the name is usually applied in derision. Only a few years passed after the death of the apostles until the majority of those of the company professing to worship Christ and God had fallen away by reason of the subtle and blinding influence of Satan. These professed worshipers of Christ and God adopted formalism and quickly indulged in hero worship, giving men great honor and praise and worship. Throughout the period of time known as the Christian era a few of those who made a covenant to do the will of God have maintained their integrity toward God, remained true and faithful to him, and worshiped him in spirit and in truth. But the great majority of so-called "Christian" people or worshipers formed themselves into companies or bodies, became active in the affairs of the world, and have since indulged in politics and other parts of Satan's organization and have become fully allied with Satan and a part of his visible organization. These organized bodies have practiced the Devil religion and falsely claimed it to be the "Christian religion". Such is the present situation throughout the nations and countries called "Christendom".

DEVIL WORSHIP

Baal worship is another name for Devil worship or Devil religion, and which Devil religion was introduced amongst the Jews. Balak was the king of the Moabites, which people practiced the Devil religion. (Num. 22:4) Balaam was a soothsayer of Mesopotamia. (Deut. 23:4, 5; Josh. 13:22) Balaam, an instrument of Satan, would do anything for hire. He belonged to that class of men that walk with their hands behind them. He hired himself to Balak to curse the Israelites. (Jude 11; 2 Pet. 2:15) Balaam taught Balak to cast a stumbling-block before the Israelites. This was a form of devilish worship by lewd rites. "And Israel abode in Shittim, and the people began to commit whoredom with the daughters of Moab. And they called the people unto the sacrifices of their gods; and the people did eat, and bowed down to their gods. And Israel joined himself unto Baal-peor; and the anger of the Lord was kindled against Israel. And the Lord said unto Moses, Take all the heads of the people, and hang them up before the Lord against the sun, that the fierce anger of the Lord may be turned away from Israel. And Moses said unto the judges of Israel, Slay ye every one his men that were joined unto Baal-peor."—Num. 25:1-5.

From the time the Devil religion was introduced amongst the Israelites there was a persistent contest between the true worshipers of God and the worshipers of Baal. Although claiming to be God's people, many of the Jews worshiped the Devil and practiced the Devil religion. "And the children of Israel did evil in the sight of the Lord, and served Baalim; and they forsook the Lord God of their fathers, which brought them out of the land of Egypt, and followed other gods, of the gods of the people that were round about them, and bowed themselves unto them, and provoked the Lord to anger. And they forsook the Lord, and served Baal and Ashtaroth."—Judg. 2:11-13.

The name "Baal" is from the primitive root which means "to be master; (hence) to marry". Therefore the name means "master" or "husband", and figuratively means "owner". Baal worship, therefore, is a religion or worship of the Devil by joining or uniting with the organization of which Satan the Devil

is master, husband and owner and by which union the
Devil is accepted as lord and master. In the practice
of this Devil religion graven images were used, which
images or statues represented or stood for the unseen.
The practice of the Devil religion still persists amongst
the nations of the earth. Today men carry on their
Devil worship and practice the Devil religion by employing such things as gold and other precious metals,
church systems, edifices, commercial and military power, and other like things which they idolize by setting
their ambitions and their affections thereon and by
worshiping them. The Devil has induced many people
to deny his existence and yet he induces them by subtle
means to worship that which he has brought into
existence.

Within ancient Jerusalem there were a few who
were faithful and true to Jehovah God and worshiped
him in spirit and in truth, and these few were hated
and persecuted by the apostate Jews who claimed to
worship God but who did not in fact. Also within
that ancient city of Jerusalem there were those who
made no pretense of worshiping the true God but who
were called "heathen" or "strangers" and who were
unfriendly to the true worshipers of God. All the nations round about the city of Jerusalem were heathen
and worshipers of the Devil or practicers of the Devil
religion, and they hated those who were faithful to
Jehovah God and who inhabited Jerusalem. Likewise
at this present day, within the land of "Christendom", which was foreshadowed by Jerusalem, there
are a few people that are true and faithful to Jehovah God and who worship him in spirit and in truth,
and these are hated by the apostate or so-called

"Christians" who have fallen away from God and are under the influence of Satan. Also within the borders of the land or nations of "Christendom" there are many who make no pretense to be worshipers of God and of Christ and who are also unfriendly to the true worshipers of God. The nations round and about "Christendom" are called "heathen", and these are unfriendly towards the true followers of Christ Jesus. With these preliminary facts before us let us now proceed to the examination of the prophecy of Ezekiel.

Ezekiel's prophecy, chapters one to twenty-four inclusive, is directed specifically against Jerusalem. When that prophecy was uttered and completed, then followed the siege of the city of Jerusalem by the Babylonians. During that siege and until the fall of the city there would be no occasion for God's prophet Ezekiel to prophesy against the city of Jerusalem; hence he is said to have been dumb during that period of time. Such 'dumbness' manifestly means that during that period of time Ezekiel the prophet was dumb so far as Jerusalem was concerned. It would not mean that he was entirely speechless. Book One of *Vindication* gives consideration to chapters one to twenty-four of Ezekiel's prophecy. Book Two of *Vindication* gives consideration to the prophecy of Ezekiel beginning with the twenty-fifth chapter, and other chapters that follow thereafter.

The siege of Jerusalem began in 608 B.C., by Nebuchadnezzar the king of Babylon. While that siege was in progress Ezekiel did not speak against Jerusalem, and therefore he is said to have been dumb;

but during that period of the siege he did speak the prophecy of Jehovah God against the nations called "heathen" and which were round and about Jerusalem. His prophecy is not spoken against Babylon; the evident reason being that the nation of Babylon was then being used by Jehovah as his instrument to enforce his judgment against the Jews. All the heathen nations or peoples practiced the satanic religion, and therefore the entire number represented the invisible ruler of this wicked world. The prophecy of Ezekiel specifically names seven of these heathen nations; and seven, being a symbol of completeness of things not seen by human eyes, evidently here is meant to include all the nations that go to make up Satan's visible organization. The entire enemy organization, both seen and unseen and which shall be utterly destroyed, is represented under the name of "Gog and Magog". The names considered in this chapter apply more specifically to those of earth who form a part of the Devil's organization aside from the professed "Christian" element or who make prominent some other part of Satan's visible organization.

Chapters twenty-five to thirty, inclusive, of Ezekiel's prophecy name seven different heathen nations, to wit, Ammon, Moab, Edom or Seir, Philistia, Tyrus and Zidon (both names applying to the same nation), Egypt, and Ethiopia. Assyria had been overthrown before the prophecy of Ezekiel began to be uttered, and probably this is the reason that no predictions are made concerning Assyria. Although Ezekiel did not directly prophesy concerning the fall of Babylon, and for the probable reason above assigned, indirectly his prophecy does apply to Babylon, and the proph-

ecy contains numerous predictions of and concerning
the restoration of God's people; which implies a deliverance from Babylon and the destruction of Babylon
as a component part of the enemies of the Most High.
The prophecy does foretell the doom of *all* the enemies
of Jehovah and therefore the enemies of Jehovah's
people.

The prophecy of Ezekiel beginning with chapter
twenty-five, and the chapters following, disclose
many features and doings of Satan's organization
and contains an illuminating description thereof.
The inference that is properly drawn from this is that
Jehovah's witnesses in the earth are first to take care-
ful note of the Devil's organization, its make-up and
its deeds against God and his kingdom, and then go
and declare God's judgment previously written
against that wicked organization and every part thereof. "Christendom" is the enemy of Jehovah God and
his kingdom. There are others, who make no pretense
of being Christian, that are God's enemies. While the
first part of Ezekiel's prophecy deals specifically with
"Christendom", his prophecy in the twenty-fifth to
the thirty-second chapters inclusive deals specifically
with other parts of Satan's visible organization all of
which is the enemy of Jehovah God. To be sure, Jehovah knows all his enemies; but manifestly one of
the primary purposes of Ezekiel's prophecy is to expose to God's covenant people now on earth every
part of the enemy Satan's organization, and this he
will do before he destroys them. "Thine hand shall
find out all thine enemies; thy right hand shall find
out those that hate thee."—Ps. 21:8.

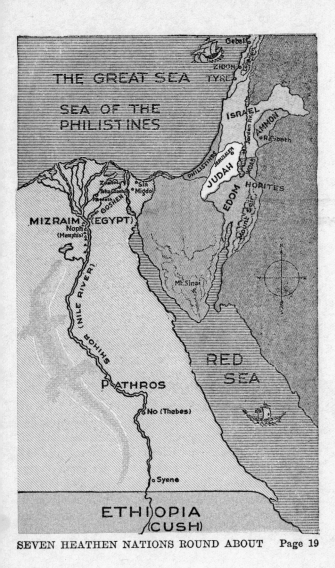

SEVEN HEATHEN NATIONS ROUND ABOUT   Page 19

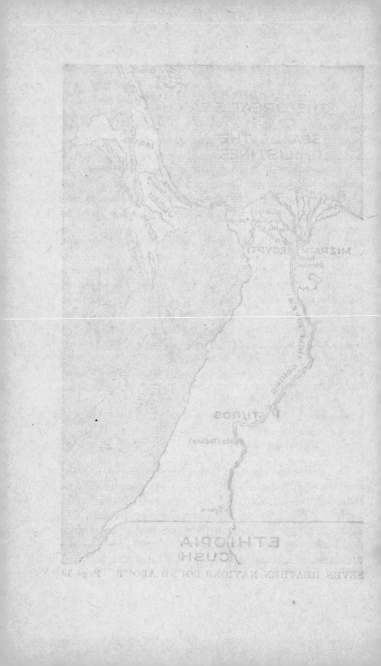

AGAINST AMMON
(EZEKIEL, CHAPTER 25)

The Revelation, chapters one to three, takes seven branches of God's organization and deals with them during the period of judgment time. The seven churches or divisions of God's visible organization clearly picture states of affairs or conditions existing in all of the companies forming God's organization at one and the same time. With the coming of the Lord to the temple of Jehovah for judgment there 'judgment began at the house of God', which judgment would include the real as well as the professed followers of Christ Jesus. Corresponding to this Ezekiel's prophecy deals specifically with seven branches of Satan's organization, which he names, and against which he prophesied during the period of his dumbness against Jerusalem. The prophecy of Ezekiel has to do with God's judgment against Satan's organization, and the prophecy here under consideration specifically pictures conditions or states of affairs that exist in all of Satan's organization, and which is symbolized by the seven nations here separately considered. The prophecy here was leveled against ancient Ammon, and it may be expected that we shall find a modern Ammon against which the prophecy is also leveled.

The prophecy against Jerusalem had been uttered, and the dumbness of Ezekiel against Jerusalem was therefore beginning, and the prophet of God then writes: "The word of the Lord came again unto me, saying, Son of man, set thy face against the Ammonites, and prophesy against them." (25:1, 2) The indisputable facts are that prior to 1918 the faithful followers of Christ Jesus specifically directed their testimony against the religious systems of "Christendom", and which work was foreshadowed by the Prophet Elijah. The prophecy of Ezekiel, beginning with the twenty-fifth chapter, evidently foreshadowed the time of change of the work of God's people from that represented by Elijah to that represented by the Prophet Elisha. This prophecy therefore points in time to the period following 1918, when the Lord came to the temple and inaugurated the day of vindication upon "Christendom" so called. It seems to point to the period marked by the formation of the League of Nations, all of which nations were and are anti-God and anti-kingdom. The prophecy, of course, refers to conditions existing long prior thereto and which conditions began to be exposed and made known from and after 1918.

The seven nations specifically named by Ezekiel, and against which nations his prophecy was directed, were hostile against one another and were all united against Jerusalem, and to that extent they were one, and were equally at all times leagued together against Jerusalem. It is written: "For they have consulted together with one consent: they are confederate against thee [God is represented by the earthly members of his organization]; the tabernacles of Edom, and the Ishmaelites; of Moab, and the Hagarenes; Gebal, and Ammon, and Amalek; the Philistines, with the inhabitants of Tyre; Assur also is joined with them; they have holpen the children of Lot [Moab and Ammon]." (Ps. 83: 5-8) Here are named five of the seven heathen powers mentioned by Ezekiel, and which are shown to be in a confederacy, or leagued, against God's true people, representing his organization. When Jerusalem fell the five heathen nations here named rejoiced, just as when God's "two witnesses" were killed the many enemies of God's people rejoiced. "And they that dwell upon the earth shall rejoice over them, and make merry, and shall send gifts one to another; because these two prophets tormented them that dwelt on the earth." (Rev. 11:10; *Light*, Book One, page 208) In both instances the rejoicing was due to selfishness and to a malicious desire to see God's people suffer. That rejoicing, however, is but temporary, as this prophecy plainly shows.

The *Revised Version* (25:2) says: "The children of Ammon, . . . prophesy against them." The name "Ammon" means "the son of my kindred, tribal (that is to say, inbred)". Ammon was a grand-nephew of Abraham. His territory bordered on the east of the territory of the tribe of Reuben. (Deut. 3:16; Gen. 19:38) The Ammonites practiced the satanic religion, worshiping the Devil under the guise of the worship of Milcom (Molech, *margin*, 1 Ki. 11:5, 7). The Ammonites were unfriendly to the Israelites during the time of the exodus of the Israelites from Egypt, and when they were marching toward Canaan. (Deut. 23:4) On a number of occasions the Ammonites committed assaults upon God's people. Also they contaminated the Israelites in a religious way. (Judg. 10:6; 11:4, 5; 2 Chron. 20:1-10; 2 Ki. 24:2) After the destruction of the city of Jerusalem the Ammonites continued to manifest their enmity against the people of Israel. When God's people were sent to rebuild the walls of the city of Jerusalem the

Ammonites conspired with the other enemies to hinder the building thereof.—Neh. 4: 7, 8.

Jehovah caused his decree to be written precluding the Ammonites from ever entering into the congregation of the Lord. "An Ammonite or Moabite shall not enter into the congregation of the Lord; even to their tenth generation shall they not enter into the congregation of the Lord for ever: because they met you not with bread and with water in the way, when ye came forth out of Egypt; and because they hired against thee Balaam the son of Beor, of Pethor of Mesopotamia, to curse thee." (Deut. 23: 3, 4) In this text "their tenth generation" manifestly means all the earthly generations of that people. "On that day they read in the book of Moses in the audience of the people; and therein was found written, that the Ammonite and the Moabite should not come into the congregation of God for ever. And I came to Jerusalem, and understood of the evil that Eliashib did for Tobiah [the Ammonite], in preparing him a chamber in the courts of the house of God." (Neh. 13: 1, 7) Furthermore, God caused the decree to be written against the Ammonites: "Therefore, as I live, saith the Lord of hosts, the God of Israel, Surely Moab shall be as Sodom, and the children of Ammon [shall be] as Gomorrah, even the breeding of nettles, and saltpits, and a perpetual desolation; the residue of my people shall spoil them, and the remnant of my people shall possess them. This shall they have for their pride, because they have reproached and magnified themselves against the people of the Lord of hosts."—Zeph. 2: 9, 10.

MODERN AMMONITES

The Ammonites therefore clearly appear to represent those whom the Lord God would never admit into the company of his true people because they neither sever themselves from Satan's organization, neither are they favorable to those who are escaping from that wicked organization, and who are pictured by the Israelites escaping out of Egypt. The modern Ammonites are a self-sufficient, inbred, evolutionistic or 'self-made by character development' class, and camp near upon the trail of God's true people for the purpose of harassing and opposing them, and have contaminated, adulterated and hindered the work of God's true people. They revile God's people while they themselves worship the Devil, practicing the Devil religion in some form.

Jehovah commanded Ezekiel to prophesy against the Ammonites: "And say unto the Ammonites, Hear the word of the Lord God; Thus saith the Lord God; Because thou saidst Aha, against my sanctuary, when it was profaned; and against the land of Israel, when it was desolate; and against the house of Judah, when they went into captivity; behold, therefore, I will deliver thee to the men of the east for a possession, and they shall set their palaces in thee, and make their dwellings in thee: they shall eat thy fruit, and they shall drink thy milk. And I will make Rabbah a stable for camels, and the Ammonites a couching place for flocks; and ye shall know that I am the Lord. For thus saith the Lord God, Because thou hast clapped thine hands, and stamped with the feet, and rejoiced in heart with all thy despite against the land of Israel."—25: 3-6.

Thus is disclosed a people that make no pretense
of being followers of Christ but who manifest a malicious and wicked spirit against the devoted people
of God. They stand by and look on while professed
"Christian religionists", so called, heap reproach and
ignominy and cruel persecution upon the faithful people of God, and when these faithful ones are taken into
the custody of the law of Satan's organization and
unjustly punished, then these modern Ammonites express delight at such acts or deeds of injustice. They
wickedly rejoice and take delight in such wickedness,
both inwardly and outwardly, all of which the Lord
God sees and takes notice of, and in due time will
give just recompense therefor.

Nothing escapes the watchful eye of Jehovah, and
in his due time he will give recompense to those who
unjustly and wrongfully treat his people. The enemies
of God may think they can ill-use his covenant people
and go unpunished, but in this they do err. Those
who love God pray: "Keep me as the apple of the
eye; hide me under the shadow of thy wings, from
the wicked that oppress me, from my deadly enemies
who compass me about. They are inclosed in their
own fat; with their mouth they speak proudly."—
Ps. 17: 8-10.

With full confidence in Jehovah, who is ever watchful, his faithful people sing: "My help cometh from
the Lord, which made heaven and earth. He will not
suffer thy foot to be moved: he that keepeth thee will
not slumber. Behold, he that keepeth Israel shall
neither slumber nor sleep." (Ps. 121: 2-4) To his
faithful followers Jesus declared the divine rule:
"Are not two sparrows sold for a farthing? and one

of them shall not fall on the ground without your Father. But the very hairs of your head are all numbered. Fear ye not therefore; ye are of more value than many sparrows." (Matt. 10:29-31) Jehovah has permitted the Devil and his crowd to exhibit their wickedness in opposition to him and his kingdom by persecuting and ill-treating his true people, but he will vindicate them, as well as his own name, in his own due time. "For thus saith the Lord of hosts, After the glory hath he sent me unto the nations which spoiled you; for he that toucheth you toucheth the apple of his eye. For, behold, I will shake mine hand upon them, and they shall be a spoil to their servants; and ye shall know that the Lord of hosts hath sent me. Sing and rejoice, O daughter of Zion: for, lo, I come, and I will dwell in the midst of thee, saith the Lord."—Zech. 2:8-10.

In corroboration of the fact that God will recompense those who have ill-treated his anointed, Ezekiel says: "Behold, therefore, I will deliver thee to the men of the east for a possession, and they shall set their palaces in thee, and make their dwellings in thee; they shall eat thy fruit, and they shall drink thy milk." (25:4) "Men of the east" here mentioned refers to the same as the "kings of the east" in Revelation 16:12. The Christ of God is the One who shall take possession of all nations and peoples of earth; hence these "men of the east" or "kings of the east" consist of Christ Jesus and the glorified members of his body now with him and also those on earth who continue faithful unto the end and who will be included in the same class. (*Light,* Book Two, page 38) God will duly recompense the enemies of his people, represented by Ammon. "Therefore, as I live, saith the Lord of hosts, the God of Israel [his covenant people], Surely . . . the children of Ammon [shall be] as Gomorrah, even the breeding of nettles, and saltpits, and a perpetual desolation: the residue of my people shall spoil them, and the remnant of my people shall possess them." (Zeph. 2: 9) "Be patient therefore, brethren, unto the coming of the Lord [to the day of executing the judgment of Jehovah against the enemy]."—Jas. 5: 7.

Jehovah's declared purpose is that the modern Ammonites shall have every reason to know that he is the Almighty God: "And I will make Rabbah a stable for camels, and the Ammonites a couching place for flocks; and ye shall know that I am the Lord." (25: 5) The meaning of the word "Rabbah" used in this verse is "great city" or "metropolis". It was the capital city of the Ammonites, and was therefore a royal city, and, says the prophet, it shall become like a camel's stable, which is a disreputable place. (Deut. 3: 11; Josh. 13: 25; 2 Sam. 11: 1; 12: 26; Amos 1: 13-15) That means that the condition of the modern Ammonites shall be that of great humiliation, and they shall know that Jehovah is God. God will not permit his covenant people to be persecuted and the persecutors to go unpunished.

Further pronouncing the divine decree against the modern Ammonites the prophet indicates that these shall be delivered up to places in the League of Nations that is anti-kingdom and then to the fate of destruction which awaits that unholy compact. "Behold, therefore, I will stretch out mine hand upon thee, and will deliver thee for a spoil to the heathen;

and I will cut thee off from the people, and I will cause thee to perish out of the countries; I will destroy thee; and thou shalt know that I am the Lord." (25:7) Because of the cruel- and hard-heartedness of the modern Ammonites, it is needful that Jehovah God literally show them who he is.—Jer. 25:17, 21.

It is interesting here to note that there appears to be no provision made or expressed in the Word of God for the recovery of Babylon, which stands primarily for hypocritical Devil religion, but there is strong proof that God will be merciful to the modern Ammonites and open their eyes to the fact that they have been captured by Satan and then give them opportunity as individuals to obey and to serve him and to have the blessings of restitution in his own due time: "Concerning the Ammonites, thus saith the Lord, Hath Israel no sons? hath he no heir? why then doth their king inherit Gad, and his people dwell in his cities? Therefore, behold, the days come, saith the Lord, that I will cause an alarm of war to be heard in Rabbah of the Ammonites; and it shall be a desolate heap, and her daughters shall be burned with fire: then shall Israel be heir unto them that were his heirs, saith the Lord. Howl, O Heshbon; for Ai is spoiled: cry, ye daughters of Rabbah, gird you with sackcloth; lament, and run to and fro by the hedges; for their king shall go into captivity, and his priests and his princes together. Wherefore gloriest thou in the valleys, thy flowing valley, O backsliding daughter? that trusted in her treasures, saying, Who shall come unto me? Behold, I will bring a fear upon thee, saith the Lord God of hosts, from all those that be about thee; and ye shall be driven out every man right forth; and none shall gather up him that wandereth. And afterward I will bring again the captivity of the children of Ammon, saith the Lord.'' (Jer. 49:1-6) Evidently this scripture means that God will not permit any of the Ammonites to be of his kingdom, but after the destruction of all his enemies the individuals that have made up the Ammonite class, who find that they have been the dupes of Satan their worst enemy, will be given an opportunity for restitution.

AGAINST MOAB

The Israelites, also called Jews, were the covenant people of God whom he punished for their unfaithfulness to him and their repudiation of their covenant with him. The people of the Jews therefore stood before the heathen world as the accredited representatives of God. Because Jehovah permitted or suffered punishment to come upon the Jews by the hand of King Nebuchadnezzar the Judeans, or Jews, were spoken of in derision by the heathen nations and these heathen said: 'The Jews are just like others of the heathen. They have claimed so much for their God and now he is unable to protect them from the assaults of Nebuchadnezzar.' Jehovah caused report of this to be made by directing Ezekiel to write: "Thus saith the Lord God, Because that Moab and Seir do say, Behold, the house of Judah is like unto all the heathen.'' (25:8) That derisive statement of the Moabites not only was a slap at the Jews, but was an insult and reproach cast upon Jehovah. It was a presumptuous interference on the part of the Moabites with the work of the Lord. It was Jehovah's exclusive prerogative to punish the Jews for wrongdoing, and it must be understood that it was none of the affair of any of Satan's organization to interfere or to speak derisively of God's work.

In like manner in these last days, the organization called "Christian", which was foreshadowed by the Judeans, or Jews, is very much in disrepute amongst those who make no pretense of serving God. They see the so-called "Christians" falling away from God and they say in substance that the Christians are no better than other people, that they are all crooks and their God is no better than any other god. They speak with like words against the true Israel as they do against the pretending Christians. It seems certain that "organized Christianity" will come into greater disrepute amongst the peoples of earth, and then after the destruction of "organized Christianity" all persons who serve God in fact, or who claim to serve him, will be in disrepute in the minds of the class represented by the Moabites. Such is and will be a great insult and reproach to Jehovah God. The name of Jehovah will be vindicated, and all must come to know that he is God; and therefore he will visit the modern Moabite and properly recompense such.

"Therefore, behold, I will open the side of Moab from the cities, from his cities which are on his frontiers, the glory of the country, Beth-jeshimoth, Baalmeon, and Kiriathaim." (25:9) "Moab" means "from my father", that is, "seed of the (mother's) father." Moab was a son of Lot by his eldest daughter. (Gen. 19:37) The Moabites were unfriendly to the Jews and ill-treated them when they were on their

trek to the land of Canaan, even hiring the soothsayer
Balaam to curse the Israelites. (Num. 22; Mic. 6:5)
The Moabites worshiped the Devil under the form of
Chemosh. (1 Ki. 11:7; Jer. 48:7, 13, 46) They as-
saulted the Jews and captured and held them in cap-
tivity for a period of eighteen years.—Judg. 3:12-14.

God has not permitted wickedness to persist in the
earth in order to teach men the evil effects thereof,
but he has permitted his covenant people to come in
contact with Satan's organization, thereby affording
them an opportunity under test to prove whether or
not they love the Lord God. The Israelites came in
contact with the heathen nations and were fully
warned aforetime to keep themselves separate from
the heathen, but they failed to do so. Their coming in
contact with the heathen afforded them an opportunity to prove their love for Jehovah. Likewise God's
covenant people who agreed to do his will and follow
in the footsteps of Jesus Christ have been in the
world but like their Master they are not of the world.
They have been duly warned to keep themselves separate from the world and to prove their faithfulness
and love for God. They have been told that friendship with the world and the mixing up with worldly
schemes is an abomination in the sight of God. The
Jews as a nation were unfaithful to God and for that
reason he punished them. At the same time there were
faithful Jews in the land who held themselves separate and distinct from their enemies and who maintained their integrity toward God. Likewise the people of "Christendom" who have covenanted to do the
will of God have in the aggregate been unfaithful to
God and have turned away to Satan's organization,

but at the same time there have been a few who have maintained their integrity and remained faithful and true to God.

Ruth was a Moabitess. She voluntarily forsook the god of Moab and became willingly and obediently the servant of the Most High, and she received God's blessing by being made a link in the genealogy of David leading up to Christ. She ceased to be a Moabitess and was adopted into the family of God. As a people or nation the Moabites were enemies of Jehovah. The Moabite Sanballat did what he could to hinder the rebuilding of the wall of Jerusalem. (Neh. 2:19) The Moabites magnified themselves against Jehovah God, and by reproaching his covenant people they reproached Jehovah, and for this reason God pronounced his decree against Moab. "The horn of Moab is cut off, and his arm is broken, saith the Lord. Make ye him drunken; for he magnified himself against the Lord: Moab also shall wallow in his vomit, and he also shall be in derision. For was not Israel a derision unto thee? was he found among thieves? for since thou spakest of him, thou skippedst for joy. . . . We have heard the pride of Moab, (he is exceeding proud,) his loftiness, and his arrogancy, and his pride, and the haughtiness of his heart. I know his wrath, saith the Lord; but it shall not be so; his lies shall not so effect it. And Moab shall be destroyed from being a people, because he hath magnified himself against the Lord." (Jer. 48:25-30, 42) "And Moab shall be ashamed of Chemosh, as the house of Israel [ten tribes] was ashamed of Beth-el their confidence. How say ye, We are mighty and strong men for the war?"—Jer. 48:13, 14.

MODERN MOABITES

The Moabites therefore were and do picture a people, whether within the confines of the land of "Christendom" or outside thereof, who do not acknowledge Jehovah as God or pretend to be Christian but who practice some form of Devil religion; a people that is self-contained, self-important; a class of people who rely upon their own strength and the strength of their organizations. There are many such in the land called "Christian", and many outside thereof, who are proud, arrogant, lofty and haughty, but despise the name of God and of his Christ, and who are against those who worship and serve God in spirit and in truth. They are closely related to the modern Ammonites. They have their lodges, clubs and leagues, and like organizations, which practice militarism, and they count much on their military strength and power, and their god is their own power and their own strength. They are like "armed soldiers" of ancient Moab. Many of these clubs, lodges and leagues made up of men and women, and to which is attached militarism, reproach professed Christians and true Christians alike; and even after the fall of "Christendom" will still reproach the true Christians with the same hatred that they now have; and they shall come to bitter sorrow, as the Lord says of them: "Therefore the armed soldiers of Moab shall cry out; his life shall be grievous unto him."—Isa. 15:4.

The modern Moabites, like the Ammonites, shall be delivered into the hand or possession of Christ: "unto the children of the east (coming) against the sons of Ammon, and I will give them in possession; in order that the sons of Ammon may not be remembered among the nations. And on Moab will I execute judgments; and they shall know that I am the Lord." (25: 10, 11, *Leeser*) The destruction of the modern Moabites is therefore closely related to that of their half brothers the modern Ammonites.—Jer. 25: 17-21.

It was "Christendom" that instigated the persecution of God's people during the World War. Foreknowing this tribulation that was to come upon them God foretold it in these words: "Take counsel, execute judgment; make thy shadow as the night in the midst of the noonday; hide the outcasts; bewray not him that wandereth. Let mine outcasts dwell with thee, Moab; be thou a covert to them from the face of the spoiler; for the extortioner is at an end, the spoiler ceaseth, the oppressors are consumed out of the land." —Isa. 16: 3, 4.

The modern Moabites there had the opportunity of furnishing some succor and help to God's covenant people then in trouble, but instead of so doing they rejoiced at the tribulation that came upon the faithful children of God during the period from 1917 to 1919 and hence these faithful ones were scattered and persecuted. No country on earth during the World War hardships furnished aid or succor to the faithful people of God, nor did these nations give heed to the truth God's faithful people had proclaimed. In all such countries those who did not even claim to be the followers of Christ or worshipers of God also manifested their ill will against God's people. These opposers of God's people did not trust in the churches of "Christendom", but they trusted in their own works and in their own treasures and practiced some form of Devil religion. They willingly cooperated, however, with the powers of "Christendom" to cut off God's people and destroy them out of the land of the living. Therefore it is written concerning the modern Moabites: "Against Moab thus saith the Lord of hosts, the God of Israel, . . . For because thou hast trusted in thy works, and in thy treasures, thou shalt also be taken; and Chemosh shall go forth into captivity, with his priests and his princes together. . . . The horn of Moab is cut off, and his arm is broken, saith the Lord."—Jer. 48: 1-25.

It is to the "men of the east", including the anointed ones on earth, that the execution of God's judgments is committed. All the saints must have a part therein even though the only part the earthly division has is to serve notice and sing the praises of Jehovah. "To execute vengeance upon the heathen, and punishments upon the people; to execute upon them the judgment written: this honour have all his saints. Praise ye the Lord." (Ps. 149: 7, 9) Any one of the anointed, therefore, who is negligent or indifferent in the performance of his duty shall be condemned by the Lord. "Cursed be he that doeth the work of the Lord deceitfully [negligently, *margin*]." (Jer. 48: 10) Jehovah's written judgment against Moab (ancient and modern) is: "But I will send a fire upon Moab, and it shall devour the palaces of Kirioth; and Moab shall die with tumult, with shouting, and with the sound of the trumpet: and I will cut off the judge from the midst thereof, and will slay all the princes thereof with him, saith the Lord." (Amos 2: 2, 3) "Therefore, as I live, saith the Lord of hosts, the God of Israel, Surely Moab shall be as Sodom." —Zeph. 2: 9, 10.

The Jews were the direct descendants of Abraham. The Ammonites and Moabites were the descendants of Lot, who was a nephew of Abraham. The Ammonites and Moabites therefore were distinctly related to the Jews and probably used a similar language, although opposed to each other. The Israelites or Jews foreshadowed the "Christians", so called, of modern times. The organizations within the borders of "Christendom", as well as outside, such as "Christian Scientists", so called, theosophists, psychologists, evolutionists and like ones, are distinctly related to "organized Christianity", and talk something like "organized Christianity". These are self-centered, self-important, and think they can by their own mental and physical efforts bring themselves up to perfection. They are the enemies of God and of his kingdom. These are the modern Ammonites and Moabites, and, like the Ammonites and Moabites of old, have been and are the dupes of the Devil; they are not willing hypocrites, but are entirely blind to God and to the truth; therefore after the destruction of their organization and systems God will have mercy upon them individually and in his own due time and way give them an opportunity for restitution blessings. "Yet will I bring again the captivity of Moab in the latter days, saith the Lord. Thus far is the judgment of Moab." (Jer. 48:47) The testimony is delivered to the modern Ammonites and Moabites within the land called "Christendom".

AGAINST EDOM

The people of Edom, otherwise called Mount Seir, picture another class of the enemies of God. "Thus

saith the Lord God, Because that Edom hath dealt
against the house of Judah by taking vengeance, and
hath greatly offended, and revenged himself upon
them." (25: 12) The Edomites picture a class of
people that reproach the name of Jehovah God because
"Seir [doth] say, Behold, the house of Judah is like
unto all the heathen". (25: 8) This class also vent
their spleen or malicious hatred against God's covenant people that serve him and give praise to his name.

Edom (which also we call Mount Seir) means
"red", and is a name of reproach because of Esau's
selling his birthright for a mess of red pottage. (Gen.
25: 30) The Edomites were descendants of Esau by
two heathen women of Canaan and by the niece of
Isaac, that is, a granddaughter of Abraham through
Ishmael. (See Genesis 36: 1-6, 43.) The Edomites
worshiped false gods; therefore they practiced the
Devil religion. (2 Chron. 25: 14, 15, 20) They inter-
married with the Horites (meaning cave dwellers,
the original inhabitants of Mount Seir). (Gen.
36: 12, 20-22) Edom is therefore addressed as "Thou
that dwellest in the clefts of the rock, whose habitation is high". (Obad. 3) The Edomites ill-treated the
children of Israel when the messengers of Moses, who
represented the Lord, requested a favor for the Israelites. (Num. 20: 21) They entered into a conspiracy
with other enemies of God against the Israelites. "For
they have consulted together with one consent; they
are confederate against thee; the tabernacles of Edom,
and the Ishmaelites; of Moab, and the Hagarenes."
(Ps. 83: 5, 6) "Remember, O Lord, the children of
Edom in the day of Jerusalem; who said, Rase it,
rase it, even to the foundation thereof."—Ps. 137: 7.

"Esau" means "rough" (that is to say, sensibly felt, because of his hairy skin). (Gen. 25:25) "Seir" means "shaggy, rugged, hairy, rough and wooded", and is another form of "sa'ir", which means "devil, satyr, goat". The name is well used to picture and applies to a part of Satan's organization. "Thus dwelt Esau in mount Seir. Esau is Edom." (Gen. 36:8, 9) The Herod who caused John the Baptist to be killed was an Edomite.

The Edomites seem clearly to picture a class of persons who claim to have been begotten of the spirit of God and are therefore classed as spiritual brothers of God's faithful sons. The opportunity was once theirs of participating in the kingdom or royal house of God, but they bartered away that opportunity or right for ever that they might gratify their selfish desires. For a mess of pottage they give up the opportunity of entering into Jehovah's organization. Soured and revengeful against those who love and serve God, they persecute and try to take vengeance upon those who do enter into the covenant with Christ Jesus to be members of Jehovah's royal house. When they see other enemies of God and of his people persecuting Jehovah's "servant" class they join themselves to the side of the enemy and take either an active or a passive position in such persecution. They are not really a part of "Christendom", although in "Christendom", because they once separated themselves from "Christendom"; and then disregarding God's commandments, and relying upon their own loftiness, they return to the elementary things of the Scriptures and forsake God's kingdom. They perch themselves very high in self-exaltation, not believing

that the Lord will bring them down to the ground as
he declares he will do. (Obad. 3, 4) They are wise in
their own conceits and past masters at deception.

They voluntarily oppose those whom they once called
their brethren. They slander these without a cause.
"Thou sittest and speakest against thy brother; thou
slanderest thine own mother's son." (Ps. 50:20)
When some of these saw there was a conspiracy against
God's covenant people who were serving him, in the
years 1917 and 1918, they lent their aid and support
to the persecutors of God's people, and have been doing so ever since. "Shall I not in that day, saith the
Lord, even destroy the wise men out of Edom, and
understanding out of the mount of Esau? And thy
mighty men, O Teman, shall be dismayed, to the end
that every one of the mount of Esau may be cut off
by slaughter. For thy violence against thy brother
Jacob, shame shall cover thee, and thou shalt be cut
off for ever. In the day that thou stoodest on the
other side, in the day that the strangers carried away
captive his forces, and foreigners entered into his
gates, and cast lots upon Jerusalem, even thou wast
as one of them. But thou shouldest not have looked
on the day of thy brother in the day that he became
a stranger; neither shouldest thou have rejoiced over
the children of Judah in the day of their destruction;
neither shouldest thou have spoken proudly in the
day of distress."—Obad. 8-12.

As the Edomites stood by and gave aid and comfort
and encouragement to those that were carrying away
the people of Israel as captives, even so the modern
Edomites or Esau crowd gave aid and comfort to the
enemy that were persecuting and carrying away God's

people during the World War distress. By thus taking vengeance and by having revenged themselves the modern Edomites put themselves in a class mentioned by the psalmist: "Out of the mouth of babes and sucklings hast thou ordained strength, because of thine enemies; that thou mightest still the enemy and the avenger." (See *The Watchtower* 1930, page 100.) In harmony with this it is written: "Whereas Edom saith, We are impoverished, but we will return and build the desolate places; thus saith the Lord of hosts, They shall build, but I will throw down; and they shall call them, The border of wickedness, and, The people against whom the Lord hath indignation for ever."—Mal. 1:4.

"SON OF PERDITION"

The description of the Edomites and the facts concerning the "evil servant" class (Matt. 24:48-51), "the son of perdition" (2 Thess. 2:3-12), exactly fit. It is this class that join themselves in a conspiracy to do injury to God's people who are faithfully endeavoring to advertise the name of Jehovah and his kingdom. "Thy terribleness hath deceived thee, and the pride of thine heart, O thou that dwellest in the clefts of the rock, that holdest the height of the hill: though thou shouldest make thy nest as high as the eagle, I will bring thee down from thence, saith the Lord." —Jer. 49:16.

In a judicial decree entered against the Edomites Jehovah says: "Therefore thus saith the Lord God, I will also stretch out mine hand upon Edom, and will cut off man and beast from it; and I will make it desolate from Teman; and they of Dedan shall fall by the sword." (25:13) Those who have once been enlightened by the Lord, and who then for envy take vengeance upon those who have been once their brethren, are far more reprehensible before God than those who have not been so enlightened. The district of Dedan was near Edom, and it is evident that those whom Dedan pictures joined with those whom Teman pictures in acts of vengeance against the people of God. It is written: "And these are the names of the dukes that came of Esau, according to their families, after their places, by their names; . . . duke Teman, duke Mibzar." (Gen. 36:40-42) These were descendants of Abraham. "Then again Abraham took a wife, and her name was Keturah. And she bare him Zimran, and Jokshan . . . And Jokshan begat Sheba, and Dedan. And the sons of Dedan were Asshurim and Letushim, and Leummim."—Gen. 25:1-3.

The adverse judgment entered by Jehovah against Esau also reaches the people of Dedan. "Flee ye, turn back, dwell deep, O inhabitants of Dedan; for I will bring the calamity of Esau upon him, the time that I will visit him." (Jer. 49:8) "And thy mighty men, O Teman, shall be dismayed, to the end that every one of the mount of Esau may be cut off by slaughter."—Obad. 9.

Jehovah will execute his vengeance against those who after having received his favor spurn his goodness, disobey his commandments, and persecute those who delight to do his will. Such are the modern Edomites. "And I will lay my vengeance upon Edom by the hand of my people Israel; and they shall do in Edom according to mine anger, and according to my fury; and they shall know my vengeance, saith the Lord God.'' (25:14) Christ Jesus, the chief executive of Jehovah, will execute his vengeance against the Edomites. All the members of the capital organization of Jehovah, including the faithful remnant on earth, are given some part in the execution of this judgment. (Ps. 149:9; Obad. 17, 18, 21) ''I shall see him, but not now; I shall behold him, but not nigh: there shall come a Star out of Jacob, and a Sceptre shall rise out of Israel, and shall smite the corners of Moab, and destroy all the children of Sheth. And Edom shall be a possession, Seir also shall be a possession for his enemies: and Israel shall do valiantly.'' —Num. 24:17, 18.

The Esau class, or modern Edomites, are those who do know better, yet who wrongfully do violence to those who praise Jehovah. God's vengeance will be specially manifested against such, and the remnant now on the earth must have to do with this in that they declare the day of God's vengeance upon his enemies. (Deut. 32:43) Those who are devoted to Jehovah will see the expression of his righteous indignation against his enemies and will rejoice in the vindication of his name. ''The righteous shall rejoice when he seeth the vengeance: he shall wash his feet in the blood of the wicked. So that a man shall say, Verily there is a reward for the righteous; verily he is a God that judgeth in the earth.''—Ps. 58:10, 11.

Jehovah further emphasized his purpose to inflict punishment upon the modern Edomites. (Jer. 25:21) ''In that day will I raise up the tabernacle of David that is fallen, and close up the breaches thereof: and I will raise up his ruins, and I will build it as in the days of old; that they may possess the remnant of

Edom, and of all the heathen, which are called by
my name, saith the Lord that doeth this.'' (Amos
9: 11, 12) ''For my sword shall be bathed in heaven:
behold, it shall come down upon Idumea [Edom], and
upon the people of my curse, to judgment. The sword
of the Lord is filled with blood; it is made fat with
fatness, and with the blood of lambs and goats, with
the fat of the kidneys of rams; for the Lord hath a
sacrifice in Bozrah, and a great slaughter in the land
of Idumea. It shall not be quenched night nor day;
the smoke thereof shall go up for ever: from generation to generation it shall lie waste; none shall pass
through it for ever and ever.'' (Isa. 34: 5, 6, 10)
''Thus saith the Lord, For three transgressions of
Edom, and for four, I will not turn away the punishment thereof; because he did pursue his brother with
the sword, and did cast off all pity, and his anger did
tear perpetually, and he kept his wrath for ever: but
I will send a fire upon Teman, which shall devour the
palaces of Bozrah.'' (Amos 1: 11, 12) These scriptures constitute strong proof that the Edomites pictured a class that is turned away to complete destruction or second death. There is no promise in the Bible of restitution of the Edomites.

AGAINST PHILISTIA

At the time of the expulsion of man from Eden
Jehovah caused to be recorded in his Word the prophecy concerning the enmity of the seed of the serpent,
Satan, against the Seed of the woman, God's organization. (Gen. 3: 15) The Philistines constituted a part
of that seed of the serpent. The Philistines harassed,
persecuted, and expressed their vengeance despitefully

against the Jews in Canaan. God through Ezekiel said: ''Thus saith the Lord God, Because the Philistines have dealt by revenge, and have taken vengeance with a despiteful heart, to destroy it for the old hatred.''—25:15.

The Philistines were the descendants of Noah's son Ham through Mizraim. (Gen. 10:6, 13, 14; Amos 9:7) The Philistines bore no close relationship to God's chosen people. The Philistines were the worshipers of the fish god Dagon and of the female god Ashtaroth, and also of Baal-zebub. (Judg. 16:23; 1 Sam. 31:8-10; Judg. 10:6; 2 Ki. 1:2, 3; Isa. 2:6) Being of the seed of the serpent they were the enemies of God's organization. They captured and imprisoned Samson. (Judg. 3:1-3; 16; Josh. 13:3; Ps. 83:7) Twice they tried to unseat David the king of Israel, moving their armies against him. In this connection the first battle of Mount Perazim was fought, which is a type of God's strange act and work.—2 Sam. 5:17-25; Isa. 28:21.

The name ''Philistine'' means ''rolling'', that is, migratory, and doubtless refers to the fact that they migrated from Egyptian territory (Mizraim) and settled on the sea coast to the north. In Exodus 23:31 the Mediterranean sea is described as the ''sea of the Philistines''. They therefore must have had harbors and ships and commercial trade by sea. The Philistines therefore seem to represent and picture those who outwardly appear to have come out of the world (that is, migrated from Egypt) and who make a pretext of worshiping God but who in fact worship the Devil under various forms and particularly oppress the ''prisoner'' class represented by Samson. They reject Christ Jesus, the Prince of peace and earth's rightful Ruler, and oppose the establishment of the kingdom of God. They reject the Stone laid in Zion, and therefore clearly include those described by the prophet of God as "the principal of the flock" and who rely upon their own strength and their military equipment and strength and are therefore under the influence of their god the Devil. During the World War practically all the clergymen of "Christendom" openly advocated the war, and supported the same in some form. Probably the wide testimony of the truth of God's Word concerning the followers of Christ Jesus engaging in the war, which testimony has been emphasized since the war ended, has caused some of the clergymen to become weak-kneed and disposed to reverse their position in regard to participating in war.

In 1931 a questionnaire was sent out to the preachers to get an expression from them concerning their advocacy of war, and in response to that questionnaire a number of clergymen expressed themselves against war. This shows that they were ashamed of their former record during the World War. During the World War these "principal men of the flock", politicians, military men and commercial men, had held the clergymen in line, but after the war some of them began to try to face about in order to gain back, if possible, the support of many people who had once thought them to be honest. About the close of 1931 a general in the United States army, and who is one of the 'principal in the flock' of the so-called "Christian church", comes forth in a printed statement in which he severely takes to task the clergymen that have

dared express themselves as opposed to war. Like his
subtle and hypocritical father the Devil, this general
in the army quotes scripture and misapplies it in
order to bolster up his position. The incident is cited
here to show the class of men who are always against
God's anointed, and who harass, unjustly criticize and
persecute them because of their faithfulness to God.
None of these "uncircumcised Philistines" get into
the real company of God's people, but they do push
their noses in, and stick out their chest, amongst the
professed Christians, and this they do in order to
make themselves appear important and great. It is
the navy and military power that backs the commercial giants at sea and makes it possible for these to
carry on their operations which result in oppressing
the people.

Great corporations have been organized and now
exist within the borders of the land called "Christendom". Many of the chief men therein have apparently
come out of the world and have associated themselves
with the so-called "Christian church" and in that
organization are made by the clergy the 'principal
ones of the flock'. These men are modern uncircumcised Philistines. They never, in fact, came out of
the world, have never had any spiritual interest in
God's kingdom, and never even claimed to have, but
have always been against it. They rely upon their own
strength and the strong arm of their so-called "law
and order force". When they can quote scripture to
apparently support their position they do so, but they
have no faith in it whatsoever. They coerce and oppress the "prisoner" class and aid the clergy in holding such as prisoners in the churches. They exercise

a cruel, oppressive military power against all that dare take a position for the right, that is to say, for God's kingdom. There is an abundance of evidence that has been brought to light during the past few years about these modern Philistines who operate, for instance, the coal fields of West Virginia, Kentucky, Pennsylvania and other places. These men persecute the men and women who make an honest endeavor to feed the starving children of the families whom they desire to keep within their power. They also persecute and oppress Jehovah's witnesses who make an effort to carry the Word of God and his kingdom amongst the people.

God's judgment is written against them; therefore he directs Ezekiel to say: "Therefore, thus saith the Lord God, Behold, I will stretch out mine hand upon the Philistines, and I will cut off the Cherethims [Cherethites, *R.V.*], and destroy the remnant of the sea coast." (25:16) "Cherethims" means "executioners", such as guardsmen, private policemen, etc. They clearly picture the element amongst the modern Philistines that are hired by their chiefs to bear military arms and to unjustly and without right execute innocent men and women. Included within this crowd are dishonest judges of courts, who owe their positions to the power and influence of the men that own and control the great corporations and who employ the force and power of the law to unjustly punish and execute those who are innocent of crime. Many an innocent man is made a "goat" to hide the wickedness of some of these "principal of the flock". These men are officers of Satan's organization posing as principals of the flock of the church organizations, and form a part of the crowd that controls and operates the commerce of land and sea, and they do it by force and violence, and are mentioned by God's prophet in these words: "Woe unto the inhabitants of the sea coast, the nation of the Cherethites! the word of the Lord is against you; O Canaan, the land of the Philistines, I will even destroy thee, that there shall be no inhabitant. And the coast shall be for the remnant of the house of Judah; they shall feed thereupon; in the houses of Ashkelon shall they lie down in the evening; for the Lord their God shall visit them, and turn away their captivity."—Zeph. 2: 5, 7.

The gross and flagrant injustices which in these days are practiced by the modern Philistine against defenseless people of the land will not go unnoticed by the Lord, and in his due time he will execute his vengeance upon such that they may know that he is the Almighty God. "And I will execute great vengeance upon them with furious rebukes; and they shall know that I am the Lord, when I shall lay my vengeance upon them."—25: 17.

Let the peoples of good will, and who are suffering oppression at the hands of these modern Philistines, consider the Word of God and take courage. The Lord's kingdom will bring them relief. All the people and the nations that have practiced the Devil religion and use various hypocritical cloaks behind which to hide their acts of unjustice, and all that oppose God and his kingdom of righteousness, shall drink of the cup of his wrath, because he has thus declared it. "Then took I the cup at the Lord's hand, and made all the nations to drink, unto whom the Lord had sent me . . . , and all the kings [wicked rulers] of the

land of the Philistines, and [the Philistines' cities of]
Ashkelon, and Azzah, and Ekron, and the remnant of
Ashdod.'' (Jer. 25:17,20) ''The word of the Lord
that came to Jeremiah the prophet against the Philistines, before that Pharaoh smote Gaza. O thou sword
of the Lord, how long will it be ere thou be quiet?
put up thyself into thy scabbard, rest, and be still.
How can it be quiet, seeing the Lord hath given it a
charge against Ashkelon, and against the sea shore?
there hath he appointed it.''—Jer. 47:1, 6, 7.

It seems certain that God's remnant on earth have
something to do with Jehovah God's judgment against
modern Philistines, and their part of the work must
be to serve notice upon such of and concerning God's
purposes and his kingdom and to tell them that his
kingdom is at hand. This work is now in progress
by the Lord's faithful witnesses. This work of wit-
nessing is not for the purpose of giving glory to the
remnant, but for the sole purpose of the vindication
of Jehovah's name, and hence that those upon whom
notice is served may know that Jehovah is the only
true God.

AGAINST TYRE
(Ezekiel, Chapter 26)

The dumbness of Ezekiel during the siege manifestly meant that it was only against Jerusalem that
he was not to speak and did not speak during that
time, but during the time of the siege he was to pronounce God's judgment against the other enemies of
God; and this conclusion is supported by the following: ''And it came to pass in the eleventh year, in
the first day of the month, that the word of the Lord

came unto me, saying." (26:1) If this was the first
month of the eleventh year, that would be three
months and nine days before Jerusalem was broken
up, and four months and seven days before the city
and the temple were burned. It is, however, not stated
by the text which month it was, but it is certain that
it was before the escaped messenger reached Ezekiel
to tell him that "the city is smitten".

Jehovah, addressing his prophet, said: "Son of man,
because that Tyrus hath said against Jerusalem,
Aha, she is broken that was the gates of the people;
she is turned unto me; I shall be replenished, now
she is laid waste." (26:2) This prophecy is directed
against Tyre. The word "Tyre" means "rock", but
not "The Rock", Jehovah. It refers to the rock of
the mimic god, the rock on which the serpent has his
way. (Prov. 30:19) It is the rock in which Satan's
seed and representatives on the earth do hide themselves "for fear of the Lord, and for the glory of his
majesty". (Isa. 2:10) It means the Devil and his
wicked organization bearing his name. The city of
Tyre was doubtless so called because it was originally
built upon the mainland and was afterwards moved
to the great island rock for defensive purposes. This
was a part of the territory of Canaan, the accursed
one. (Gen. 10:15, 19; 9:25) Even in ancient times
it was a strong city. (Josh. 19:29) It was called the
"strong hold of Tyre". (2 Sam. 24:7) The prophet
speaks of it as the "city whose antiquity is of ancient
days". (Isa. 23:7, 8) Tyre is spoken of as "the
strength" of the ships of Tarshish or a "fortress".
(*Roth.*) According to the *Revised Version* it is called
"the strong hold of the sea". (Isa. 23:4) The ships

of Tarshish were the carrier vessels of Tyre, being
so called because of being a certain type peculiar to
Tyre rather than because of being of Tarshish or
built or owned by Tarshish. Proof of this is found
in the following text: "Jehoshaphat made ships of
Tharshish to go to Ophir for gold; but they went
not; for the ships were broken at Ezion-geber." (1 Ki.
22:48) During the rebuilding of the walls of Jerusalem there were in Jerusalem traders from Tyre.
(Neh. 13:16) At one time there was friendship between the king of Tyre and Jerusalem's rulers, but
this changed to hostility.

Tyre seems to specifically refer to the mercantile-
marine division of Satan's organization, that is to
say, the business interests which exploit the people
by ships at sea. It finds its highest expression in the
seventh world power, to wit, the dual empire of
Britain and America. This marine power once at
least pretended to be friendly to God's people, but
in the latter times has become very unfriendly. Ger-
many did at one time bid fair to be a powerful con-
tender for the shipping of the world, but her power
was broken. The Bible attributes no commercial fleet
to ancient Egypt. Tyre therefore seems to represent
a special division or part of Satan's organization,
whereas it appears that Egypt more particularly represents the commercial or Big Business power on the
land, backed by military power, and which appears
more prominently in the great financial and trust
companies which juggle with the produce of the land
and control the means of public transportation. While
most of these organizations and powers operate within
the borders of the land called "Christendom", yet

many of them do not even pretend to be of "organized Christianity". Among the powerful men who control the commerce of the sea are many Jews, so called, yet who are against God and against Christ and against the kingdom of God. This is probably the reason why God by his prophet speaks of them separately and distinctly from Jerusalem, both ancient and modern. All are representatives of the Devil, to be sure, and form a part of his organization, but the Lord is pointing them out as separate and integral parts of Satan's organization and gives his people a vision of them from different standpoints.

It was in 1917 to 1919 that the seventh world power, particularly the mercantile empire of Satan's organization, succeeded in scattering the people of God, and which is mentioned by Ezekiel as saying "against Jerusalem, Aha, she is broken that was the gates of the people; she is turned unto me". Jerusalem, that is, God's covenant people, were "the gates of the people" God-ward, and Satan evidently reasoned that now the way toward God is broken by reason of the falling down of God's people during the World War. Then Satan would and did say, "Aha, she is broken . . . ; I shall be replenished now she is laid waste." This would also be the language of that part of Satan's organization here specifically pictured.

The World War was really a contest for the control of the commerce of the earth. The seventh world power was perfectly willing and even glad that divine truth, which is the way of the people to God, should be cast down and trodden under foot just so she was not impeded in her efforts to win the World War and to control the great commerce of the seas of the earth.

It would be natural, then, for this world power, seeing God's people go down and herself winning, to say, as it is put by another translator: "I shall be made full, now she is laid in ruins." (26:2) "Now the commerce of nations will be turned to me." (*Margin, Rashi*) Satan would and did rejoice when God's people were in distress in 1918 because these had impeded his progress in getting everything on earth for himself. Many heard the Word of God and believed it but were overcome by the deceitfulness of the riches of commerce: "He also that received seed among the thorns, is he that heareth the word; and the care of this world, and the deceitfulness of riches, choke the word, and he becometh unfruitful."—Matt. 13:22.

But now when the World War came Satan and his chief instruments in the commerce of the sea observed the faithful witnesses of Jehovah go down and become apparently dead, they would reason, Now we shall have the whole thing to ourselves and without opposition. This was too much for the weak faith of some of those who professed to be God's people and they turned aside from following after the Lord; but not so with the true ones. Jehovah God will supply the necessities of his faithful people, and those who are devoted to him will not be overreached by the commercial or rich influence of the world.

The big men of the seventh world power who control the commerce of the seas are doubtless the proudest that have lived on the earth. They are really rulers or princes of the seventh world power and together with their allies at land control the politics or politicians who are the more tangible rulers. These princes are really Devil worshipers, because they worship things such as money power and their own bellies, and they consult with the wicked angels and by this means are in communication with the Devil and are directed by him. God declares himself against them, which means both ancient and modern Tyre, and he so writes his judgment in these words: "Therefore thus saith the Lord God, Behold, I am against thee, O Tyrus, and will cause many nations to come up against thee, as the sea causeth his waves to come up. And they shall destroy the walls of Tyrus, and break down her towers; I will also scrape her dust from her, and make her like the top of a rock. It shall be a place for the spreading of nets in the midst of the sea: for I have spoken it, saith the Lord God; and it shall become a spoil to the nations. And her daughters which are in the field shall be slain by the sword; and they shall know that I am the Lord."—26:3-6.

NEBUCHADNEZZAR

No man could be a type of Christ Jesus, the King of kings, unless that man was fully devoted to Jehovah God. A man, although not devoted to God, might be used as an illustration of God's manner of accomplishing his purposes. Nebuchadnezzar the king of Babylon destroyed Jerusalem. He was the head of the world power of Babylon. He was a representative of Satan, the god of this world, and, being the chief one in the world, he was therefore the king of kings. He was an illustration of the mighty One whom Jehovah will use for his destructive work against Satan's organization; therefore he illustrated or pictured Christ Jesus, who at the end of the period of waiting becomes the universal ruler of the world and whose right it is to rule, and who therefore is the King of kings. (Ps. 110:1,2) Prior to that time Christ Jesus had no kingdom although he was anointed as King. Satan had offered to give him the kingdoms of this world, and thus Satan was recognized by the Lord as ruling the world. Jehovah now takes away from Satan the right to rule the world and gives it to Christ, and this is according to the rule announced by the Lord.—Matt. 25:29; see *Light,* Book Two, page 321.

Jehovah therefore used Nebuchadnezzar as an illustration of his power that would be exercised against Satan's organization. Nebuchadnezzar destroyed Jerusalem and then laid siege to Tyre, and thus he illustrated the fact that Jehovah will first destroy "Christendom" and then all of Satan's organization, and that he will do so by the King of kings, Christ Jesus. Jehovah caused Ezekiel to prophesy against ancient Tyre, and which prophecy applies to modern Tyre, in the following language: "For thus saith the Lord God, Behold, I will bring upon Tyrus Nebuchadrezzar king of Babylon, a king of kings, from the north, with horses, and with chariots, and with horsemen, and companies, and much people. He shall slay with the sword thy daughters in the field; and he shall make a fort against thee, and cast a mount against thee, and lift up the buckler against thee. And he shall set engines of war against thy walls, and with his axes he shall break down thy towers. By reason of the abundance of his horses their dust shall cover thee; thy walls shall shake at the noise of the horsemen, and of the wheels, and of the chariots, when he shall enter into thy gates, as men enter into a city wherein is made a breach. With the hoofs of his horses shall he tread down all thy streets: he shall slay thy people by the sword, and thy strong garrisons shall go down to the ground. And they shall make a spoil of thy riches, and make a prey of thy merchandise; and they shall break down thy walls, and destroy thy pleasant houses: and they shall lay thy stones, and thy timber, and thy dust, in the midst of the water.''—26:7-12.

History states that Nebuchadnezzar besieged Tyre for thirteen years but did not succeed in reducing it as described in the foregoing words of the prophet. Later Alexander assaulted it and in seven months captured the city. This would indicate that the prophecy was not completely fulfilled in the day of Nebuchadnezzar, but must be completely fulfilled 'in that day which the Lord has made'; and must be fulfilled upon that great organization, which Tyre represented. The fulfilment of the prophecy, therefore, must be the great act of Jehovah by and through Christ Jesus in destroying this and other parts of Satan's organization. The antitypical city or organization must suffer complete destruction, because Jehovah by his prophet further says: "And I will cause the noise of thy songs to cease; and the sound of thy harps shall be no more heard. And I will make thee like the top of a rock; thou shalt be a place to spread nets upon; thou shalt be built no more; for I the Lord have spoken it, saith the Lord God.''—26:13, 14.

Jesus visited Tyre in his day, thus showing that the city existed then. (Matt. 15:21) In this present century it has about 6,500 inhabitants. This shows that the complete fulfilment of the prophecy setting forth the judgment written against antitypical Tyre must be fulfilled against the organization pictured by ancient Tyre and fulfilled in ''the last days''. Therefore that must mean the complete destruction of the seventh world power, particularly with reference to the maritime Big Business, which has dominated and ruled commerce, and which shall be built no more after Armageddon. However, it shall be more tolerable for the men of Big Business after the fall and during times of restitution than it will be for those ecclesiastical hypocrites of modern Jerusalem.—Matt. 11: 21, 22.

''Thus saith the Lord God to Tyrus, Shall not the isles shake at the sound of thy fall, when the wounded cry, when the slaughter is made in the midst of thee?'' (26: 15) ''The isles'' here mentioned seem clearly to represent the small maritime-mercantile or commercial dealers in the seventh world power having favorable treaties and relationships with the giants or Big Business crowd. At the fall of the latter the isles or smaller ones shall also be shaken. The exalted leaders and magnates or commercial giants are referred to as ''princes'' whose policy is to exploit the seas of humanity and concerning which the prophet of God says: ''Then all the princes of the sea shall come down from their thrones, and lay away their robes, and put off their broidered garments; they shall clothe themselves with trembling; they shall sit upon the ground, and shall tremble at every moment, and be astonished at thee. And they shall take up a lamentation for thee, and say to thee, How art thou destroyed that wast inhabited of seafaring men, the renowned city, which wast strong in the sea, she and her inhabitants,

which cause their terror to be on all that haunt it!"
—26:16, 17.

Britain, the head and seat of the seventh world
power, has refused to recognize the freedom of the
seas. Her navy is a shield and protector of her big
commerce and has been and is a terror to all who
have sought to do or to carry on business in great
waters. The merchant marine of the seventh world
power has made possible its Big Business, both at sea
and on land. Tyre, however, more particularly represents Big Business that has operated by means of
the waterways, but the relationship is close to that
of commerce that is carried on at land. The prophecy of Ezekiel, however, treats the two from two different viewpoints.

Jehovah God will make a clean-up of that which
has brought a curse upon mankind, and only the glory
of the Lord will remain to fill the earth. The commerce of the seas, as well as of the land, has been made
a curse to mankind and has been a means of glorify-
ing men, but God's judgment is written against it
and it shall not rise the second time. "For thus saith
the Lord God, When I shall make thee a desolate city,
like the cities that are not inhabited; when I shall
bring up the deep upon thee, and great waters shall
cover thee; when I shall bring thee down with them
that descend into the pit, with the people of old time,
and shall set thee in the low parts of the earth, in
places desolate of old, with them that go down to the
pit, that thou be not inhabited; and I shall set glory
in the land of the living." (26:19, 20) "For the day
of the Lord of hosts shall be upon every one that is
proud and lofty, and upon every one that is lifted

up, and he shall be brought low; . . . and upon all
the ships of Tarshish, and upon all pleasant pictures.
And the loftiness of man shall be bowed down, and
the haughtiness of men shall be made low: and the
Lord alone shall be exalted in that day." (Isa.
2: 12-17) The God of battle will make a complete
wreck of oppressive commercialism, which has been
a terror to humankind, and concerning which the
prophet says: "I will make thee a terror, and thou
shalt be no more; though thou be sought for, yet shalt
thou never be found again, saith the Lord God."—
26: 21.

In the time of the resurrection, when men who have
been adherents of Big Business, and who have operated the same, are brought forth they will be surprised
to learn that commerce for the purpose of exploiting
the people will never again exist. That fact will be
a great consolation to those who have been exploited
and gouged and oppressed by Big Business. "And
Tyrus did build herself a strong hold, and heaped up
silver as the dust, and fine gold as the mire of the
streets. Behold, the Lord will cast her out, and he
will smite her power in the sea; and she shall be
devoured with fire."—Zech. 9: 3, 4.

Christ Jesus, the great King of kings, will destroy
this oppressive agent of the Devil and will deliver
the needy. "The kings of Tarshish and of the isles
shall bring presents; the kings of Sheba and Seba shall
offer gifts. Yea, all kings shall fall down before him;
all nations shall serve him. For he shall deliver the
needy when he crieth; the poor also, and him that
hath no helper." (Ps. 72: 10-12) During the time of
restitution Satan will be dead. His organization will

also be destroyed. Satan shall never build another organization. During restitution men who have had to do with Big Business, the Scriptures seem to indicate, will seek to know how they might again carry out their schemes. Concerning this, according to another rendering of the text, the Lord says: "An unsubstantial thing will I make thee, and thou shalt pass away." "Suddenly will I annihilate thee, but thou shalt never be found any more."—26:21, *Leeser*, marginal reading.

This applies both to Satan and the maritime Big Business that he has organized and carried on to oppress the people. It is only those who have willfully sinned against the light of God's kingdom that will not be resurrected until the end of the thousand-year reign and suffer complete destruction with the Devil. Those who have been dupes of the Devil, and have sinned ignorantly concerning God's kingdom, will have an opportunity during the thousand-year reign of Christ.

STRATEGIC POSITION
(EZEKIEL, CHAPTER 27)

The twenty-seventh chapter of Ezekiel's prophecy continues against Tyrus or Tyre. The seventh world power, to wit, Britannic-American empire, and particularly the mercantile commerce of the seas, has held a strategic position among and power over the peoples of the nations in all commercial transactions, and this world power has made the most of it. Foreknowing this Jehovah caused Ezekiel to take up a lamentation against Tyre, but which applies particularly against the product of the Devil, to wit, the seventh world power: "And say unto Tyrus, O thou that art situate at the entry of the sea, which art a merchant of the people for many isles, Thus saith the Lord God, O Tyrus, thou hast said, I am of perfect beauty." (27:3) According to another translator the language is: "I am the perfection of beauty!" (*Roth.*) Although within the borders of the land fraudulently called "Christendom" the Big Business crowd that has controlled the seas make gold their god, strut about arrogantly, and greatly admire themselves. Jehovah has caused to be written of his own organization: "Out of Zion, the perfection of beauty, God hath shined."—Ps. 50:2.

Modern Tyre disputes this and, at the instance of the Devil, says: "I am the perfection of beauty." So great is the vanity and self-admiration of the maritime Big Business of Britain and America that those in control have constituted themselves the dictators of what the people shall hear and even think about, and they carefully exclude the message of truth concerning God and his kingdom. The radio is the God-given channel for the instruction of the people in matters of interest and convenience. In Britain Big Business controls the radio and absolutely refuses to permit even a word to be broadcast by Jehovah's witnesses concerning his kingdom. Big Business absolutely controls the radio messages by sea or from ship to shore, and shore to ship, or internationally. In the United States wing of the seventh world power the same element controls all the choice radio frequencies or channels and refuses to use any of these, or to permit their facilities to be used, for broadcasting the message of God's kingdom. No message is welcome or acceptable to these vain princes that informs the people truthfully as to what is the cause of the world distress or how it can be remedied. Although these dictators must know that man has no adequate remedy for the terrible conditions existing amongst the nations, yet Jehovah God's Word of truth concerning the same is excluded from the people by them as far as it is possible, and the exclusion is put upon the ground that it might offend some others. The real purpose, however, is to prevent the people from hearing and therefore from being informed concerning Satan, that he is the god of this world, and that the maritime power is one of the strong instruments he uses against the interests of the people. The people are learning that the advertising of Big Business as the sole stay and help for the people is purely a propaganda scheme and is intended for the gullible public to swallow that they might be kept quiet while Big Business continues to rifle the pockets of the people.

The prophet, continuing to address both ancient and modern Tyre, with words of sarcasm says: "Thy borders are in the midst of the seas, thy builders have perfected thy beauty." (27:4) Commerce claims that its rightful field of exploitation is the people; that it has all the rights, and that this right is represented in the power it possesses and that "the public be damned".

The seventh world power not only denies the freedom of the seas, but in the language of its father Satan it says: 'These waters are mine, and I have made them for myself.' The master builder of modern Tyre is, of course, the Devil himself, and in this work there have been employed the most efficient and expert men, such as planners and builders, and these are the ones that it is claimed have "perfected thy beauty". Today this same Big Business or commercial power not only controls the ships and commerce of the waterways, but has engaged and employed and controls the keenest financial experts, the most brilliant lawyers and technical men that the world produces, for the purpose of carrying out her selfish schemes. She has spared nothing in her efforts to perfect the organization. All just and rightful privileges of the home, family and country are disregarded and even human life counts for nothing when these would prevent the carrying out of the selfish and devilish schemes to exploit the people to the profit of the few.

Furthermore the prophet, concerning this devilish organization, by verses five to seven continues to describe the divers means employed by these instruments of Satan to make his organization to appear beautiful, that it might dazzle and confound the peoples of the earth.

Zidon preceded Tyre as the master of the seas and then gave way to the latter. "The inhabitants of Zidon and Arvad were thy mariners: thy wise men, O Tyrus, that were in thee, were thy pilots. The ancients of Gebal, and the wise men thereof, were in thee thy calkers: all the ships of the sea with their mariners were in thee to occupy thy merchandise." (27: 8, 9) Arvad is an island near Zidon which was also Canaan territory. (Gen. 10: 15, 18) The Canaanites under the curse of the Lord became the "rowers" (*Roth.*) of the ships of Tyre. Likewise those under the curse of sin, and under the control of their master the Devil, have been compelled to push and row the ships of Big Business, the Devil's organization, both at land and at sea. Those who are in God's kingdom and wholly devoted to it refuse to pull or boost for any part of Satan's organization.

In the world a man is considered wise if he is able to "put over" some big scheme. "Thy wise men, O Tyrus, that were in thee, were thy pilots." These worldly-wise men now monopolize and control and manage the commerce of the earth, and hence are the pilots thereof, and exploit the whole business upon the people. These wise men are on the boards of directors, and see to it that things in their organizations are done according to their selfish wishes; but even in the present day, because of distress, many of them are turning black in the face.

Ancient Tyre had her rough sea work done by foreigners. Likewise the pilots of modern Tyre have their rough and dirty work done by hirelings while the pilots themselves hold themselves aloof as the very pink of beauty and as the preservers of the business interests of the world. Many of these workers in modern Tyre now recognize that they are foreigners and no longer free but that they are held where they are because with them it is to "do what you are told to do or starve".

It is thrilling in this day to observe that Jehovah long ago foreknew and foretold the present oppressive conditions existing in the world by reason of the operation of Satan and his tools in modern Tyre. The fact that these things are now coming to light is proof that we are now in the day of deliverance and therefore in a time to feed upon truths that the Lord is giving us and to rejoice.

In the ninth verse of this prophecy above quoted Gebal is mentioned. Gebal means "hilly, mountain, border", and refers to the sharp-sighted, far-seeing ones of the commercial part of Satan's organization. The wise men thereof are not novices, but are experienced, astute, far-seeing and shrewd. These are employed as calkers (that is, preventers of leaks) to keep Satan's commercial ships afloat. Business panics, business depression, slack trade, and such like, must not be permitted if they can avoid it. To that end great holding companies have been organized, giant mergers accomplished, that a few might control almost everything. Special legislation has been enacted, public officers are influenced and even wars are produced, in order to keep the old ship of commerce afloat. These "wise men" have thought to completely control the business of the world by sea and by land, but even now they are becoming very much frightened at what they see coming upon the world.

"They of Persia, and of Lud, and of Phut, were in thine army, thy men of war: they hanged the shield and helmet in thee; they set forth thy comeliness [splendour, *Roth.*]." (27:10) Ancient Tyre hired soldiers from other countries to protect her ships from pirates and other marauders. The great wealth resulting from her commerce enabled Tyre to hire outsiders to do her fighting. The controllers of commerce, which we commonly call Big Business and, to wit, modern Tyre, have not put their cultured and rich sons to the front to fight the battles amongst the nations and peoples, or in the navies and the armies, to do the rough work, but they have sent the men and boys of the people from the common walks of life to fill the trenches and to man the battleships and to shed their blood. The rich favored ones have stayed behind the lines to help work out the schemes to reap big profits and to get rich quick. The military and the navy are really the arm of force for Big Business but are camouflaged as the defenders of the nations. The fact is that the common people of no nation on earth would force a war between nations. These wars are always forced by the selfish interests of those who control the commerce. There would never be a war if it were left to the rank and file of the common people.

What has made the seventh world power appear so strong and beautiful in the eyes of all the peoples of the earth? The prophet answers: "The men of Arvad, with thine army, were upon thy walls round about, and the Gammadims [valorous, *Roth.*] were in thy towers: they hanged their shields upon thy walls round about; they have made thy beauty perfect." (27:11) The navies, the marine corps, and the supporting armies have been required to keep the things looking rosy or beautiful for the big commercial interests of the seventh world power operated at sea and upon land. By reason of the navy and the army and the marine corps the seventh world power has dominated the sea and kept the people helpless and in subjection while the experts of Big Business have gone through their pockets and have extracted whatsoever was found there.

Ancient Tyre had a profitable business or commercial connection with all parts of Satan's mighty empire, that is to say, with all the nations of the world. It did not handle things of the Lord by trying to carry his message to the ends of the earth for the glory of God. Likewise modern Tyre, the seventh world power, has had profitable or commercial or business relationships with the entire human race and has dominated the business of the world. These use the so-called "Christian religion" as a camouflage, sending missionaries along with their fleets into all parts of the earth, and backing these up with the guns and bayonets of the navy and the army, and by this means Big Business or commerce has been enabled to accomplish many of her selfish purposes. The Devil has thus made a powerful instrument out of this part of his organization. The seventh world power has given herself over to the traffic of this world which says: 'What shall we eat or drink, or wherewith shall we be clothed?'

Verses twelve to twenty-five of the twenty-seventh chapter describe the marine or commercial marts of the three great branches of the human race with which ancient Tyre had dealings and therefore picture modern Tyre, which likewise has commercial relationships with the entire world. Verses twelve to fifteen inclusive describe particularly the Japhetic, that is to say, the European race. (Gen. 10:2-5) Verses eighteen to twenty-one describe the Shemites. In the nineteenth verse Dan is mentioned, but this is not Dan of the tribe of Dan, but "Vedan" (*R.V.*), or "Wedan" (*Roth.*). Verses twenty-two and twenty-three describe the Hamitic.—Gen. 10:6, 7.

It is noted that Judah and the land of Israel had commercial intercourse with Tyre, and doubtless from Tyre the Jews learned how to cheat their fellow man. This may also picture how some of God's covenant people permit themselves to be choked by the weeds and thorns of the cares of this world, and the deceitfulness of riches, and who therefore resort to improper commercial schemes to gain such ends.—Matt. 13: 22.

It is not wrong for God's people to engage in an honest and just barter where the rules are observed that were laid down by Jesus, but anyone who engages in commerce and willingly takes advantage of opportunities to cheat others could not be pleasing to the Lord. Some of the consecrated in modern times have been drawn into deals with Big Business for pecuniary interest, which is always unprofitable spiritually to those who are seeking the Lord's approval. To be sure, God's people must come in contact with Big Business for the bare necessities of life; otherwise they must "go out of the world", as the apostle suggests. (1 Cor. 5: 9, 10) Those, however, who are truly devoted to God, and who are children of his woman Zion, are seeking the things of the kingdom, and God according to his promise adds things that are necessary for their existence.

Big Business has by means of hire and also by coercion induced many men to do menial service and to be pushers and pullers or rowers of their schemes. These pushers or pullers or rowers have brought Big Business into deep waters, and the next step will be the breaking up of the oppressive crowd. "Thy rowers have brought thee into great waters: the east wind hath broken thee in the midst of the seas."—27: 26.

Big Business has gained control of big preachers, big lawyers, big doctors, and big engineers, and all of the various machinery of the governments, all of which are resisting and opposing earth's rightful King, Christ Jesus, the Stone which Jehovah God has laid in Zion. Big Business attempts to prevent the message of the kingdom from being published by the radio and by the public press. This wing of the Devil's organization continues to heap injustice upon those who serve God and those who try to do right. "Ye have lived in pleasure on the earth, and been wanton; ye have nourished your hearts, as in a day of slaughter. Ye have condemned and killed the just; and he doth not resist you."—Jas. 5:5, 6.

"ACT OF GOD"

The "east wind" that breaks Tyre in the midst must refer to the power of Christ, the King from the sun rising, to whom is given all power in heaven and in earth. "Thou breakest the ships of Tarshish with an east wind. As we have heard, so have we seen in the city of the Lord of hosts, in the city of our God; God will establish it for ever." (Ps. 48:7, 8) Such breaking is "an act of God", that is to say, the divine visitation of Jehovah God upon this part of Satan's organization and which Big Business cannot successfully resist. Jehovah has commanded his King to proceed to the breaking-up work, and the commercial wing of Satan's organization is in for her share in due time. "They that go down to the sea in ships, that do business in great waters; these see the works of the Lord, and his wonders in the deep. For he commandeth, and raiseth the stormy wind, which lifteth up the waves thereof. They mount up to the heaven, they go down again to the depths; their soul is melted because of trouble." (Ps. 107:23-26) "He stretched out his hand over the sea; he shook the kingdoms; the Lord hath given a commandment against the mer-

ROWERS BROUGHT THEE INTO GREAT WATERS Page 71

chant city, to destroy the strong holds thereof.'' (Isa. 23:11) The nations composing the seventh world power have been the places for the chief operation of the commercial wing of Satan's organization, and these are in for their part of a complete drubbing.

The doom of every part of Satan's organization is written, and there is no escape for Big Business. ''Thy riches, and thy fairs, thy merchandise, thy mariners, and thy pilots, thy calkers, and the occupiers of thy merchandise, and all thy men of war, that are in thee, and in all thy company which is in the midst of thee, shall fall into the midst of the seas in the day of thy ruin.'' (27:27) Those who have been used by the Devil to build this mighty machine of oppression must, by the power of Jehovah exercised against them and the organization, be brought to know that Jehovah is God. He has power and resources vast and deep like unto the sea, and which will engulf the entire organization of Big Business and its military and naval equipment, and make it disappear from the sight of heaven and earth, even as the Egyptians were engulfed in the Red sea. ''And a mighty angel took up a stone like a great millstone, and cast it into the sea, saying, Thus with violence shall that great city Babylon be thrown down, and shall be found no more at all.'' (Rev. 18:21) And then the wicked organization shall completely fall. (Ezek. 27:34) The sea, or ''depths of the waters'', in this text pictures Jehovah's power under the lash of the ''east wind'', The Christ dashing to pieces the enemy organization.

Fear has now taken hold of the mighty men of this wicked organization, but the worst is yet to come. Verses twenty-nine to thirty-one inclusive describe the

distress of those who have put their trust in riches,
making gold their god, and who therefore have worshiped this part of the Devil religion. These have
looked upon the commerce of the seventh world power
as that which could not be broken, but they shall see
that mighty organization go down. "And in their
wailing they shall take up a lamentation for thee, and
lament over thee, saying, What city is like Tyrus,
like the destroyed in the midst of the sea?" (27:32)
This conclusion is further supported by the following texts: Ezekiel 26:15-17; Revelation 18:17-19.
Every part of Satan's organization shall be destroyed,
and these texts specifically refer to the commercial
division thereof. All shall drink of the wrath of God.
"And all the kings of Tyrus, and all the kings of
Zidon, and the kings of the isles which are beyond the
sea."—Jer. 25:22.

The prophetic picture here given is for the special
benefit and instruction of God's faithful covenant people. Those who love God now will stay clear of Big
Business and devote themselves exclusively to the
kingdom and will do "this one thing". Some who
heard the call to the kingdom committed the fatal
error of going after wealth and riches and were
'drowned in the sea'. "But they that will be rich, fall
into temptation, and a snare, and into many foolish
and hurtful lusts, which drown men in destruction
and perdition. For the love of money is the root of
all evil; which while some coveted after, they have
erred from the faith, and pierced themselves through
with many sorrows. But thou, O man of God, flee
these things [of Tyre]; and follow after righteousness,
godliness, faith, love, patience, meekness." (1 Tim.

6:9-11) Those who have made a covenant with the Lord, and who have then become negligent thereof and become entangled with Big Business, will have more cause for weeping and wailing than the worldly merchants. Not only will they lose their earthly possessions, but they will lose their hope of life everlasting.—Rev. 20:13.

It appears strange to many that a man poor in this world's goods who enters politics and is elected to a public office and receives a reasonable salary, as fixed by law for his services, yet, in spite of all this, within a few years is a man of great material wealth. What is the reason? Big Business provides the wealth for such in consideration of special services in behalf of their selfish and oppressive schemes. Men in public office who render these services are described as "kings", that is to say, the earthly visible rulers of Satan's organization, and concerning which the Lord says: "When thy wares went forth out of the seas, thou filledst many people; thou didst enrich the kings of the earth with the multitude of thy riches and of thy merchandise." (27:33) For this reason public office has become a private grab and office-holders are corrupted by the ill-got gains of the commercial wing of Satan's wicked organization operated on sea and on land.

Today the small mercantile shippers who take note are astounded at the grip hold Big Business has on every thing. The small trader has attempted to carry on a legitimate business separate from and independent of the big giants, but the mighty ones who control the commerce have almost completely crushed the life out of all small traders. Foreseeing this great

act of injustice practiced by a few, the Lord caused
Ezekiel to write: "All the inhabitants of the isles
shall be astonished at thee, and their kings shall be
sore afraid, they shall be troubled in their counte-
nance. The merchants among the people shall hiss at
thee; thou shalt be a terror, and never shalt be any
more." (27:35, 36) But the day of these giant commercial oppressors is about at an end, and their big
machines, together with all other parts of Satan's organization, shall go down; and then the people, small
dealers and others will hiss contemptuously at the
bare mention of these commercial giants, and never
again will God permit such pernicious things to trouble the peoples of earth.

During the World War God's earthly organization
was made "desolate" and a perpetual hissing at the
instance of the clergymen, and Big Business, represented by Tyre, stood by and concerning God's faithful company said: 'Aha, she is broken and will trouble
us no more.' For this wickedness Jehovah in due time
will recompense Tyre with some of her own medicine.
"Yea, and what have ye to do with me, O Tyre, and
Zidon, and all the coasts of Palestine? will ye render
me a recompence? and if ye recompense me, swiftly
and speedily will I return your recompence upon your
own head: because ye have taken my silver and my
gold, and have carried into your temples my goodly
pleasant things: the children also of Judah and the
children of Jerusalem have ye sold unto the Grecians,
that ye might remove them far from their border.
Behold, I will raise them out of the place whither ye
have sold them, and will return your recompence upon
your own head: and I will sell your sons and your

daughters into the hand of the children of Judah, and
they shall sell them to the Sabeans, to a people far
off: for the Lord hath spoken it." (Joel 3:4-8) God
will vindicate his name and his organization.

God has provided the things of the earth for the
benefit of obedient mankind. Therefore not only is
the day of relief for the people coming, but the time
when the product of the earth, which Big Business
has used to exploit the people to enrich themselves,
God will take away from them and give to the people
that obey and serve him, that they may with these
natural resources glorify the name of the great Creator who has made them. Then shall be fulfilled the
words of the prophecy: "And her [Tyre's] merchandise and her hire shall be holiness to the Lord: it
shall not be treasured nor laid up; for her merchandise shall be for them that dwell before the Lord, to
eat sufficiently, and for durable clothing."–Isa. 23:18.

LEADERS OF TYRE
(Ezekiel, Chapter 28)

Then the prophet of God addresses the leaders or
rulers of the commercial division of Satan's organization. "Son of man, say unto the prince of Tyrus,
Thus saith the Lord God, Because thine heart is lifted
up, and thou hast said, I am a God, I sit in the seat
of God, in the midst of the seas; yet thou art a man,
and not God, though thou set thine heart as the heart
of God." (28:2) The word here rendered "prince"
is the same as that in Daniel 9:25 rendered in "Messiah the Prince". It refers to one that stands boldly
out to the front and makes announcement of the public policies of the people, therefore the leader. The

prince of Tyre is clearly distinguished in this chapter
from the king of Tyre, and therefore the prince seems
to clearly picture or have reference to the visible
ruling factors or dictators of the policies of Satan's
commercial system of the world and who are hence
spokesmen on earth for Satan in this division of his
organization. These mighty ones control the big newspapers, the colleges, the universities of various kinds,
including the theological, technical, medical and law
schools; they control the greater part of the radio
facilities and other means of communicating to the
people, the purpose being to prevent anything's being
carried to the people that might reflect upon Big
Business.

This crowd is proud and haughty, and of them
the prophet says: "Thine heart is lifted up." They
are a self-admiring, self-important, dominating and
arrogant class, and because of their riches consider themselves gods, and they therefore assume that
position amongst the people. The great banking giants
that control the commerce of the seas and the land,
and who operate within the borders of the seventh
world power today, assume this very attitude. These
mighty men are set forth as models for the youth of
the land, particularly for those young men who spend
their early days in the colleges and universities where
they are taught to learn everything that is anti-God
and anti-kingdom. These strong men of commerce
and finance are idolized by the younger and weaker
elements among them. Their own selfishness is their
god and they believe that "money is power". They
heap it up regardless of the amount of suffering which
this entails upon the common people. These men as-

sume the positions of gods and claim themselves to
be benefactors of the world, and they demand respect
and veneration and claim that they are justly entitled to rule and to dictate the policy of the nations.

As an example of this, recently a newspaper reporter attempted to have an interview with one of
these big financial bosses at a railway station in the
city of London, where he had just arrived, and that
self-appointed god denounced the poor reporter because he had the audacity to even speak to him. But
let the people take note that the prosperity of these
visible agents of Satan draws near to an end, when
God's indignation shall be openly expressed against
them. The Lord by his prophet tells this self-
admiring crowd who claim to be gods: "Thou art
a man, and not God." This strongly proves that
the "prince of Tyrus" refers to the visible representatives of Satan's organization who by reason of their
wealth dictate the policy of the nations of earth, and
particularly by and through the seventh world power.
At Armageddon these will come to fully realize the
meaning of the statement: "Thou art a man, and not
God." "Arise, O Lord; let not man prevail; let the
heathen be judged in thy sight. Put them in fear, O
Lord; that the nations may know themselves to be but
men." (Ps. 9: 19, 20) "Neither their silver nor their
gold shall be able to deliver them in the day of the
Lord's wrath; but the whole land shall be devoured
by the fire of his jealousy: for he shall make even a
speedy riddance of all them that dwell in the land."
—Zeph. 1: 18.

These cold-blooded, conscienceless, commercial representatives of Satan think themselves wiser than all

other men, and even deny the very existence of the
prophets, such as the Prophet Daniel; therefore the
Lord in derision says to them: "Behold, thou art wiser
than Daniel; there is no secret that they can hide from
thee." (28:3) Daniel gave all credit to Jehovah God
for the deep and secret things about which he spoke.
(Dan. 2:22) The "wise men" of Satan's commercial
organization, and who are wise therefore in their own
conceits, regard themselves as incomparably greater
than the prophets of Jehovah. They are past masters
at manipulating schemes and making secret agree-
ments and in detective operations, which they call
secret service, and which is used to oppress the peoples in humble walk. They are exceedingly wise in
making deals, compromising, and in giving bribes and
corrupting public officials, and in operating secret
and subtle schemes to obtain control of patents and
inventions, and of laboratories and research work, and
financing the same for their own selfish aggrandizement. They scour the seas and scrape the land to
obtain control of the commerce and the markets, of
the mineral deposits, power sites and power plants,
and every thing of whatsoever kind that might be
used to produce material wealth. They are of the
opinion that no secret, even of Jehovah God, is hidden
from them, because they deny God and think themselves to hold all the secrets of the world.

With the cunning and sagacity of their father Satan these mighty men have greatly enriched themselves, and because they have been able to do so they
lift up their own eyes and in the eyes of their under-
studies they are great. The Lord says to them: "With
thy wisdom and with thine understanding thou hast

gotten thee riches, and hast gotten gold and silver into thy treasures: by thy great wisdom, and by thy traffic, hast thou increased thy riches, and thine heart is lifted up because of thy riches." (28:4, 5) These words of the prophet are exactly in harmony with the utterances of James the apostle. (5:1-6) These men, the visible representatives of Satan, the commercial wing of his organization, rely upon the power of their wealth, "and they say, How doth God know? and is there knowledge in the Most High? Behold, these are the ungodly, who prosper in the world; they increase in riches." (Ps. 73:11, 12) They depend upon their power and their riches to make the earth a suitable place for man and that they have the ability thus to robe the earth with their own glory and beauty. But the Lord says: "They that trust in their wealth, and boast themselves in the multitude of their riches; none of them can by any means redeem his brother, nor give to God a ransom for him. For he seeth that wise men die, likewise the fool and the brutish person perish, and leave their wealth to others." (Ps. 49:6, 7, 10) "He that trusteth in his riches shall fall."—Prov. 11:28.

The Lord then tells these representatives of Satan why they must go down: "Therefore thus saith the Lord God, Because thou hast set thine heart as the heart of God; behold, therefore, I will bring strangers upon thee, the terrible of the nations; and they shall draw their swords against the beauty of thy wisdom, and they shall defile thy brightness. They shall bring thee down to the pit, and thou shalt die the deaths of them that are slain in the midst of the seas." (28:6-8) With reference to ancient Tyre the 'strangers of the terrible nations' were Nebuchadnezzar and his armies; and thus is illustrated the Lord's means of performing his "strange act", which will strike terror to the heart of the prince of Satan's commercial organization that rules and dominates the people. The mighty princes of Tyre will die like those of a storm-wrecked ship at sea. The wide distribution of the booklet *The Kingdom, The Hope of the World*, amongst these financial giants is notice of what they may expect to come to pass, but they will not take heed to it.

Jehovah says to the proud and arrogant: "Wilt thou yet say before him that slayeth thee, I am God? but thou shalt be a man, and no God, in the hand of him that slayeth thee." (28:9) The braggadocio of the "prince of Tyre", Big Business and leaders, will come to naught and these will fall before the assault of the King of kings, who is Jehovah's Executive Officer, and who at Jehovah's command does these terrible things: "Gird thy sword upon thy thigh, O most Mighty, with thy glory and thy majesty. And in thy majesty ride prosperously because of truth and meekness and righteousness; and thy right hand shall teach thee terrible things." (Ps. 45:3, 4) Jehovah will rise, as he says, and shake terribly the earth, that is, the organization of Satan that is visible to man, and the power of that wicked organization will cease. "In that day a man shall cast his idols of silver, and his idols of gold, which they made each one for himself to worship, to the moles, and to the bats; to go into the clefts of the rocks, and into the tops of the ragged rocks, for fear of the Lord, and for the glory of his majesty, when he ariseth to shake terribly the earth. Cease ye from man, whose breath is in his

nostrils." (Isa. 2:20-22) "But the Lord is with
me as a mighty terrible one; therefore my persecutors shall stumble, and they shall not prevail;
they shall be greatly ashamed; for they shall not
prosper; their everlasting confusion shall never be
forgotten." (Jer. 20:11) In that terrible day their
riches will avail them nothing: "Riches profit not in
the day of wrath; but righteousness delivereth from
death." (Prov. 11:4) These proud ones have spurned
the words of wisdom recorded in God's Book, the Bible, and have relied upon their own wisdom and the
strength of their own organization. They have not
given any heed to the advice: "Be not rash with thy
mouth, and let not thine heart be hasty to utter any
thing before God; for God is in heaven, and thou upon
earth: therefore let thy words be few." (Eccl. 5:2)
"God is not a man, . . . neither the son of man . . . :
hath he said, and shall he not do it?"—Num. 23:19.

Jehovah is now sending forth his witnesses to bear
testimony of warning to those branches of Satan's
organization. These witnesses need expect no comfort
from such now; nor when they appear before them,
shall they fear or tremble, and surely they should not
assume an apologetic attitude when presenting to them
the message of truth. Those who trust in the Lord
will be calm, firm, and speak the truth in kindness.
Therefore Jehovah says to his witnesses that when
they come in contact with the princes of modern Tyre
"I, even I, am he that comforteth you; who art thou,
that thou shouldest be afraid of a man that shall die,
and of the son of man which shall be made as grass;
and forgettest the Lord thy maker, that hath stretched
forth the heavens, and laid the foundations of the

earth; and hast feared continually every day because of the fury of the oppressor, as if he were ready to destroy? and where is the fury of the oppressor?" —Isa. 51: 12, 13.

These princes of modern Tyre, to wit, leaders in Britain and America's sea commerce or Big Business, hold themselves forth as the honorable men of the earth to whom the common people should bow down and beg their favor; but the days of their arrogance draw near to an end, because the Lord says to them, "I am against thee, O Tyrus." (26:3) "Who hath taken this counsel against Tyre, the crowning city [the bestower of crowns, *Roth.*], whose merchants are princes, whose traffickers are the honourable of the earth? The Lord of hosts hath purposed it, to stain the pride of all glory, and to bring into contempt all the honourable of the earth. He stretched out his hand over the sea; he shook the kingdoms: the Lord hath given a commandment against the merchant city, to destroy the strong holds thereof. Howl, ye ships of Tarshish; for your strength is laid waste."—Isa. 23: 8, 9, 11, 14.

Jehovah's decree is written and cannot be reversed. "Thou shalt die the deaths of the uncircumcised by the hand of strangers; for I have spoken it, saith the Lord God." (28:10) "Thus saith the Lord, For three transgressions of Tyrus, and for four, I will not turn away the punishment thereof; because they delivered up the whole captivity to Edom, and remembered not the brotherly covenant: but I will send a fire on the wall of Tyrus, which shall devour the palaces thereof."—Amos 1: 9, 10.

Whomsoever of God's people the princes of modern
Tyre captured they delivered up. Modern Tyre and
her princes shall die the death of the unclean. (Gen.
17: 11, 13) These have lived wantonly and luxurious-
ly in utter disregard of the rights of other men. They
have trafficked in human flesh and blood for their own
selfish gain and have taken away from their hired
laborers that which was justly due the babies of the
poor. They have burned the property of the poor,
destroyed their food, persecuted and oppressed men
and women of good will who dared render aid and
comfort to the poor and their children. The coal
operators of West Virginia and Kentucky and other
places are glaring examples of such cruelty. They
have carried on their wicked operations within the
borders of the land called "Christendom", and mis-
labeled "the land of the free and the home of the
brave". These princes of Tyre have marked America
with the inscription: "The land of the thieves and the
home of the slaves." They disregard the Word of
the Lord and his warning message brought to them
by his witnesses, and their end draweth nigh.

THE DEVIL

The master and chief ruler carrying on all the
wickedness upon the earth is the Devil himself. The
princes of Tyre are merely his tools and visible representatives. At the command of Jehovah Ezekiel
speaks concerning the Devil: "Son of man, take up a
lamentation upon the king of Tyrus, and say unto
him, Thus saith the Lord God, Thou sealest up the
sum, full of wisdom, and perfect in beauty." (28: 12)
He is superior to the 'princes of Tyrus', therefore

the invisible ruler and god of the world. (John 12:31; 16:8, 11) Jehovah is the King of His organization. (Jer. 10:10) The mimic god Satan is the king or god of his organization. (2 Cor. 4:4) It has been said by the ecclesiastical commentators that the language of Ezekiel here used refers to the man Hiram, who was king of Tyre, because he made a league with Solomon and manned his ships. (1 Ki. 9:11-14, 26-28) But this conclusion could not be correct, because God could not say to Hiram: "Thou sealest up the sum, full of wisdom, and perfect in beauty." These words are certainly addressed to the invisible ruler of Tyre, that is, Satan the Devil, and refers to the time when he was created and when his name was Lucifer. He was the glorious work of Jehovah God by and through Jehovah's Son the Logos. It is likely that Lucifer was the first creative work of Jehovah, by his Son, in the creation of creatures, and was the final word or seal in the realm of proportions and beauty and showed forth the wisdom of God's creative power and not the wisdom of Lucifer. Jehovah therefore says to him: "Thou hast been in Eden the garden of God; every precious stone was thy covering, the sardius, topaz, and the diamond, the beryl, the onyx, and the jasper, the sapphire, the emerald, and the carbuncle, and gold: the workmanship of thy tabrets and of thy pipes was prepared in thee in the day that thou wast created."—28:13.

Modern commentators limit the application of this text to the king of the ancient city of Tyre. The words of description do apply to ancient Tyre, but that is not the limit of the application. Under Hiram Tyre attained unto its greatest glory. It appears that the dominion of this king extended over the west slopes of Mount Lebanon, famous for its great cedar trees. In Ezekiel 31: 3 it is recorded: "Behold, the Assyrian was a cedar in Lebanon . . . , and of an high stature; and his top was among the thick boughs." In verses eight and nine of the same chapter these cedars are spoken of as being in the garden of God, in the garden of Eden. The broader application of these texts, however, is to the real garden of Eden, the garden of God. (Gen. 2: 8) It is not necessary to conclude that Lucifer was bodily in Eden, but that his attention was there to things of Eden because Jehovah had appointed him to that position and to exercise power there. The statement of his being in Eden is to be understood as a favorable and beautifying background or setting for Lucifer. Eden manifestly was in the jurisdiction of Lucifer to which Jehovah God had assigned him.

The precious stones mentioned in the thirteenth verse were doubtless available to the king of Tyre, because the merchants of Sheba and Raamah exhibited in the fairs and doubtless offered for sale "all precious stones". (27: 22) It must be presumed that the king of Tyre arrayed himself with these precious stones that his beauty might be enhanced and that the people might behold his glory. These precious stones would cause him to appear in a blaze of multicolored light. The Scriptures do not say that God covered Lucifer with such precious stones, and in view of his subsequent actions we may well presume that the precious stones as applied to Lucifer are really descriptive of his original pride. He gave attention to his personal appearance as a means of adding to his brilliancy, and thus he began to develop vanity, which led him to desire the worship of creatures.

Men who are children of the Devil have frequently done this very thing, and it is natural for the sons to follow the example of the father. Kings and high dignitaries in the church organizations, such as the pope of Rome, bishops, cardinals and others, employ precious stones and deck themselves therewith for the purpose of enhancing their outward beauty and therefore that they might influence others to give them honor and worship.

According to *Rotherham* this language is used: "And of gold was the work of thy timbrels and thy flutes within thee." The tabret or timbrel was used by the Israelites to praise Jehovah. "And Miriam the prophetess, the sister of Aaron, took a timbrel in her hand; and all the women went out after her with timbrels and with dances." (Ex. 15: 20) "Praise him with the timbrel and dance; praise him with stringed instruments and organs." (Ps. 150: 4) It thus appears that Lucifer was outfitted or fully equipped with the means of praising the Lord, and he should have employed these means to that end. He was without doubt one of the "morning stars" that did praise the Creator on one occasion. (Job 38: 7) These musical instruments or means of praise to the Lord are spoken of as an ornament. "Again I will build thee, and thou shalt be built, O virgin of Israel: thou shalt again be adorned with thy tabrets [*margin*, timbrels], and shalt go forth in the dances of them that make merry." (Jer. 31: 4) The Hebrew word for "tabret" is *toph*. Instead of using the timbrel or tabret (*toph*) to give praise to Jehovah his Creator, Lucifer employed it to prepare *Tophet* for the worship of himself, the mimic, and therefore the false, god. He inveigled the Jews to thus practice the Devil religion. "And they have built the high places of Tophet, which is in the valley of the son of Hinnom, to burn their sons and their daughters in the fire; which I commanded them not, neither came it into my heart."—Jer. 7:31.

"Pipes," used in the foregoing text, denotes something pierced, and may refer either to instruments or to perforated gems. In either event Lucifer used the "pipes" with which he was supplied to pierce, curse and blaspheme Jehovah God, instead of giving praise to him. (Lev. 24:11; Num. 23:8, 25) Jehovah equipped Lucifer for useful service. "In the day thou wast created were they prepared." (*Roth.*) Thus equipped, Lucifer perverted the use of his equipment and used the same to dishonor God's name.

ANOINTED CHERUB

That Lucifer was an officer in God's organization is shown by the following verse: "Thou art the anointed cherub that covereth; and I have set thee so: thou wast upon the holy mountain of God; thou hast walked up and down in the midst of the stones of fire." (28:14) Other translators render the first part of this verse thus: "Thou wast a cherub with outspread covering (wings)." (*Leeser*) "Thou wast the anointed cherub that covered." (*Roth.;* also *R.V.*) This statement of God's Word shows that the prophecy here given is applicable to that which is far higher than the visible, earthly king of ancient Tyre, and, therefore, that its application properly is to the invisible ruler Satan the Devil.

Translators differ as to the meaning of the name "cherub"; but according to the meaning of the term, as used in the Scriptures, cherub or cherubs are ministers of God's appointment to guard and keep and maintain the justice and judgment of Jehovah. Cherubims were placed on guard to keep the way of the tree of life in Eden. (Gen. 3: 24) Cherubims with wings covered the mercy seat of the ark of the covenant. (Ex. 37: 9) Probably the term applies both to the office and to the creature in that office appointed by Jehovah and assigned to the sacred duties of the office. Jehovah is said to dwell among the cherubims. (Ps. 99: 1) The Hebrew word literally means cherubim, and it is reasonable to conclude that in the beginning Lucifer was the only cherub having to do with the garden of Eden, and that he was charged with covering or guarding "the tree of life also in the midst of the garden", in order that man might not partake thereof until God's due time. When Lucifer became a traitor he would no longer keep the way covered, or guard the way to the tree of life, but evidently he advised Adam and Eve to go and eat of that tree. The eviction of man from Eden immediately followed, and Jehovah placed faithful officers on guard to keep the way and to close up access by man to the tree of life. It is certain that if Lucifer had continued to cover that way, and to duly perform his official duties, there would have been no necessity for Jehovah to appoint other officers to perform that duty.

Lucifer was appointed to his office by Jehovah, and concerning this the Scriptures are quite clear: "When I appointed thee in the holy mount of God." (*Roth.*) "I set thee, so that thou wast upon the holy mountain of God." (*R.V.*) The statement here made could not possibly have reference to the fact that Hiram the king of Tyre furnished cedar timber for the building of the temple on the holy mount Moriah at Jerusalem. It must mean that Jehovah God had extended his universal kingdom or organization to include the earth with his creatures Adam and Eve upon it and had given Lucifer the office of cherub to cover or look after God's interests on the earth. Jehovah assigned him to this distinctive position. His official position permitted Lucifer to have access to God in his heavenly courts. (Job 2: 1, 2) Had Lucifer been grateful for his position he would have covered it faithfully. His ingratitude for favors received is proof of his selfishness, and ingratitude for such favors always opens the way to disaster.

The walking of Lucifer up and down in the midst of the stones of fire, as stated in the fourteenth verse, must mean more than merely walking about amid a fiery blaze of precious stones. He could communicate with other spirit creatures who were glorious as blazing stones, and he could walk amidst these, and he did induce many of such spirit creatures to join him in his rebellion. God's chosen people on the earth, and anointed in Christ, are designated as "living stones". Satan has walked up and down in the earth amidst these people of God and has used his power to interfere with them and to cause them to fall while undergoing fiery tests or purging, and he has succeeded in causing many to deflect and fall away. He has appeared as an angel of light amongst them. God says to him, "I will destroy thee, O covering cherub, from the midst of the stones of fire," meaning that he may no more have access to these stones of fire, or creatures of light.

Continuing to address the king of Tyrus God's prophet says: "Thou wast perfect in thy ways from the day that thou wast created, till iniquity was found in thee." (28:15) These words could not possibly apply to Hiram or to any other earthly king, because no one of such was ever perfect. Adam was the only perfect man on the earth, and he was never a king. Jehovah God created Lucifer, and God's work is perfect. "[Jehovah] is the [great] Rock, his work is perfect; for all his ways are judgment: a God of truth and without iniquity, just and right is he." (Deut. 32:4) "As for God, his way is perfect." (Ps. 18:30) It is therefore certain that at the time of his creation Lucifer was perfect, and he was bound to be in harmony with God at the beginning; thus he continued 'perfect until [unrighteousness, *R.V.*; wickedness, *Leeser*; perversity, *Roth.*] was found in thee'. Becoming selfish and ambitious he corrupted his moral existence and the purpose for which he was created. He distorted the truth about the creation of God and caused man to fall away from Jehovah's favor and to be put to death. "He was a murderer from the beginning, and abode not in the truth." (John 8:44) That does not mean from the beginning of Lucifer, but from man's beginning, because it was man that he murdered. The perversity of Lucifer began after he was assigned to his official position by Jehovah.

Lucifer began the commercial enterprise of the earth, and this is proven by the words: "By the multitude of thy merchandise they have filled the midst

of thee with violence, and thou hast sinned: therefore
I will cast thee as profane out of the mountain of God:
and I will destroy thee, O covering cherub, from the
midst of the stones of fire.'' (28:16) He yielded to
the willful desire to make merchandise of man. He
foresaw a vast earthly sea of humanity which would
flow from this perfect man and perfect woman. He
determined that he would begin at the fountain head
and exploit that sea of humanity. When the human
race had increased to multitudes like unto the sea,
then the Devil out of the symbolic sea brought forth
the beastly thing of his own creation, and which thing
or organization he has used to oppress and kill mankind. He began by resorting to violence, and his
ambitious desire has filled his beastly organization
with great violence. He incited Cain to commit murder by violence. He filled the earth with violence that
prevailed in Noah's day. Satan, therefore, is the
creator of the wicked system of commerce that oppresses humankind, and he has practiced this from
the beginning of man. Therefore the great marine-
commercial kingdom of Tyre fitly pictures that part
of the wicked organization of Satan, and which is
manifested specifically in the seventh world power,
and which is extended over the earth, and which has
exploited and oppressed the human race. Nothing
could more fitly picture the mighty commerce that
controls the affairs of earth. As ancient Tyre extended
her commerce to the ends of the earth, so modern
Tyre has extended her commerce to the utmost parts
of the earth, and which commercial operations by sea
have been marked and continue to be marked with
great violence. It has been the mighty navies of the

countries composing the seventh world power in particular that have controlled the commerce of the seas for such world powers.

The pursuit of great wealth by means of commercial enterprise is always accompanied by great violence, selfishness, pride and ambition, and the men or giants of commerce permit nothing to stand in the way of accomplishment of their desired ends. The commerce by sea and land has been the most effective part of Satan's organization for exploiting and oppressing the peoples of earth. The fact that Jehovah has given so much attention thereto in his Word is proof of its power for wrongdoing and its operation in the way of wickedness. Concerning these selfish men who have operated in the earth as Satan's tools the Lord says: "Therefore pride compasseth them about as a chain; violence covereth them as a garment. Their eyes stand out with fatness: they have more than heart could wish. They are corrupt, and speak wickedly concerning oppression: they speak loftily. They set their mouth against the heavens; and their tongue walketh through the earth. Behold, these are the ungodly, who prosper in the world; they increase in riches." (Ps. 73: 6-9, 12) Such is a description of the mighty men who have controlled the commerce of the seas. "For the rich men thereof are full of violence, and the inhabitants thereof have spoken lies, and their tongue is deceitful in their mouth." (Mic. 6: 12) These mighty and rich men are generally put in a place of prominence in the church organizations of the seventh world power, and are designated "the principal of the flock", but they have no faith in God nor in his Word. It was the

ANOINTED CHERUB—Commercial Iniquity Begins   Page 95

spirit of violence that stirred up Tyre to say "Aha" when Jerusalem was by violence overthrown. It was the same spirit of violence and wickedness that caused the mighty and the rich and their tools to say "Aha" when God's people were by violence thrown down by the seventh world power in 1914 to 1918. To these commercial giants in and about "Christendom" Jehovah's witnesses must now testify.

CAST OUT

Lucifer sinned against light; therefore he committed the unpardonable sin, and for such there is no forgiveness or pardon; hence God said to him: "Thou hast sinned; therefore I will cast thee as profane out of the mountain of God." That sin brought great reproach upon the name of Jehovah. Satan has since used religion and the commercial wing of his organization in particular to bring reproach and violence upon the people of God.

God then announces his purpose concerning Satan, saying: "I will cast thee as profane out of the mountain of God." The more literal rendering is: "I profaned thee out of the mountain of God." (*Roth.*, margin) Lucifer profaned the name of God and the name of Christ; and he has profaned God's sanctuary class by using the seventh world power to cast it down to the ground and to tread it under foot, which was done during the period of the World War. Jehovah now deals with Satan as the profaned thing, and likewise he deals with those who knowingly and willingly resort to Satan's methods of profaning the name of God. No more is Satan permitted to continue in heaven even to make reports, but he is cast out of heaven because he is a defiled and a defiling thing. Satan has now set up his astonishing abomination on the earth in the holy place, to wit, the League of his nations. He still appears to keep ground space, but soon both Satan and his organization shall go into the abyss. To him God says: "I will destroy thee . . . from the midst of the stones of fire." Jehovah therefore becomes an Abaddon or destroyer unto Satan. (Rev. 9: 11; see *Light*, Book One, page 145) This means the end of Satan in heaven and no longer shall his rod rest upon the lot of the righteous people of God on the earth and soon he shall be killed. (Ps. 125: 3) Notice must be served on his representatives.

Regardless of all the advantageous things with which a creature is endowed, if he does not fear God and serve him he is certain to come to a bad end. This is proven by the course Lucifer took. "Thine heart was lifted up because of thy beauty; thou hast corrupted thy wisdom by reason of thy brightness; I will cast thee to the ground, I will lay thee before kings, that they may behold thee." (28: 17) Without a doubt Lucifer was originally a creature of beauty. But God did not make him "perfect in beauty" to cause him to fall. Lucifer should have appreciated the fact that all he possessed was a gift from Jehovah God and he should have given God the credit and honor therefor. The proper rule for the creature is stated in these words: "I will praise thee; for I am fearfully and wonderfully made: marvellous are thy works: and that my soul knoweth right well."—Ps. 139: 14.

Men have made the same grave mistake at all times by attempting to search out and exhibit their own glory and beauty to others. "For men to search [out] their own glory is not glory." (Prov. 25:27) When one revels in his own beauty and his own attainments he is deceiving himself. For one to seek to shine as beautiful in the eyes of others is a dangerous course for him. Says the Proverb (31:30): "Favour is deceitful, and beauty is vain." The only safe course is for one to give glory to God for whatever he has and to fear him and to serve him with gladness of heart. Lucifer sought his own glory and therefore he is doomed to a disastrous end. The same must be true of every creature who seeks his own glory. Jesus told his disciples that the exaltation of creatures is an abomination in God's sight; and manifestly the reason is that such is the course that Satan took and has induced other creatures to take. (Luke 16:15) Paul warned those of the early church of the same danger, but many who claimed to be followers of Christ have ignored the warning. In this day, when the light of truth from God's temple is shining upon his people, there is absolutely no excuse to give praise and exaltation to men. To seek praise for oneself or to willingly receive praise from others for one's own attainments and one's beauty, is dangerous and will lead to disaster, if persisted in. Lucifer was proud because of his beauty and thereby corrupted himself. He ceased from the fear of God which is the beginning of wisdom and which course the wise always pursue. His wisdom possessed in the beginning he corrupted, and turned it to cunning subterfuge, conscienceless diplomacy, and to artfully hiding darkness in his heart but outwardly appearing with brightness.

The diplomacy of the seventh world power exceeds that of all other peoples that ever lived on the earth, and it came through Satan's coaching. Diplomacy is another name for fraud and deceit. Honesty must be had and practiced by the creature that pleases God. Lucifer should have appreciated that fact and given God the glory, but he glorified himself. Men have followed in his course from the beginning of time till now, but Jehovah's witnesses will now put into actual practice the truism long ago written, to "learn . . . not to think of men above that which is written, that no one of you be puffed up for one against another. For who maketh thee to differ from another? and what hast thou that thou didst not receive? Now if thou didst receive it, why dost thou glory, as if thou hadst not received it?"—1 Cor. 4: 6, 7.

Because of his pride and self-glory God says to Lucifer: "I will cast thee to the ground." According to another translator: "Upon the earth did I cast thee, before kings did I set thee, that they might look at thee." (*Roth.*) This statement is exactly in harmony with that of Revelation that the Devil 'was cast out of heaven onto the earth', and thus he is humiliated to the ground. The "kings" here mentioned are the kings who shall be with Christ Jesus in his kingdom. (Rev. 1: 6) God is now setting the Devil before the remnant by opening the eyes of their understanding to the hideousness of this creature the Devil and giving to them a vision of his wicked organization. Now they behold Satan as the king of Tyre who has organized the great commercial system of the sea, as well as of the land, and by which he has exploited the people and which he has used in conjunction with the hypocritical and fraudulent religious systems within said land.

It must be humiliating to the Devil now to be exposed to the gaze and contempt of those whom he has abused and falsely accused and whom he would now immediately destroy except for the protection provided them by Jehovah God. The kings of earth do not now recognize that Satan rules the world, and Satan hates Jehovah's witnesses who are now calling the attention of the rulers and of the people to the fact that Satan is the wicked and invisible ruler of the world, and that his destruction approaches. Those of the remnant who remain on earth during Armageddon will see the complete humiliation of Satan and the men of the earth who are the rulers under the direction of Satan. These rulers will also see the humiliation of Satan, because God has decreed that they shall know that Jehovah is God, and that he will humiliate the wicked one in the eyes of all.

Lucifer was created perfect and made a part of God's organization, even as Adam was made perfect and was a part of God's organization which is clean and pure. Jehovah further pronounced his denunciation against Satan the wicked one in these words: "Thou hast defiled thy sanctuaries by the multitude of thine iniquities, by the iniquity of thy traffic: therefore will I bring forth a fire from the midst of thee, it shall devour thee; and I will bring thee to ashes upon the earth, in the sight of all them that behold thee." (28:18) Other renderings of the text illuminate it somewhat. "In the unrighteousness of thy traffic thou hast profaned thy sanctuaries." (*R.V.*)

"In the perversity of thy traffic thou didst profane thy sanctuaries." (*Roth.*) "Through the wickedness of thy commerce didst thou profane thy sanctuaries." —*Leeser*.

The basic thought of "sanctuary" is 'to be clean'. In Psalm 68:35 it is written: "O God, thou art terrible out of thy holy places [sanctuary, *Roth.*]." It represents the place where the creature does worship to the Creator God. He must worship in purity and in cleanness. Originally Lucifer was assigned to a place that was clean, pure and holy, and there it was his privilege and duty to render worship to Jehovah God. When he was assigned to give attention to the garden of Eden as the covering cherub that sphere of office became one of Lucifer's sanctuaries, in which he was duty-bound to worship God in purity and in holiness to the Lord. There Lucifer became profane; and for the selfish purpose of trafficking in the human family, exploiting and making merchandise of mankind, he defiled his sacred office and trust, which he held by appointment from Jehovah, and that particular part of God's organization was profaned and defiled by Lucifer. That holy sanctuary, where thought should have been given to the honest, pure and holy things unto God, and where Jehovah alone should have been worshiped, Lucifer turned into a place of merchandise for his own selfish purposes. Satan has ever directed his dupes along the same unrighteous lines. He has established many religions and has captured "organized Christianity", and his religious services are marked by the same merchandising spirit, and these have defiled God's earthly sanctuary. It was so with the Jews, and for this reason Jesus said to them that had turned the temple into a place of merchandise: "Take these things hence; make not my Father's house an house of merchandise." (John 2: 14-16) "And [he] said unto them, It is written, My house shall be called the house of prayer; but ye have made it a den of thieves." (Matt. 21: 13) The church of "Christendom", where God should be worshiped in holiness, is turned into a house of merchandise, and the giants of big commerce boss the proceedings; and the worship is carried on in a formal way, that these may not be offended.

Satan's course leads him to destruction; hence God in his decree says: 'I will bring fire from the midst of thee, and it shall devour thee.' This fire pictures a spontaneous combustion, a self-bursting into flames, hence the course of a suicide, and which course Satan has taken since he began his wicked work. The Devil is as sulphur or pitch, and the Lord will apply the heat and cause that wicked one Satan to burst into flames of destruction, as it is written: "And the streams thereof shall be turned into pitch, and the dust thereof into brimstone, and the land thereof shall become burning pitch."—Isa. 34: 9, 10.

Jehovah by his beloved King has ousted Satan from heaven and has cast him down to the earth and thus He causes Satan to be filled with burning rage and therefore he 'hath great wrath and a short time'. (Rev. 12: 12) The words "to ashes upon the earth" picture the destruction of Satan which takes place after he is cast out of heaven. Both Satan and his wicked organization shall suffer destruction. "And ye shall tread down the wicked; for they shall be ashes under the soles of your feet in the day that I shall do this, saith the Lord of hosts." (Mal. 4:3) Satan is responsible for his own destruction, but God destroys him.

The killing of Satan and the destroying of his organization will be one of the means of teaching other creatures that Jehovah is the supreme and only true and almighty God. "All they that know thee among the people shall be astonished at thee; thou shalt be a terror, and never shalt thou be any more." (28:19) For many centuries Satan has been a terrifying creature. He has used his preachers of hell-fire and brimstone to terrify many and to cause them to seek refuge in the hypocritical organization of "churchianity" and to join in defaming God's name. He has used his commercial agents to terrify men and compel them to yield to all manner of oppression. The men of earth today are afraid to oppose his wicked commercial organized power. The terrible destruction that shall come upon Satan and his organization will give astonishment to the peoples of earth and will inspire fear in all who come to know God, so that they will shudder even at the thought of the course Satan has taken and of his disastrous end. Those creatures that have willingly pursued a like course of Satan after having received some light and learned that Jehovah is God shall likewise be destroyed. Concerning Satan and his followers it is written: "And they shall be an abhorring unto all flesh [that shall be given life upon the earth]."—Isa. 66:24.

Religion has ever been the chief means by which Satan has deceived the people and caused them to blaspheme God's holy name. Commerce or merchandise is the chief means employed by Satan whereby

the people are oppressed and devoured. By religion
he has exhibited his serpentine qualities, and by his
merchandise or commerce he has more fully exhibited
the qualities symbolized by the dragon or devourer.
Within the borders of the seventh world power Satan
has worked with much success his fraudulent and de-
ceptive religious schemes. Within the seventh world
power Satan has builded the greatest commercial machine of all time, and which has brought the greatest
amount of sorrow to the people, and the greatest
amount of reproach to Jehovah God's name. Within
the borders of the seventh world power crime has
abounded as nowhere else under the sun. Violence
and wickedness within these borders has gone to seed.

Jehovah God, knowing the end from the beginning,
used Jerusalem to foreshadow ''Christendom'' and
Tyre to foreshadow the commercial division of Satan's mighty organization, and more specifically that
part of the commercial organization that operates upon the seas. With oppressive Big Business at an end
there would be no more inducement for wars, hence
no more reason for the building of mighty navies.
With false religion destroyed the people will turn to
the worship of the true God. Let the people now take
courage and rejoice that Satan and his entire organization soon shall perish and God will then bless all
who love and serve him in spirit and in truth. Let
all the people of good will, and who desire righteousness, now take their stand on the side of Jehovah God
and get in line for the blessings that God has in store
for them. Let them learn now to measure up to the
requirements which the Lord has prescribed for those
whom he will approve.—Mic. 6: 8.

AGAINST ZIDON

Jehovah does not disclose all of Satan's organization in one picture. He shows it to his people from different viewpoints, which enables those who love him to discern the hideous thing that has so long defamed the name of Almighty God. While there are three general divisions of Satan's organization, to wit, religious, commercial and political, there are subdivisions of these which show the minute workings of Satan's wicked machine.

The commercial giants are the men behind the screens whom Satan employs to carry forward his dark and powerful schemes, while religionists act as the hypocritical smoke-screen by which the people are blinded to the truth, and the politicians talk long and loud making many false pretenses and promises as to what shall be done for the people and thus to hold the people in line. The mighty mind of Satan the Devil directs the entire machine. God's day has come to show up the whole wicked organization, that the people may know the truth and that the name of Jehovah God may be vindicated. Manifestly this is the reason why Jehovah exhibits this hideous organization in detail and from many viewpoints.

The prophet of God now directs his prophecy against Zidon. "Son of man, set thy face against Zidon, and prophesy against it, and say, Thus saith the Lord God; Behold, I am against thee, O Zidon; and I will be glorified in the midst of thee; and they shall know that I am the Lord, when I shall have executed judgments in her, and shall be sanctified in her." (28: 21, 22) Zidon was an older city than Tyre, but Tyre surpassed it in importance; and this is indicated by the lesser mention of it in the Scriptures. It was doubtless at one time a great city, since Joshua calls it "great Zidon". (Josh. 11:8) The inhabitants practiced the Devil religion under the form of Baal or Ashtoreth worship. (1 Ki. 11:5,33) Zidon furnished mariners for its neighbor city Tyre. (Ezek. 27:8) Zidon means "fortress". (*Young*) Another author also says the name is from the Hebrew word meaning "to lie alongside, that is to say, to watch, to catch in the sense of catching fish". Another author (Gesenius) says the word means "fishing or fisheries".

Zidon therefore seems to picture or represent a special division of Satan's organization that is a tool or ally of the commercial part of that organization operating particularly by sea and also exploiting the people. It represents a tool or ally that fishes for those who will bite at their bait and come into the nets or traps set for them. The description therefore fits the advertising agencies or tools of commerce. It is a propaganda organization that lays nets and sets baited hooks with beards on them for the unsuspecting. Therefore it must represent the publishing agencies, the newspapers and magazines, and in these more modern days the radio, which commerce or Big Business seeks to control and uses almost exclusively to advertise its commercial schemes. The newspapers, magazines, or radio stations that do not want to yield to the dictates of Big Business can scarcely survive. The broadcasting of the truth concerning Big Business is inimical to its interests, and only the Lord can make it possible for the truth to reach the people by means of radio. These various means of communicating to the people Satan desperately attempts to control for his organization. The public press is especially used, always in an effort to mold public opinion to suit the side of the commercial powers.

Jehovah has declared that the message of truth shall reach into Zidon, and hence unto that which Zidon represents. (Jer. 25: 15, 22) ''For I will send into her pestilence, and blood into her streets; and the wounded shall be judged in the midst of her by the sword upon her on every side; and they shall know that I am the Lord.''—28: 23.

The public press would have furnished a splendid channel for the publication of the truth of and concerning Jehovah and his kingdom, but the Big Business heads, aided and abetted by other wings of the Devil's organization, to wit, the clergy and conscienceless politicians, have kept the message of truth out of the papers and out of the magazines. The public press makes various excuses, saying that this publication is not news or this might offend some big preachers. Radio stations make the same excuse, although the law governing the same declares that they shall be used for public convenience, public interest and public necessity. Nothing could be more convenient or upbuilding to the people than the truth. Satan desperately attempts to keep this away from the people. God therefore declares against this wing of the Devil's organization: ''Behold me! against thee, O Zidon, therefore will I get myself glory in thy midst.'' —28: 22, *Roth*.

The glory which Jehovah will get will be his righteous victory over this powerful instrument in the wicked organization of Satan. When Jehovah's judgments are executed against Satan's organization, Big Business will no longer be able to hide from the people the fact that Jehovah is the only true God and that his kingdom is the one and only hope for the world. They will no longer be able to use the public press to blind the people to their own unrighteous schemes. When the Lord says, "I will send into her pestilence, and blood into her streets," this would mean death to the powerful ally of Big Business, so that no longer could the truth be kept back from the people. The Lord God is now proceeding with the publication of his message of truth, which shows that his pestilence is already upon Zidon. God's purpose is that those who handle the public press, as well as others, shall know that he is the Almighty One.

Satan, by the various divisions of his organization, attempts to prevent the people from knowing that Jehovah is God, but he is now "reckoning without his host". "And there shall be no more a pricking brier unto the house of Israel, nor any grieving thorn of all that are round about them, that despised them; and they shall know that I am the Lord God."— 28: 24.

The Zidonians and other Canaanites in Palestine were left there as a test to God's covenant people "to prove Israel by them, to know whether they would hearken unto the commandments of the Lord, which he commanded their fathers by the hand of Moses". (Judg. 3: 1-4) Likewise God has permitted his covenant people in these days to be in the midst of the enemy organization, yet not a part of it, and many who have made a covenant to do the will of God have failed to prove their love and devotion to Jehovah but have hearkened and yielded to the enemy because of selfish fear that they might lose some earthly favor. Big Business and its subsidized press has certainly "despised" God's faithful people and caused God's kingdom, which they represent, to be misrepresented and reproached. Like briers and thorns, the press has scratched, pricked and pierced the Lord's true people when it would have been much easier for the press to state the truth. These giants of the enemy have followed the same course as that of Satan and have resorted to lies.

But the arm of the Lord Jehovah is not shortened. He has organized his people and sent them forth as his witnesses. He has provided them with printing machines and factories for the publication of the message in the form of books and magazines and other papers, and he has employed the radio as another means of informing the people of the truth. Jehovah's witnesses are now formed into a service organization and go to the homes of the people and tell them the truth, and thus the Lord is getting the message to the people and that to his own honor. Jehovah's witnesses go forward regardless of the pricks and scratches that are inflicted upon them by the various instruments of Satan. The public press, owned or subsidized by Big Business, has refused to learn from the present proclamation of the truth that Jehovah is God; hence God declares his purpose to compel them to know his power and his justice and of his destructive acts.

"THE HOLY LAND"

It has been thought that Jehovah is speaking concerning the Jews in Palestine when he says: "Thus saith the Lord God, When I shall have gathered the house of Israel from the people among whom they are scattered, and shall be sanctified in them in the sight of the heathen, then shall they dwell in their land that I have given to my servant Jacob." (28:25) This is not the correct conclusion. The Jews that are now gathered to Palestine are not there to the glory of God, because they are gathered in unbelief and they do not believe or serve God. The reference in this last-quoted scripture is to God's anointed remnant.

Jacob especially foreshadowed the remnant of the Lord. These God has taken out from the Gentile powers as a people for his name and has gathered them unto Zion, his own organization. This is now being done "in the [very] sight of the heathen"; because God's remnant are neither keeping out of sight nor keeping their mouths closed, but they are constantly proclaiming the name and the praise of the Most High. Jehovah is now sanctified in them in that he has called them into his active service and they extol his name and declare his mighty works. The faithful remnant do now 'dwell in their land given to Jacob', because they are God's "servant" class, and are now dwelling in the condition pictured by 'the land shadowed with wings' of Jehovah. (Isa. 18:1, 2) The birthright has been taken from Esau and given to this "servant" class, and they are God's servants. They are therefore "in the holy land" or condition rather than in the literal land of Palestine, which is now under the control of the seventh world power. It is therefore certain that this verse applies to God's chosen people now upon the earth.

Further speaking of the security and prosperity of his favored "servant" class the Lord says: "And they shall dwell safely therein, and shall build houses, and plant vineyards; yea, they shall dwell with confidence, when I have executed judgments upon all those that despise them round about them; and they shall know that I am the Lord their God." (28:26) This is a figurative expression showing how God's remnant people are now safely placed in God's organization. There they dwell in the house of the Lord and abide in the true vine, Christ Jesus, and bring forth the fruit of the kingdom, and partake of the wine of joyful proclamation of the kingdom of God and of his Christ. When the Lord has thus brought his people into this favored position this is evidence that the fall of Satan's organization is near at hand.

Every part of Satan's organization despises God's remnant, even as Moab, Ammon, Edom, Philistia, Tyre and Zidon hated Israel. Since 1919 Jehovah's judgments are being declared against the despisers of his people and of his kingdom. God has gathered his anointed ones into their "home land", that is to say, into God's organization, in order that they might be secure while delivering the message of his kingdom and serving notice upon the enemy nations. This message of the Lord is being declared by men and women, and hence the mighty satanic organization refuses to believe it even though the Lord has declared: "Beware, therefore, lest that come upon you, which is spoken of in the prophets; Behold, ye despisers, and wonder, and perish: for I work a work in your days, a work which ye shall in no wise believe, though a man declare it unto you.'' (Acts 13:40, 41; Isa. 29:14; Hab. 1:5) Even after Armageddon some of the remnant may be used for the further fulfilment of this prophecy. Even now God's remnant people know that they dwell in security in his organization, and they know that his promised blessings to them are sure and true. This is a vindication of God's name now in the eyes of these faithful ones, and they know now that they are the servants of Jehovah, the true and only God. They will, by his grace, continue to make known the message of Jehovah and his kingdom regardless of the opposition by the Zidonians.

AGAINST EGYPT
(Ezekiel, Chapter 29)

Jehovah's great opposer is Satan. For centuries he has pitted himself against Jehovah God and boasted of his ability to thwart God's purposes. Before destroying him Jehovah makes a show of Satan, that is to say, he exhibits to his people Satan and his organization from various viewpoints, and when the enemy goes down all will know that Jehovah is the Almighty God; and this is the chief reason for the giving of the testimony and for the battle of Armageddon. Just one year and two days after Nebuchadnezzar laid siege to Jerusalem, and Ezekiel's dumbness toward Jerusalem began, Jehovah directed his prophet to further speak against the enemy: ''In the tenth year, in the tenth month, in the twelfth day of the month, the word of the Lord came unto me, saying, Son of man, set thy face against Pharaoh king of Egypt, and prophesy against him, and against all Egypt: speak,

and say, Thus saith the Lord God, Behold, I am against thee, Pharaoh king of Egypt, the great dragon that lieth in the midst of his rivers, which hath said, My river is mine own, and I have made it for myself.''
—29: 1-3.

This is a prophecy against the Devil and his organization. ''Pharaoh,'' meaning ''shepherd'', refers to Satan who shepherds his own organization and for his own selfish purposes. The Hebrew word for Egypt is *Mizraim*, meaning ''the encloser or embanker of the sea'' and user of the same for traffic. (See *Prophecy*, page 139; *The Watchtower*, 1929, pages 206, 279.) Satan has banked up the ''sea'' or humanity and turned it into channels for the carrying on of his wicked and oppressive merchandise or commercial schemes. The third verse above quoted refers to Satan as ''the great dragon''. Both *Leeser* and *Rotherham* render the Hebrew word as ''crocodile''. Such is a great water monster with scales, and a mouth having strong jaws, and it also has feet. (32: 2) Pharaoh king of Egypt, which stands for or represents Satan the Devil, claims the river for his own. The river here claimed is the stream of human creatures. Satan concludes that because mankind is turned to sin now the human race belongs to him, and that God has no proper claim on the race. Although man enclosed the sea with dikes, and turned the waters of the Nile into certain channels, yet neither man nor Satan made the waters of the Nile, nor the rain nor the springs that feed the headwaters thereof. Satan did not create the human race, nor can he give life to any one thereof. He merely turned the stream of humanity aside from following toward God; and he concludes that because

I WILL BRING THEE OUT OF THY RIVERS   Page 119

he turned them from God they are his. Satan has made the human race what it now is both mentally and morally, and he is the god of this wicked world. Jehovah now informs his covenant people of his purpose concerning Satan and directs them to make these facts known to all others in and about Jerusalem who will hear, and therefore he says by his prophet: "But I will put hooks in thy jaws, and I will cause the fish of thy rivers to stick unto thy scales; and I will bring thee up out of the midst of thy rivers, and all the fish of thy rivers shall stick unto thy scales."— 29: 4.

The "hooks" [Hebrew, *chach*] mentioned in the foregoing verse are the kind used on captives or to capture animals and by which those when caught are led or compelled to follow. "Because thy rage against me, and thy tumult, is come up into mine ears, therefore will I put my hook in thy nose, and my bridle in thy lips, and I will turn thee back by the way by which thou camest." (Isa. 37: 29; see also Ezek. 38: 4) The same Hebrew word *chach* is also rendered "chains": "The nations also heard of him; he was taken in their pit, and they brought him with chains [*chach*] unto the land of Egypt. And they put him in ward in chains, and brought him to the king of Babylon; they brought him into holds, that his voice should no more be heard upon the mountains of Israel." (19: 4, 9) These hooks correspond with the "great chain" with which Christ Jesus binds the Devil.—Rev. 20: 1-3.

"I will cause the fish of thy rivers to stick unto thy scales," says the Lord. Members of the "beast" and "false prophet" system, that is to say, members

of Satan's organization, are here the fish that stick
to the Devil: "even Pharaoh, and all them that trust
in him." (Jer. 46:25) For selfish reasons these fish
line up on Satan's side and in his organization and
they trust in Satan's power. The giant Goliath, who
is a picture of Satan, was covered with a coat of
mail (Hebrew, scales) which corresponds to the scales
of the old dragon, Satan. (1 Sam. 17:5) Satan's coat
of mail, or scales, will furnish no protection for him
against the assault of Jehovah's mighty Executive
Officer whom David foreshadowed when he smote Goliath. The Lord will bring Satan out of the rivers, in
this, that he will destroy his control of the people and
cause him to cease his operations amongst the people.
(Rev. 20:2) "The fish of thy rivers," meaning the
official members of his organization, will go to Satan;
but the rest of the people who take their stand on the
side of the Lord will no longer 'lie under the wicked
one'. (1 John 5:19) Those who take their stand on the
side of Jehovah will flow unto the mountain of the
house of the Lord.—Isa. 2:2, 3.

God declares his purpose to humiliate Satan to the
very dust. "And I will leave thee thrown into the
wilderness, thee and all the fish of thy rivers; thou
shalt fall upon the open fields; thou shalt not be
brought together, nor gathered: I have given thee for
meat to the beasts of the field and to the fowls of the
heaven." (29:5) Satan and his organization must be
and will be dragged out into the open and put to a
violent death and made food for the carrions of the
open field. The Devil has for a long time kept his
identity a secret from most people and has used the
so-called "Christian Scientists" to this end, and now

he does not like God's faithful witnesses to point him out and expose him to others by telling the truth about him and his wicked, oppressive organization. He hates Jehovah's witnesses because these, by the grace of God, are now proclaiming the truth which exposes Satan and his agencies. They are participating in and delivering the testimony of truth of Christ Jesus, the Chief Witness, and for this reason that old Dragon in the modern waters is desperately attempting to destroy them. God will shield and protect all those who love him.

All shall know that Jehovah is God. "And all the inhabitants of Egypt shall know that I am the Lord, because they have been a staff of reed to the house of Israel." (29:6) The Big Business element of Satan's organization has assumed that it was indispensable to the unholy and so-called "organized Christianity". Those who have claimed to serve God and who have done so merely in name, and those who have been unfaithful to the Lord, have time and again applied to Big Business for aid. It was the commercial interests that financed the movement to unite the churches. The Interchurch World Movement announced its purpose to raise three hundred and thirty million dollars to carry forward its scheme, and Big Business furnished most of the money. Big Business is now using its powers and finance to erect skyscraper church buildings and cathedrals, and claims to do this in behalf of "Christianity" or for "organized Christian religion". In due time Jehovah God will convince even those of Big Business that he can accomplish his work without them, and then these oppressors of humanity will be forced to know that Jehovah is

God. Big Business has been a staff and a reed to the professed house of Israel, and that staff and reed shall be broken.

Jehovah has never blessed any attempt of his people in adopting Big Business methods to acquire money for his witness work. In fact, every one who has attempted to resort to such methods upon the pretext of getting money to carry on the Lord's work has failed. "When they took hold of thee by thy hand, thou didst break, and rend all their shoulder: and when they leaned upon thee, thou brakest, and madest all their loins to be at a stand. Therefore thus saith the Lord God, Behold, I will bring a sword upon thee, and cut off man and beast out of thee." (29: 7, 8) Commercialism has been a bane to God's people. Whoever has become entangled therewith has received injury, and many have been 'drowned in the sea'. Jehovah God alone is the sure support of his people and his cause. It is not proper for any of God's people to lean upon any creature of Satan's organization. Big Business must be taught this lesson, as well as the professed people of God. Jehovah's witnesses have, by the grace of the Lord, learned the lesson. "Woe to them that go down to Egypt for help; and stay on horses, and trust in chariots, because they are many; and in horsemen, because they are very strong; but they look not unto the Holy One of Israel, neither seek the Lord! Yet he also is wise, and will bring evil, and will not call back his words: but will arise against the house of the evil doers, and against the help of them that work iniquity. Now the Egyptians are men, and not God; and their horses flesh, and not spirit. When the Lord shall stretch out his hand [for judgment], both he [Egypt] that helpeth shall fall, and he [God's covenant people] that is holpen shall fall down, and they all shall fail together.''— Isa. 31: 1-3.

The faithful have learned to trust in the Lord, and not in man. (Ps. 118: 8) We are now in the day which Jehovah has made, and in that day the Lord with his sore and strong sword shall slay the dragon that is in the sea. (Isa. 27: 1) Satan and his organization must go down, because Jehovah has thus made his decree. ''And the land of Egypt shall be desolate and waste; and they shall know that I am the Lord: because he hath said, The river is mine, and I have made it. Behold, therefore, I am against thee, and against thy rivers, and I will make the land of Egypt utterly waste and desolate, from the tower of Syene even unto the border of Ethiopia.'' (29: 9, 10) Otherwise stated, Satan and his organization shall be rent from end to end. This harmonizes with James 5: 1-6.

By his prophet Jeremiah God declares that all nations of earth shall be made desolate, and this includes Egypt. (Jer. 25: 15, 26) It includes the king of Egypt and his servants. ''No foot of man shall pass through it, nor foot of beast shall pass through it, neither shall it be inhabited forty years. And I will make the land of Egypt desolate in the midst of the countries that are desolate, and her cities among the cities that are laid waste shall be desolate forty years: and I will scatter the Egyptians among the nations, and will disperse them through the countries.'' (29: 11, 12) Satan's organization, particularly the commercial part thereof here emphasized, shall be completely wiped out.

Forty years was the length of the period of time of the reign of David, and also that of Solomon, both of which foreshadowed the reign of Christ Jesus. 'Forty years of the desolation of Egypt' above mentioned therefore seems to correspond with the reign of Christ, the antitypical David, over the period of a thousand years, during which antitypical Egypt must be in captivity to Christ Jesus. During that time must be fulfilled the prophecy of Isaiah 19:21, to wit: "And the Lord shall be known to Egypt, and the Egyptians shall know the Lord in that day, and shall do sacrifice and oblation; yea, they shall vow a vow unto the Lord, and perform it." This will prove how impotent the Devil or any part of his organization is to carry through his purposes. It will prove how foolish it is for Satan or any creature to think he can pursue his own selfish and wicked course forever. The forty years also corresponds with the period of time Satan will be dead. He will never be permitted to again build his organization.

During the reign of Christ the people who have been under Satan and unwillingly held there will be permitted to reform. Those who are obedient to Christ will be brought to God and restored and reconciled to him. "Yet thus saith the Lord God, At the end of forty years will I gather the Egyptians from the people whither they were scattered: and I will bring again the captivity of Egypt, and will cause them to return into the land of Pathros, into the land of their habitation; and they shall be there a base kingdom." (29:13, 14) The loving-kindness of Jehovah is shown to the dupes of Satan by giving them an opportunity for restitution, and those who obey will become the people of God. "In that day shall Israel be the third with Egypt and with Assyria, even a blessing in the midst of the land; whom the Lord of hosts shall bless, saying, Blessed be Egypt my people, and Assyria the work of my hands, and Israel mine inheritance." (Isa. 19 : 24, 25) When Satan is brought out of the pit at the end of the thousand years he will never be restored to anything, but, like the Dragon, he will be completely destroyed. Obedient people under the reign of Christ will be returned to the land of their habitation, the garden-of-Eden condition, and, continuing obedient to God, they will live.

TRADING

Buying and selling is not in itself wrong, but it must be done in honesty. (Lev. 25 : 15, 16) The law of God permitted his people to buy and sell. Barter and trade between the people of things that they have and which they can spare to their neighbors is entirely proper. The great wrong is caused, however, from exploiting the people and employing the mercantile schemes to pile up great amounts to be used for selfish, oppressive purposes. The kingdom of God will never permit commercialism in any such form as it is now practiced. Even legitimate trade will be the basest part of the kingdom of God: "It shall be the basest of the kingdoms; neither shall it exalt itself any more above the nations: for I will diminish them, that they shall no more rule over the nations." (29 : 15) What buying and selling will be done in the realm of God's kingdom will be merely subsidiary to the life of the people and used to the service of God.

The consideration of men so far as trading is concerned will then be "What shall we eat? or, What shall we drink? or, Wherewithal shall we be clothed?" That is, they will barter and trade only in things that are necessaries of life, and never for pecuniary profit. In such trading the people will measure to each other honestly and fairly. They will be merciful, even as God is merciful, and will give good measure, pressed down and shaken together. (Luke 6: 36-38) This rule now shows that the proper course of dealing for God's people is to be open, square and absolutely honest, and not resort in their trades to fraudulent schemes, such as the world uses. No true child of God could be excused for willingly cheating or defrauding anyone.

In the kingdom of God commercialism shall not be the confidence of the people. "And it shall be no more the confidence of the house of Israel, which bringeth their iniquity to remembrance, when they shall look after them [calling to mind iniquity, by their turning to follow them, *Roth.*]; but they shall know that I am the Lord God." (29: 16) The remnant of God's people even today are fulfilling this scripture. They do not put confidence or reliance upon Big Business, but they clearly discern that commerce is one of the chief factors of Satan's wicked organization. The Lord is calling his people out of commercial pursuits and calling them to enter the service of publishing his great name and the message concerning his kingdom. This they are doing by building printing plants and supplying the people with the printed message of the truth and at the very lowest cost. The remnant of God's people on earth are now

in a measure carrying out the divine rule announced
by this scripture.

REWARDING THE INSTRUMENT

The miniature fulfilment of the prophecy hereby
considered was delayed apparently for a time, but
God did not forget the instrument he employed in its
fulfilment. "And it came to pass in the seven and
twentieth year, in the first month, in the first day of
the month, the word of the Lord came unto me, saying." (29:17) This was sixteen years, two months,
and eighteen days after the prophecy against Egypt
was spoken, and fifteen years, six months and twenty-
three days after the destruction of Jerusalem and its
temple, that the Lord spoke to his prophet and said:
"Son of man, Nebuchadrezzar king of Babylon caused
his army to serve a great service against Tyrus: every
head was made bald, and every shoulder was peeled:
yet had he no wages, nor his army, for Tyrus, for the
service that he had served against it." (29:18) Doubtless the soldiers of Nebuchadnezzar's army became
baldheaded and sore of shoulder by reason of carrying
heavy loads and being exposed to the elements during
the time of their hard service when besieging Tyre.
The army had served thirteen years in besieging Tyre
but had failed to take it. God's prophecy, therefore,
must have complete fulfilment later, which complete
fulfilment is at the end of the world, this present day.

The heathen king Nebuchadnezzar did not worship
Jehovah, and therefore was not justly entitled to any
favor from God. Nebuchadnezzar was pursuing a selfish course in attacking Tyre, but this served God's
purpose in a measure in the fulfilment of the prophecy

against Tyre; hence it pleased God to not restrain
Nebuchadnezzar, but to permit him to transfer his
military operations against Egypt and thus fulfil
God's judgment against that nation in a measure:
"Therefore thus saith the Lord God, Behold, I will
give the land of Egypt unto Nebuchadrezzar king of
Babylon; and he shall take her multitude, and take
her spoil, and take her prey; and it shall be the wages
for his army." (29:19) God would not have permitted Nebuchadnezzar to subjugate Egypt if he had
not served Jehovah's purpose. God did not bless
Nebuchadnezzar in a spiritual way, but permitted him
to be paid in his own kind or value, and such that he
would appreciate, for the efforts he had expended
against Tyre. Therefore the Lord's prophet was directed to say: "I have given him the land of Egypt
for his labour wherewith he served against it, because
they wrought for me, saith the Lord God."—29:20.

In his campaign against Egypt Nebuchadnezzar
was further used as God's means of carrying out his
purpose against Satan's organization. It is in this
connection written in Ezekiel 30:10-12: "Thus saith
the Lord God, I will also make the multitude of Egypt
to cease by the hand of Nebuchadrezzar king of Babylon. He and his people with him, the terrible of the
nations, shall be brought to destroy the land: and
they shall draw their swords against Egypt, and fill
the land with the slain. And I will make the rivers
dry, and sell the land into the hand of the wicked;
and I will make the land waste, and all that is therein,
by the hand of strangers: I the Lord have spoken it."

Nebuchadnezzar was not a type of Christ; but he
did serve Jehovah's purposes, and for that reason he

is called Jehovah's servant. (See *Vindication*, Book One, pages 282, 283.) The name "Nebuchadnezzar" means "Nebo (that is, the prophet) is the protector against misfortune". The name properly applies to Christ Jesus, who is the great Prophet of God and who is the protector of his people against their foes, especially when warring against Satan's organization, which Egypt represented. Nebuchadnezzar pictures the manner in which God will use Christ Jesus, the one "terrible" to Satan's organization, and will use him for the purpose of destroying that organization. Jehovah's 'elect servant' is a stranger to and unfriendly to Satan's organization. Jehovah gave Nebuchadnezzar Egypt as pay for his services; and so in a similar way he gives to Christ Jesus all the world for his possessions. "Ask of me, and I shall give thee the heathen for thine inheritance, and the uttermost parts of the earth for thy possession. Thou shalt break them with a rod of iron; thou shalt dash them in pieces like a potter's vessel." (Ps. 2:8, 9) As Nebuchadnezzar went from Tyre to Egypt, even so Christ Jesus goes from one victory to another, and before his onward march all of Satan's organization must flee and fall.

JEHOVAH'S ANOINTED

The house of Israel represents God's covenant and anointed people. "In that day will I cause the horn of the house of Israel to bud forth, and I will give thee the opening of the mouth in the midst of them; and they shall know that I am the Lord." (29:21) Jesus Christ is particularly "the horn of the house of Israel"; and Jehovah caused it to bud or shoot forth in the year 1914, when he placed his King upon his throne. "The Lord shall send the rod of thy strength out of Zion: rule thou in the midst of thine enemies." (Ps. 110: 2) Since the arrival of God's Messenger at his temple the strength of the remnant has budded and continues to increase. "For the Lord hath chosen Zion: he hath desired it for his habitation. There will I make the horn of David to bud: I have ordained a lamp for mine anointed. His enemies will I clothe with shame; but upon himself shall his crown flourish."—Ps. 132: 13, 17, 18.

The Prophet Ezekiel represented Jehovah's witnesses now on earth, and to Ezekiel Jehovah said: "I will give thee the opening of the mouth in the midst of them." This foreshadows how the Lord God is now using the mouth of his "servant" class to give testimony for him to all the nations round about, as well as to those who are begotten of the spirit of God; and thus these faithful ones speak to each other, "and [say] unto Zion, Thy God reigneth." "Open thy mouth wide, and I will fill it." (Ps. 81: 10) "And I have put my words in thy mouth, and I have covered thee in the shadow of mine hand, that I may plant the heavens, and lay the foundations of the earth, and say unto Zion, Thou art my people." (Isa. 51: 16) "And he hath made my mouth like a sharp sword; in the shadow of his hand hath he hid me, and made me a polished shaft: in his quiver hath he hid me." (Isa. 49: 2) "And it shall come to pass in that day, that the mountains shall drop down new wine, and the hills shall flow with milk, and all the rivers of Judah shall flow with waters, and a fountain shall come forth of the house of the Lord, and shall water the valley of Shittim. Egypt shall be a desolation, and Edom shall be a desolate wilderness, for the violence against the children of Judah, because they have shed innocent blood in their land. But Judah shall dwell for ever, and Jerusalem from generation to generation. For I will cleanse their blood that I have not cleansed; for the Lord dwelleth in Zion." (Joel 3:18-21) The Lord's faithful people had to be brought to a better knowledge of Jehovah and of who he is and what his name signifies and what are his purposes, and so the Lord is fulfilling upon them the promise that "they shall know that I am the Lord".

WARNING
(EZEKIEL, CHAPTER 30)

As God commanded Ezekiel, so now he commands his remnant people: "The word of the Lord came again unto me, saying, Son of man, prophesy and say, Thus saith the Lord God, Howl ye, Woe worth the day! For the day is near, even the day of the Lord is near, a cloudy day; it shall be the time of the heathen." (30:1-3) The day of God's wrath is come upon all nations and upon all operations of Satan's organization, and the Devil himself knows that fact. (Rev. 12:12) It seems strange that there are now on the earth many spirit-begotten ones who claim to love God and yet who do not see or appreciate the fact that the day of God's wrath is quickly to be expressed against all the nations. Those who fail to see this are missing a great opportunity to proclaim the truth. It is a dark day on Satan's organization, and its being "a cloudy day" portends that Jehovah is

present and is very near to the time of the execution
of his vengeance upon Satan's organization and to
the vindication of his name. "The burden of Egypt.
Behold, the Lord rideth upon a swift cloud, and shall
come into Egypt; and the idols of Egypt shall be
moved at his presence, and the heart of Egypt shall
melt in the midst of it." (Isa. 19:1) It is the time
for the visitation of God upon the nations, hence the
time of their misfortune or punishment, the description of which is given by the prophet in Jeremiah
25:15-28.

AGAINST ETHIOPIA

Egypt and Ethiopia were neighbors and sometimes
allied themselves with or served each other. Ethiopia
is frequently mentioned in the Scriptures in connection with Egypt. Ethiopia was never a world power
such as Egypt was, and hence pictures some ally of
Satan's commercial element, just as Zidon was a subsidiary of Tyre. Ethiopia seems to fitly picture the
"gun" element or "strong-arm squad" of Big Business that is employed by Big Business to carry out
its contemptible and wicked purposes. When Big
Business wants something accomplished, and cannot
accomplish it otherwise, it employs what it calls 'strike
breakers' or 'special police' which inflict all manner of
cruel punishment upon those who will not do the
bidding of Big Business. For instance, the coal mine
operators, owned and controlled by the big commercial wing of Satan's organization, employ men with
deadly weapons to oppress, harass and kill those who
get in the way of the schemes of Big Business. This
same commercial element also employs military force

when their selfish schemes seem to require it, and they take advantage of what they call "law and order" to overrun and shoot down men and women who are defenseless. The seventh world power would not be pursuing her wicked and heartless course against the peoples of India right now were it not for the purpose of maintaining the commerce of that world power. The Ethiopians therefore seem well to represent the employees of the commercial wing of Satan's organization to inflict punishment upon others. "Come up, ye horses; and rage, ye chariots; and let the mighty men come forth; the Ethiopians and the Libyans, that handle the shield; and the Lydians, that handle and bend the bow."—Jer. 46: 9.

The prophet of the Lord tells of the "cloudy day" of God's wrath, and then says: "And the sword shall come upon Egypt, and great pain shall be in Ethiopia, when the slain shall fall in Egypt, and they shall take away her multitude, and her foundations shall be broken down." (30:4) Jehovah will not permit to go unnoticed, and hence unpunished, those men who have hired themselves to Big Business and cooperate with Big Business to oppress, harass and kill the defenseless.

As a means of identifying some of this class: Recently in the coal fields of Kentucky, operated by Big Business interests, a peaceful farmer committed the 'grievous offense' against Big Business of making a bail bond for a poor woman of the laboring class who had been arrested on some charge at the instance of the mine operators, and whom the mine operators were persecuting. Within a few minutes after he had signed the bond some agent of Big Business warned the farmer. For the offense of signing a bail bond this farmer had his barn and store building burned to the ground within twenty-four hours. This is just one minor incident, and there are many others committed throughout the realms of the seventh world power and at the instance of the commercial wing of Satan's organization.

Furthermore the Lord says of this "strong-armed bludgeon squad": "Ethiopia, and Libya [Put, *R.V., Leeser*], and Lydia [Lud, *R.V., Leeser*], and all the mingled people, and Chub [Cub, *R.V., Leeser*], and the men of the land that is in league, shall fall with them by the sword." (30:5) Put (meaning "bow") was a brother of Cush and Mizraim. (Gen. 10:6) Lud (meaning "tortuous, full of writhings", like a snake) was a son of Mizraim. (Gen. 10:13) Chub (Cub) probably means Nubians, a black and ferocious people. "Mingled people" (*arab*) more particularly applies to those wild and ferocious people that hire themselves out to commit devilish deeds. All together this element pictures the helpers or hired tools of Big Business who by violent methods carry out the schemes of the commercial powers. Concerning the 'leagued men' (*Leeser*) the text, according to *Rotherham,* means "the sons of the land of the covenant". This latter translation of the text shows that it applies to the sons of the land of Israel who were in a covenant with God but who at the time of the fall of Jerusalem fled for refuge to Egypt. Against such the Lord said: "So shall it be with all the men that set their faces to go into Egypt, to sojourn there; they shall die by the sword, by the famine, and by the pestilence; and none of them shall remain or

escape from the evil that I will bring upon them.''
(Jer. 42:17) In modern times there are those who,
contrary to the Lord's instruction, violate their covenant with the Lord by seeking aid or refuge in the
Devil's organization and who therefore will go down
with the Devil's organization when the Lord Jesus
Christ makes his assault upon it. One having been
favored by the Lord and who then turns to any part
of Satan's organization, whether out of fear or for
any other reason, will be counted in as a part of Satan's organization and meet the same fate.

All allies of Big Business shall fall, according to
the words of God's prophet. ''Thus saith the Lord,
They also that uphold Egypt shall fall; and the pride
of her power shall come down: from the tower of
Syene shall they fall in it by the sword, saith the Lord
God. And they shall be desolate in the midst of the
countries that are desolate, and her cities shall be in
the midst of the cities that are wasted. And they
shall know that I am the Lord, when I have set a
fire in Egypt, and when all her helpers shall be destroyed.'' (30:6-8) These necessarily include men
of big politics, militarism, and the big League of Nations, the commercial and all other supporters and
allies thereof. Big Business prides herself upon the
fact that politicians and big preachers are under the
control of the commercial power and do the bidding of
that wing of Satan's organization, and that therefore
their gold is sufficient to protect them and their allies.
Their gold will not be able to deliver them or any of
that crowd at Armageddon. (Zeph. 1:18) The great
financial institution will be wrecked, and its ''strong-
arm squad'' or ''military bludgeon crowd'' and its

armies and navies will be destroyed; and since the
seventh world power contains most of this, the seventh
world power will come in for the worst part of the
expression of God's indignation. This is but a corroboration of Ezekiel 29: 8-10 (see comments there).
Members of Satan's organization have been and are
so hard-hearted and cruel, and so hard-headed in refusing to receive any knowledge of or concerning Jehovah God, that the Lord God will break up the devilish organization from end to end, that is to say, "from
Migdol to Syene," as is stated in the margin of the
text. This the Lord will do in order to drive it into
their heads that Jehovah is supreme. His word and
name must be vindicated.

HIS WITNESSES

Jehovah gives encouragement and comfort to his
witnesses to press the battle to the gate. Such is one
of the reasons for making known his purposes by the
unfolding of these prophecies. (Rom. 15:4) "In that
day shall messengers go forth from [before] me in
ships, to make the careless Ethiopians afraid, and
great pain shall come upon them, as in the day of
Egypt; for, lo, it cometh." (30:9) The word "messengers" is from the Hebrew word *malach,* meaning
ambassadors of the Lord God. These ambassadors go
forth with the message of God's Word. 'Going forth
from before the Lord' shows that these messengers
must be the ones to whom God gives first an understanding of his prophecy "in that day" of God's
vengeance and vindication and who are the first to
discern the Devil's organization and to give testimony
against it. The word "ships" in this text is from

the Hebrew *tsi*, meaning "something set up, a fixture". These ships are not the ships of the enemy, but the Lord God's battle ships. They therefore seem to correspond to the Lord's war chariots. (Nah. 2:3) They well picture the world-wide organization of Jehovah God's people which by his grace and power has been "set up" for the purpose of giving testimony to the people of God, and to others of the nations, and which organization has been set up in various companies of the Lord's people for conveying the message to others according to God's commandment.

In these organizations and in an orderly manner God's remnant, who are his ambassadors, ride upon the seas, that is, upon the people, bringing the message of the kingdom of God and of the fact of the vindication of his name. As the Lord was with his servant Paul in the ship (Acts 27:22-24), so the Lord is with his ambassadors or witnesses in their ships or organizations who are doing an organized and orderly service in the name of Jehovah. It is therefore certain that those who oppose these ambassadors who are giving testimony are opposing Jehovah God. Those who claim to be in a covenant with God and who fail and refuse to perform the duties of an ambassador or witness of Jehovah show that they do not have on the wedding garment (Matt. 22:11, 12) and that they are therefore not in the covenant for the kingdom.

According to *Rotherham* the latter part of this verse reads, "to cause dread unto Ethiopia so confident." The hireling strong-arm military squad of Big Business, who oppress the people, and who persecute and arrest and maltreat God's people, have

been and are bold-faced against the Lord and rely
upon Satan's organization for protection, but even
these show in their faces some dread when laying hold
upon God's witnesses. The testimony of the truth
when stated to them frightens them. The navy and
military forces of Big Business are in the same pre-
dicament of dread, and this is evidenced by the many
naval and disarmament conferences that are now being
held. The message of truth has stirred up some fear
and dread amongst the chief ones of Big Business
operations and they have considered this at their
meetings, and especially the message that is contained
in the *Kingdom* booklet. Fear has taken hold upon
them because of what they may lose, but they do not
fear God or give their allegiance to him. Their fear
is for the loss of what they have. "Great pain [trem-
bling, *Leeser*] shall come upon them." The Lord gives
assurance to his messengers or witnesses that the
burden of their message which he has given them shall
not fail. For this reason the faithful company of Jehovah's witnesses are not at all disturbed by reason
of the scoffers and opposers. These scoffers and opposers are afraid now, but they continue to scoff at
the messengers of God. But these faithful witnesses
go straight forward in the performance of their God-
given duties and privileges.—2 Pet. 3: 3, 4.

Jehovah announces his purpose to destroy Egypt
by the hand of Nebuchadnezzar. "Thus saith the
Lord God, I will also make the multitude of Egypt
to cease by the hand of Nebuchadrezzar king of Babylon. He and his people with him, the terrible of the
nations, shall be brought to destroy the land: and they
shall draw their swords against Egypt, and fill the

land with the slain. And I will make the rivers dry, and sell the land into the hand of the wicked; and I will make the land waste, and all that is therein, by the hand of strangers; I the Lord have spoken it." (30:10-12) Nebuchadnezzar here foreshadowed Christ Jesus, he that is the "terrible one" to Satan's organization. God will dry up the rivers which Satan has claimed for himself and "sell the land into the hand of the wicked". The word "wicked" here, according to the *Revised Version* and also *Leeser,* is rendered "evil men"; hence the word wicked in the *Authorized Version* does not mean morally wicked, but it does mean the power used to bring distress and affliction upon Satan's organization. God created evil, that is to say, that which he uses to bring affliction upon his enemies. (Isa. 45:7) Thus the "evil men" here represent Christ and his army that bring afflictions and punishment upon Satan's organization. Christ and his armies are indeed strangers and unfriendly to Satan's commercial organization, not at all allied with it, and will destroy it and all other parts of Satan's organization.

IDOLS

The prophecy here resumes prediction against the commercial and military powers of Satan's organization. "Thus saith the Lord God, I will also destroy the idols, and I will cause their images to cease out of Noph [Memphis]; and there shall be no more a prince of the land of Egypt: and I will put a fear in the land of Egypt." (30:13) This means that commercialized religion will be abolished; also the god of war, together with sacrifices unto the god of war, will be destroyed. When the Lord has executed his judgments there will be no more any captains of the commercial wing of Satan's organization, such as billionaires, aristocrats, admirals, and such like that have ruled and oppressed the people and who have been regarded as and called 'princes'.

Continuing his denunciation against Egypt the prophet says: "And I will make Pathros desolate, and will set fire in Zoan, and will execute judgments in No." (30:14) Southern Egypt around Thebes is here described as Pathros, from which the Egyptians expanded northward down the course of the River Nile. Concerning Zoan and Noph it is written: "The princes of Zoan are become fools, the princes of Noph are deceived; they have also seduced Egypt; even they that are the stay [margin, governors] of the tribes thereof. The Lord hath mingled a perverse spirit in the midst thereof: and they have caused Egypt to err in every work thereof, as a drunken man staggereth in his vomit. Neither shall there be any work for Egypt, which the head or tail, branch or rush, may do." (Isa. 19:13-15) The men who have manipulated the commerce of the world have been unfaithful stewards of the material wealth of the earth and have done great violence to the interests of the people, causing them much distress and suffering; therefore the fiery judgment that awaits them. Zoan was the place where Moses confronted Pharaoh and where Jehovah demonstrated that he is God.—Ps. 78:12, 43.

"And I will pour my fury upon Sin [margin, Pelusium], the strength [R.V., stronghold] of Egypt; and I will cut off the multitude of No. And I will set

fire in Egypt; Sin shall have great pain, and No shall
be rent asunder, and Noph shall have distresses
daily." (30:15, 16) Sin, in Egyptian meaning "sun",
was a place of entrance into Egypt; hence it needed
to be a stronghold. It is not strong enough, however,
to resist the entering of Jehovah's Executive Officer
when he proceeds to break up Satan's organization.
No was the seat of worship of the god Amon (meaning
"the hidden or unseen one"). Neither the Devil nor
any of his associates can resist the attack of the great
Warrior, Christ Jesus.

Satan's organization shall be assaulted "daily"
(*R.V.*, in the daytime), that is to say, when the light
of the new day shines. The attack of the Lord Jesus
against Satan's wicked organization will be open and
aboveboard, and not secret. Now the Lord is having
his witnesses serve notice upon the Devil's organization in advance of the open assault against it by Christ
and his organization.

"The young men of Aven and of Pibeseth shall fall
by the sword; and these cities shall go into captivity."
(30:17) "Aven" means "vanity, wickedness", and
"the young men of Aven" seems to refer to the strong
ones of Big Business giving worship to the selfish and
wicked things which are vain. Pibeseth (margin,
Pubastum) was "the abode of the goddess Bast (the
lion-headed or cat-headed or lioness-faced goddess)".
She represents Satan's wife or organization which
brings forth the false seed of promised blessings.
Cat-faced or lioness-faced women are often the ready
instruments of Satan and exercise a subtle and wicked
influence over those about them and demand and receive homage to which they are not entitled. Of

course the Devil is back of all this unrighteous course.
Big Business assumes to be the seed that will give to
the people what they need, and, like their mother, the
cat-faced, lioness-faced goddess, it is sly, cunning and
wicked. Logically they would worship their mother,
who is in covenant with the Devil; hence the Devil's
organization is their goddess or object of worship.
All of these wicked elements of Satan's organization
shall be destroyed.

"At Tehaphnehes also the day shall be darkened,
when I shall break there the yokes of Egypt: and the
pomp of her strength shall cease in her: as for her, a
cloud shall cover her, and her daughters shall go into
captivity. Thus will I execute judgments in Egypt;
and they shall know that I am the Lord." (30:18,19)
Tehaphnehes, also called Daphne, means "laurel",
and was sacred to the sun god. It was there that the
people were guilty of assaulting God's chosen people
the Israelites. (Jer. 2:16) After the fall of Jerusalem some of the Jews fled to this place of Tehaphnehes
for refuge. (See Jeremiah 43:7.) Jeremiah himself
was forced to go there against his will. This pictures
that it is vain for any of God's people to flee to the
citadel of commercialism or any other part of Satan's
organization for refuge, because all of Satan's organization shall go down. Christ Jesus, the Executive
Officer of Jehovah, whom Nebuchadnezzar pictured,
shall destroy the enemy organization. "And I will
kindle a fire in the houses of the gods of Egypt; and
he shall burn them, and carry them away captives;
and he shall array himself with the land of Egypt,
as a shepherd putteth on his garment; and he shall
go forth from thence in peace. He shall break also

the images of Beth-shemesh, that is in the land of Egypt; and the houses of the gods of the Egyptians shall he burn with fire."—Jer. 43:12, 13.

ARM BROKEN

For his own purposes Jehovah keeps an accurate time schedule. "And it came to pass in the eleventh year, in the first month, in the seventh day of the month, that the word of the Lord came unto me." (30:20) This was five months and three days before the sack of Jerusalem and her temple. King Zedekiah had appealed to Egypt for help and Egypt had come to Jerusalem's aid, and the Chaldeans under Nebuchadnezzar withdrew from the assault. (Jer. 37:5, 11) Jeremiah told the Jews that Pharaoh's army would return to Egypt and that the Chaldeans would come back to destroy Jerusalem. The Egyptian campaign failed and they were compelled to return to Egypt, and then the Chaldeans began the final assault upon the city of Jerusalem. This well illustrates how Satan by the use of his commercial and military force would save "Christendom" from the assault of Jehovah's Executive Officer, and foreshadows his certain defeat.

"Son of man, I have broken the arm of Pharaoh king of Egypt; and, lo, it shall not be bound up to be healed, to put a roller to bind it, to make it strong to hold the sword." (30:21) When Christ Jesus went forth to cast Satan out of heaven Satan would know that the earthly part of his organization, and particularly "Christendom", would be and was in immediate danger. He therefore plunged the nations of "Christendom" into the World War, using Big

Business, the military and political forces to more fully solidify the three elements of his earthly organization and to strengthen his invisible and visible power of control over the people. The clergy of "Christendom" quickly acted with the other branches of Satan's organization to get into the war. By hurling Satan out of heaven the Lord, in the language of this text, 'broke his arm.' His heavenly power was completely destroyed. Satan must now confine his operations to the earth, pictured by Egypt, which place he had been forced to occupy; and now he is gathering all of his forces to make his last desperate stand at Armageddon. Christ continues to send his witnesses forth into "Christendom" and to all parts of Satan's organization, to serve notice and warning.

In due time "Christendom", together with all other parts of Satan's organization, will fall at the hands of Christ; which will mean the complete destruction of Satan's power. Satan has attempted to heal his broken arm or broken power by applying the "roller" or long bandage thereto in the form of the League of Nations compact (or splint) into which League he has brought the spiritual (or religious), commercial and political elements of his organization in an attempt to prevent another fracture. His heavenly power cannot be healed, and his earthly power is in no wise strengthened. He desperately pushes his commercial agencies forward in the formation of gigantic financial or commercial mergers, and attempts to have the religious and political elements of his organization to support the commercial factor. His political forces of the governments of the earth, and particularly those in the League, aided by the clergy or religious elements, which are constantly cooperating with Big Business forces, are acting against the interests of the people in general in trying to prepare for the assault at Armageddon. These three elements, commerce, politics and religion, try to bind up or heal the injury already inflicted upon the organization and to make it strong, so that it can hold the power of the sword. The desperate efforts of Satan's agents fail to better conditions, and the cries of the oppressed people continue to increase.

Jehovah God hears the cries of the oppressed and takes note of the desperate and wicked acts of Satan to strengthen his organization, and his prophet speaks: "Therefore thus saith the Lord God, Behold, I am against Pharaoh king of Egypt, and will break his arms, the strong, and that which was [already] broken; and I will cause the sword to fall out of his hand." (30:22) God gives full assurance now to those that love him that both of Satan's arms will be broken; that is to say, his entire power shall fail and his sword shall be knocked out of his hand, and his entire fighting equipment, together with his organization, shall be destroyed.

There are millions of people on earth who are properly called "hangers-on" to Satan's organization and who therefore support that organization. These have the "mark of the beast" in their foreheads and in their hands (Rev. 13:16, 17), and hence they are Egyptians. To be sure, most of them are deceived; but regardless of all the oppression and suffering of the people, and regardless of all testimony that is being given by Jehovah's witnesses as to the cause thereof and the remedy God has provided, only a few hear and give heed to such testimony. Even those of good will who do hear and heed fail to take their stand wholly on the Lord's side. Armageddon will be required to cause the people to know that Jehovah is God and that his kingdom is their only hope. Therefore says the Lord: "And I will scatter the Egyptians among the nations, and will disperse them through the countries." (30:23) The complete downfall of Satan's organization at Armageddon and the scattering of the people throughout the nations will awaken them to the real solution of the world's troubles.

The great issue of supremacy must now be settled once and for ever. "And I will strengthen the arms of the king of Babylon, and put my sword in his hand: but I will break Pharaoh's arms, and he shall groan before him with the groanings of a deadly wounded man. But I will strengthen the arms of the king of Babylon, and the arms of Pharaoh shall fall down; and they shall know that I am the Lord, when I shall put my sword into the hand of the king of Babylon, and he shall stretch it out upon the land of Egypt. And I will scatter the Egyptians among the nations, and disperse them among the countries; and they shall know that I am the Lord."—30:24-26.

"The king of Babylon" here mentioned pictures Christ Jesus, the great Executive of Jehovah God who will wield the sword of his divinely-given power to dash to pieces Pharaoh, that is, Satan and his organization. Jehovah's witnesses now on earth constitute a part of The Christ because they are members of his body. Jehovah God has put all power and authority in the hands of Christ Jesus and sent him forth to execute his judgment. (Ps. 110:2) This same psalm states that God's faithful ones are willing in the day of the Lord; which means that they participate in the assault upon Satan's organization. The clear implication is that Jehovah will now strengthen his faithful witnesses to do their part in the great vindication work that is proceeding. Now these can truly say, as is written: "Blessed be the Lord my strength, which teacheth my hands to war, and my fingers to fight."—Ps. 144: 1.

Those who know God and faithfully obey his commandments "shall be strong, and do exploits". (Dan. 11: 32) "For the arms of the wicked shall be broken: but the Lord upholdeth the righteous." (Ps. 37: 17) That which is of paramount importance now is the vindication of Jehovah's name. Both the friends and the enemies of God will have it proven to them beyond all doubt that Jehovah is supreme. "They shall know that I am the Lord." Jehovah's witnesses now know this great truth and they are telling it to others. When Armageddon is done all will know that Jehovah is God. That trouble will kill many and will scatter those who survive. "Then shall ye return, and discern between the righteous and the wicked; between him that serveth God, and him that serveth him not."—Mal. 3: 18.

SATAN AND HIS TREES
(EZEKIEL, CHAPTER 31)

Ezekiel was still dumb as against Jerusalem, but he spoke under God's direction to the king of Egypt and his supporters. This seems clearly to teach that after the message of God is made clear and positive against "Christianity", so called, the witnesses whom Ezekiel foreshadowed will continue to speak to Satan and other parts of his organization. According to God's expressed will it was first necessary that the religious element be exposed; but now the attack must be made, and is being made, upon all branches of Satan's organization. The thirty-first chapter continues to expose Satan and his organization to view and to predict its fall: "And it came to pass in the eleventh year, in the third month, in the first day of the month, that the word of the Lord came unto me, saying."—31:1.

This was two months and six days before the firing of the temple that the prophecy here considered was uttered. Jeremiah prophesied at the direction of the Lord: "For, lo, I begin to bring evil on the city which is called by my name, and should ye [the enemy nations, the other part of Satan's organization] be utterly unpunished? Ye shall not be unpunished: for I will call for a sword upon all the inhabitants of the earth, saith the Lord of hosts." (Jer. 25:29) That prophecy must have been some consolation to those of Jerusalem who heard it, to know that God will also deal with the enemies of God's chosen people. Even so now, those who hear the testimony given to them by Jehovah's witnesses must find some consolation in the fact that, while God will punish those who have taken his name in vain, he will also punish all his enemies that have defamed his name and have persecuted his chosen people.

God directed his prophet Ezekiel to speak unto the king of Egypt and unto his multitude. "Son of man, speak unto Pharaoh king of Egypt, and to his multitude; Whom art thou like in thy greatness? Behold, the Assyrian was a cedar in Lebanon with fair branches, and with a shadowing shroud, and of an high stature; and his top was among the thick boughs." (31:2, 3) Satan and his organization are inseparable. The "king of Egypt" here refers specifically to Satan, whereas "his multitude" refers to all of those who are members of his organization and hence his supporters.

The third verse says: "Behold, the Assyrian was a cedar." The word "was" is an interpolation. According to *Rotherham,* marginal reading, the text is: "Lo! a sherbin cedar in Lebanon." The text is therefore not comparing Pharaoh to the "Assyrian", but to a tree. (Isa. 41:19) Cedars of Lebanon are first mentioned in Judges 9:15. They are used as a symbol of Satan and the official members of his organization because of the pride, hauteur, prominence, strength, ambition and exaltation of such as lift themselves up high. "For the day of the Lord of hosts shall be upon every one that is proud and lofty, and upon every one that is lifted up, and he shall be brought low; and upon all the cedars of Lebanon, that are high and lifted up, and upon all the oaks of Bashan, and upon all the high mountains, and upon all the hills that are lifted up. And upon all the ships of Tarshish, and upon all pleasant pictures. And the loftiness of man shall be bowed down, and the haughtiness of men shall be made low; and the Lord alone shall be exalted in that day." (Isa. 2:12-14, 16, 17) The application is to Satan and his creatures or representatives, both invisible and visible to man, and therefore it applies to his entire organization.

"Lebanon" means "white" or "snowy". As Satan's mountain or organization calls itself white and righteous, so is this the particular claim of the seventh world power on the borders of the land called "Christendom". By its own laws, enacted by the representatives of Satan, his organization legislates righteousness unto itself. This is particularly made manifest in the Prohibition laws of the United States and some other parts of "Christendom", and in the claim made by the British Empire that it is God's kingdom on earth.

The seventh world power has produced the most extensive and powerful commercial machine that has ever existed. When the prophet speaks of this tree in Lebanon "with fair branches" and its "shadowing shroud", or "forest-like shade", it is easy to see how it pictures Satan and his organization. Satan, by and through his organization, and particularly the commercial element thereof, has spread his branches out and taken in a vast territory. His boughs or branches are well represented by his great banking institutions, with their many branches; the navy and military, with its various branches; the marine organization; the bases for the operation of naval and military powers; and its great political organizations. All these organizations cast shadows that hide that which properly belongs to the people, as the boughs of a great tree hide the things that are under it. The commercial part of Satan's organization is the most prominent and therefore the most powerful part of the organization. The enemy and his organization rises up into the clouds because of its self-exaltation and extensive power. Satan and his enormous and far-reaching organization is described by the prophet in these words: "The waters made him great, the deep set him up on high with her rivers running round about his plants, and sent out her little rivers unto all the trees of the field. Therefore his height was exalted above all the trees of the field, and his boughs were multiplied, and his branches became long, because of the multitude of waters, when he shot forth." —31: 4, 5.

The peoples of earth, alienated from God and pictured here as the waters and coming under the influence and control of Satan, have made Satan and his organization great. Satan began his commercial operations in Eden, and as the peoples of earth have increased he has extended his mercantile operations. It has reached a climax in the end of the world. He created Big Business and has manipulated it for his own selfish purposes. By means of special class legislation enacted by purchased politicians he has fixed the laws to suit Big Business, and the common people have been compelled to depend upon Big Business. Satan has therefore made his visible organization very great by his exploitation of the people. He has caused Big Business to tower above all other things of the world. The waters of the seas and the rivers have furnished trade channels for Big Business to carry on its operations. The waters (symbolic of the peoples) have furnished opportunities for Satan to build his powerful commercial organization, and this he has done, and has used big religion and big politics to aid his commercial power to grow great and wax fat.

Birds and fowls hang on to the branches of trees, nest and roost there, and beasts of the field find shelter under the boughs of the trees. In symbolic language the Lord speaks of Satan and his organization and says: "All the fowls of heaven made their nests in his boughs, and under his branches did all the beasts of the field bring forth their young, and under his shadow dwelt all great nations." (31:6) Those hangers-on among the people of the world are such as desire to have an attractive place, one of ease, where they can roost and feather their own nest. These have put themselves under Satan, and particularly under the control of the commercial wing of his organization. The "sky-pilots", who according to their own estimate fly above the things of the earth, light in the branches of Satan's big tree and are borne up by the commercial part thereof, and there they roost and bring forth their young, and befoul those who come to rest under the trees. The beastly politicians and military officers make their roosting places and their beds under the boughs of Satan's commercial branches and there bring forth their children, that is to say, their wicked schemes. Thus the Lord in symbolic phrase shows Satan and his mighty organization, particularly the commercial part thereof, bringing all the power of the great nations under Satan's control. Only those who put themselves wholly on the side of the Lord God are freed from such wicked influence. These latter ones, being God's chosen people, neither hang on to Satan's organization nor seek rest or shade or shelter thereunder.

Then the Lord speaks of the greatness of Satan and his organization and says: "Thus was he fair in his greatness, in the length of his branches: for his root was by great waters. The cedars in the garden of

God could not hide him: the fir trees were not like his boughs, and the chestnut trees were not like his branches; nor any tree in the garden of God was like unto him in his beauty.'' (31: 7, 8) God's anointed people, who are made a part of his capital organization, are called "trees of righteousness, the planting of the Lord". (Isa. 61: 3) The chief one amongst those trees is Christ Jesus. In contrast with God's organization it is noted that when God made the earth and created man upon it, and assigned the things of the earth to Lucifer's domains, the things pertaining to the earth, including man, constituted a part of the organization over which Lucifer was made chief. As a living creature symbolized by a tree, Satan is fair in his domain, and he was great compared to other creatures in that domain. There was no other tree, that is, a living creature in his organization, that was like him for beauty and strength.

When Lucifer rebelled, and became Satan, the opposer of God, he turned all his power and his organization to wickedness. The most potent part of his visible organization consists of the commercial wing thereof, because by it Satan has erected a power that dominates and controls all the other portions of his earthly organization. Since trees symbolically represent Satan and other creatures of his organization, they also symbolically picture the organization in its entirety. As Lucifer towered above other trees in the garden of God, so now Satan towers above all other parts of his organization, and Big Business, or commerce, is the greatest part of his organization in its size and power and towers above the other branches of Satan's earthly organization. The political trees and the clergy trees and the military trees of Satan's company cannot control the commerce, or Big Business, but, on the contrary, Big Business dictates the policy of the others, and Satan, to be sure, is the chief one in the entire organization. The seventh world power has become Satan's greatest; and that which dominates the seventh world power is its commerce by sea and by land, and all other trees must come under or be subservient to Satan and the commercial wing of his organization.

The earth belongs to the Lord Jesus Christ, and the fullness thereof is his, because Jehovah has given into his hands all things; and since Christ Jesus has taken his power it is a "holy place" unto Jehovah. Now Satan and his organization illegally occupy the earth and the things thereof, and thus 'the abomination of desolation stands in the holy place'. This is particularly represented by his combined power united in the League of Nations. Let those who discern Satan's wicked organization, composed of religious, commercial and political divisions, and who long to see the earth made a fit place for man to dwell in, put themselves now wholly on the side of Jehovah God. (Matt. 24: 15, 16) Jehovah by his prophet then speaks further concerning the Devil and his organization: "I have made him fair by the multitude of his branches; so that all the trees of Eden, that were in the garden of God, envied him."—31: 9.

Pharaoh the king of Egypt pictured Lucifer, who is now the Devil. God made Lucifer fair and beautiful and by the multitude of his commercial branches the Devil has made his appearance in the eyes of men to be beautiful. Satan has directed his organization, and particularly making the commercial part thereof fat and bulging and powerful and therefore the envy of every other tree or every other part of his visible organization. This he has done by reason of using the God-made natural resources of the earth to carry out his own selfish and wicked purposes. Satan has caused his selfish agents, particularly within the realm of the seventh world power, to seize the natural resources of the earth and use them to exploit and oppress mankind in general. As Satan is great, likewise is his instrument Big Business a great or big tree, that is to say, a moving, going thing, and is envied by all other branches of Satan's organization. This envy induces men of similar calibre to try to imitate the giants of Big Business and has led many to create and operate "get rich quick" schemes. Big Business advertises itself in all the big newspapers and by radio and on the billboards, so that the people will be impressed by its importance. The politicians bow to it as their dictator, and the preachers and story writers frame it up as being the highest attainment of man, and therefore, according to them, the commercial power of the world is and must have divine approval.

Satan has thus lifted up himself and his commercial Big Business power over all the other creatures of his organization, and in these latter days he has especially magnified commerce, or Big Business, by seizing and controlling all the inventions, the waterways, the means of transportation by land, and machinery of every kind. The divine rule never changes; and Satan's exalted power must now be made low, because it is written: "Whosoever shall exalt himself, shall be abased." (Matt. 23:12; Dan. 5:18-21) Jehovah then announces his judgment against this wicked and oppressive one and his wicked and oppressive organization: "Therefore thus saith the Lord God, Because thou hast lifted up thyself in height, and he hath shot up his top among the thick boughs, and his heart is lifted up in his height; I have, therefore, delivered him into the hand of the mighty one of the heathen, he shall surely deal with him: I have driven him out for his wickedness." (31:10, 11) The wickedness of Satan's organization must come to an end.

UPROOTED

Jehovah God has planted his royal family with Christ Jesus the Head and Chief One thereof. This constitutes the capital of Jehovah's organization, and is likened unto the mighty and new cedar tree. Before the onward march of this mighty One, who is earth's rightful Ruler, Satan and all his trees must fall. To Satan and his trees Christ is "terrible". (Joel 2:11) Christ Jesus, the fresh, new and green cedar tree, and full of life, is placed in full possession of all things of the earth: "Thus saith the Lord God, I will also take of the highest branch of the high cedar, and will set it; I will crop off from the top of his young twigs a tender one, and will plant it upon an high mountain and eminent. And all the trees of the field shall know that I the Lord have brought down the high tree, have exalted the low tree, have dried up the green tree, and have made the dry tree to flourish: I the Lord have spoken, and have done it." (17:22, 24; see Vindication, Book One, pages 232, 233) In harmony with this statement God's prophet here again says concerning Satan and his wicked or-

ganization that it shall be taken by Christ the terrible
One and shall be broken. "And strangers, the terrible
of the nations, have cut him off, and have left him;
upon the mountains and in all the valleys his branches
are fallen, and his boughs are broken by all the rivers
of the land; and all the people of the earth are gone
down from his shadow, and have left him." (31:12)
All the natural resources of the earth which Satan has
misused shall be taken away from him and given to
earth's rightful Ruler and then all shall know that
Jehovah is God.

In this thirty-first chapter of Ezekiel's prophecy
the commercial part of Satan's organization is given
special prominence, but it must also be kept in mind
that the picture applies both to Satan and to his organization. The destruction of Big Business corresponds with the picture concerning the Dragon's being hauled out of the rivers and scattered over the
fields. (29:4, 5; 32:3-6) "Upon his ruin shall all the
fowls of the heaven remain, and all the beasts of the
field shall be upon his branches: to the end that none
of all the trees by the waters exalt themselves for their
height, neither shoot up their top among the thick
boughs, neither their trees stand up in their height,
all that drink water: for they are all delivered unto
death, to the nether parts of the earth, in the midst
of the children of men, with them that go down to
the pit." (31:13, 14) All the beasts of the field, that
is to say, every class of men forming Satan's organization, will be witnesses to the fall of the commercial
powers; and this is likened unto the great monarch of
the forests falling down and attracting the attention
of all about. The Lord will thus teach all worshipers

and servers of predatory wealth to suffer a lasting lesson.

The prophetic lesson is here given in advance for the benefit of those who have agreed to do the will of God, and affords them an opportunity to prove their love for God rather than for riches and ease. Those who by preference turn to things commercial or to industrial work and neglect the Lord's service, to which they have been once assigned, may expect to lose what they have once gained. Some may be compelled, because of obligation to children, for instance, to still labor with their hands for pecuniary profit, but all those who can do so, and who love the Lord and appreciate their privilege of service, will now delight to bear testimony to the name of Jehovah God.

The people of the seventh world power in particular, and which are pictured by the waters, have prided themselves in and boasted of the gigantic trees, to wit, the great commercial giants, Big Business, and its chief men, which they, the people, have irrigated, nourished, supported and borne up. They have put their trust in Satan and in his creation, and not in the Lord God, and therefore the Lord God will see to it that they have cause to mourn. "Thus saith the Lord God, In the day when he went down to the grave I caused a mourning. I covered the deep for him, and I restrained the floods thereof, and the great waters were stayed; and I caused Lebanon to mourn for him, and all the trees of the field fainted for him." —31:15.

Many have long ago concluded that the prosperity of the people in general depends upon Big Business, but even now there is widespread business depression

and many complain and mourn. With the complete
fall of the commercial power of the world there will
be much mourning amongst the small as well as the
great dealers pictured by the many trees of the forests
that faint and mourn. That this prophecy refers specifically to Big Business is proven by the fact that it
mentions Mount Lebanon, the site of the primeval
forests which God caused to take root and grow, and
which was turned into wickedness and oppression.
"So caused I gloom over him unto Lebanon, and all
the trees of the field for him were covered with a
shroud." (31:15, *Roth.*) Many of the clergy have
forsaken the Lord to engage in a commercial business,
which commerce has become the welcome ally of "organized Christianity" and is the mainstay of big
politics. This shows that all these trees (living creatures that envy the big tree of the forest, to wit, Big
Business) have for selfish reasons tried to imitate the
big tree and profit thereby and will mourn when their
great idol falls.

It is a common saying that when the commercial
power goes down the governments will go with it.
This must be true now because Big Business controls
the governments of the nations. "I made the nations
to shake at the sound of his fall, when I cast him
down to hell with them that descend into the pit: and
all the trees of Eden, the choice and best of Lebanon,
all that drink water, shall be comforted in the nether
parts of the earth." (31:16) If the commercial element of the British-American empire falls, therefore,
the seventh world power falls, and all other nations
in the League will be able to do nothing. They cannot
cope with the world situation. Even when Russia went

to the pot the other nations were frightened; but when
God uproots the commercial elements of Satan's visible
organization, particularly made manifest in the
seventh world power, everything else in the way of
politics and militarism will go with it. According to
Rotherham the text reads: "At the sound of his fall
I made nations tremble, when I caused him to descend
into hades with them who descend into the pit; then
were grieved, in the earth below, all the trees of
Eden, the choicest and best of Lebanon, all who had
drunk the waters." The words Lebanon and Eden
are here used to refer to the same thing, which shows
that the text has reference particularly to the commercial organization of the world; and when this commercial power goes down all that have drunk at her
waters shall go to the grave with it. That every
branch of Satan's organization must go down is further supported by the words of the prophet: "Even
they with him descended into hades among them who
were thrust through with the sword, even his seed
who dwelt in his shade in the midst of the nations."
(31:17, *Roth.*) Thus the systems or organizations
perverted by Satan and that have leaned upon him
or associated with or depended upon the chief tree,
Big Business, must find their final resting place in
hell or oblivion. Everything cooperating with or giving support to Satan's big business commercial power
will fall before the forward march of Christ Jesus,
the terrible One to Satan.

Both Satan and his organization are pictured in
this prophecy: "To whom art thou thus like in glory
and in greatness among the trees of Eden? yet shalt
thou be brought down with the trees of Eden unto

the nether parts of the earth: thou shalt lie in the midst of the uncircumcised with them that be slain by the sword. This is Pharaoh, and all his multitude, saith the Lord God." (31:18) Some authorities claim that the Egyptians practiced circumcision as the Hebrews did. Probably they learned it from the Hebrews, and that to accomplish some selfish beneficial results to themselves thereby. "Organized Christianity," particularly the clergy, which stands in a position similar to that of the Jews, has tried to circumcise Big Business and make it appear as a clean thing. For this reason the clergy have made the men of Big Business the "chief ones in their flocks". The man who financed the Interchurch World Movement was the world's then richest man and the big boss of Big Business. "Organized Christianity" yields to the wishes of Big Business. The clergy and others who claim to serve God refuse to say anything that might reflect upon the 'purity' of Big Business, and which might induce the people to believe that it is unclean. Big Business and its operators are not circumcised of heart. (Rom. 2:29; Jer. 4:4) These are unclean, and the Lord declares that they shall die the death of the unclean. The Lord God will clean the earth of everything that defiles, and his kingdom will make the earth a fit place in which obedient men may live in happiness for ever.

END OF OPPRESSION
(EZEKIEL, CHAPTER 32)

Jehovah's promise to his "faithful servant" class is that he will show to them things that must speedily come to pass as well as the fulfilment of prophecy al-

ready taken place. (Isa. 42: 9) This promise is sure,
and when we see events coming to pass that exactly fit
the prophecy we may be able to tell somewhat of the
things that are speedily to follow; thus the Lord permits his faithful people to look into the immediate
future. He has revealed to these the hideousness of
Satan's organization and given his people assurance
that soon it shall be destroyed. (Ps. 74: 14) Big Business is the chief element or power by which Satan has
oppressed and is now oppressing the people. The facts
well known, and the light which the Scriptures throw
upon these, strongly intimate that the complete downfall of Big Business and other parts of the oppressive
system, together with Satan himself, is in the very
near future. The thirty-second chapter of Ezekiel begins with the prophecy uttered one year, six months
and twenty-three days after the fall of Jerusalem and
the destruction of its temple. This suggests that Satan's controlling and oppressing power comes to a
disastrous end after "organized Christianity" meets
its fate. Jehovah God first exposes and makes known
to his people the hypocritical religious element that
has deceived the world, and then discloses and points
out the fate of the powerful commercial wing of Satan's organization that has dominated and oppressed
the people.

TYRE AND EGYPT

The ancient city of Tyre was a mercantile-marine
power. She carried on her commerce by her ships
that plied the seas and other waterways. She traded
with all the nations of the then known world. Ancient
Egypt was a world power, builded a great political

machine, and controlled the commerce that was carried on by land. Ancient Tyre maintained a navy to protect her ships and commerce. Ancient Egypt maintained a powerful military organization by land to protect her commerce and to prosecute her commercial schemes. Both Tyre and Egypt practiced the Devil religion and were under the control of Satan. The peoples of both Tyre and Egypt were alienated from God by Satan, and the peoples thereof bore up, sustained and supported the ruling organization, which was a beastly thing. Both Tyre and Egypt represented the Devil in his world-wide visible organization. Satan's commercial organization by sea and by land finds its chief expression in the seventh world power, to wit, Britain-America alliance. Therefore modern Tyre and modern Egypt consist of the commercial power, both by sea and by land, that dominates the nations of the earth, and which is the chief part of Satan's visible organization.

The commercial power of modern times, both on the sea and on the land, constitutes what is termed Big Business. Jehovah uses ancient Tyre to picture the commerce or Big Business that exploits the people and controls the trade of the peoples by sea or other waterways. He uses Egypt to picture the commerce or Big Business that exploits the people and controls the trade of the world by land. By sea and land Big Business controls the world. This dominating, ruling factor is the offspring or seed of Satan. The king of Tyre therefore represents Satan himself, and Pharaoh of Egypt also represents Satan himself. The princes and supporters in this prophecy picture the chief ones in Satan's visible organization. Tyre represents the commercial factor of Satan's organization that dominates the sea. Egypt represents Satan's commercial organization that dominates the land. Satan's organization commercial, from the viewpoint of the sea and land, constitutes Big Business that controls the world.

The seventh world power, as the indisputable facts show, dominates the seas. The greatest shipping interests on earth belong to the seventh world power, and her navy is the most powerful of all. Whatsoever reason may be assigned for maintaining the great navies of the Britannic-American empire, or the navy of any other nation, for that matter, the real reason is to protect and support commerce, or Big Business. The people are burdened with excessive taxes to maintain these mighty navies, which in turn are used to exploit the people and to keep them in subjection and under the control of the ruling factors, particularly Big Business. Big Business owns and controls the merchant marine, the cable lines, the wireless that operates from ship to shore and shore to ship, and all other means of communication between the nations. Big politicians, who ride the ships of the sea, are the tools of Big Business and make convenient laws for and do the bidding of the owners of the ships. The clergy support the Big Business of the sea, and there is such a complete understanding between them and the owners of the ships that only orthodox clergymen of "organized Christianity" are permitted to hold religious services or deliver Biblical lectures aboard these ships. No shipping crew dares permit any aside from an authorized "organized Christianity" clergyman to publicly address the people aboard the ships. While the seventh world power is the greatest of all, it has accredited and brought into its folds the other leading nations under the compact of the League of Nations.

Commerce, or Big Business, dominates everything on the land. It is in the saddle, and dictates the terms to the people. Big Business owns practically all the banks and the money in them. It receives on deposit what little cash the common people have, and then uses that cash for its own selfish purposes. Big Business owns and controls the newspapers, the magazines, and other means of advertising itself to promote and carry on its propaganda schemes for exploiting the people and creating public opinion. Big Business owns and controls the armies and all of their equipment, including the air fleets. Big Business owns and controls the legislative and executive branches of the governments. It manipulates, elects and selects its own men to public office. It owns and controls the big lawyers, the judges, the courts, and the officers and servants that serve thereat. It owns and controls the big scientists, the engineers, the planners, architects and constructors of public works. Big Business owns and controls the majority of the colleges and the universities, and even the public or common schools. It owns the radio and controls the music that goes on the air, and the musicians that play. Big Business owns and controls "organized Christianity", and in particular the clergy that serve the same, and also other religions that Satan operates amongst the people and causes them to practice. Big Business owns and controls the natural supply of raw material out of which the clothing for the people is made and the fuel and facilities by which the people are furnished

heat and light. Big Business owns and controls the
patent rights for all the important machinery used
for commerce or trade and also which the people have
occasion to use. Big Business owns the people and
tells them what they may drink, what they may wear,
where they may educate their children, and what they
may study, and what they must hear and believe. All
of this is Satan's organization, visible to human eyes.

It must be concluded that Satan knew about what
time God would send his beloved Son forth to rule the
world, because Satan can read the Scriptures. Therefore, as the time drew nigh Satan would use all power
at his disposal to quicken the minds of his astute dupes
to bring forth labor-saving machines and devices by
which commerce has grown to such gigantic proportions and controls the labor as well as the material
that is in the world. Satan's purpose would be to con-
centrate all wealth and visible power in the hands of
a few in order that he might keep the people under
control and compel them to bear up and support his
visible organization. His chief objective at all times
has been to turn the people away from God and to
have them support him and his organization. By Big
Business he has controlled the religions and the
preachers, and by these has induced the people to
believe the slanders against God and the reproaches
put upon His name. Satan has consolidated the religions, the commerce and the politics of the world,
and has made this unholy combine a mighty and powerful machine for wickedness. These three elements,
working today under the direction and master-mind
of Satan, have heaped up great treasures by exploiting and robbing the people. Instead of labor's being

able to war against capital, Big Business owns both capital and labor and has made the common people mere serfs, and yet the masses of the people bear up and support the satanic organization.

The small number of people on earth who are faithful and true to Jehovah God are, in the eyes of most people, so completely overshadowed by Satan's great organization that they appear as nothing. Even many who have once made a covenant to do the will of God are now so overawed by Satan and his powerful organization that they refuse to say anything about it. In the eyes of Satan's chief agents on earth Jehovah's faithful witnesses amount to nothing but pestiferous things to annoy Satan's princes in the world. When the little company of God's faithful ones fell under the persecuting hand of "Christendom" during the World War all portions of Satan's organization rejoiced and felicitated one another. Jehovah does not permit such to go unnoticed. Jehovah, foreknowing this, directed Ezekiel to take up a lamentation against Pharaoh king of Egypt, meaning Satan and his organization, and now he directs the Ezekiel class on earth to proclaim this lamentation against the Devil and his organization. Hence he directed Ezekiel to write: "Son of man, take up a lamentation for Pharaoh king of Egypt, and say unto him, Thou art like a young lion of the nations, and thou art as a whale in the seas; and thou camest forth with thy rivers, and troubledst the waters with thy feet, and fouledst their rivers."—32:2.

This prophecy, according to *Rotherham,* speaks of Pharaoh the king of Egypt as "the young lion of the nations thou didst deem thyself". According to

Leeser: "Thou didst deem thyself like a young lion among the nations." In other words, Big Business, under the direction of its father Satan, deemed itself the proper ruler and dictator of the peoples of the nations of the earth. Such has been literally true for years and is true even at this day. Big Business, like its father Satan, has tried to hide itself behind the screens while carrying on its nefarious work. It has always likened itself, however, to the young lion, that is to say, the king of the beasts that dominates and rules. For instance, recently in the city of New York announcement was made by the political department that it was the purpose of the city to market a large amount of bonds to finance public works and other grafts. The big bankers of the city offered to float this bond issue provided the government of the city was fully given over into their hands. This was rather open and bold, but it is in keeping with what Big Business has been doing indirectly in that city for years. The same is true of the nations, particularly of the seventh world power. Space would not permit a review of the many wicked things that have been done by the dominating power of the world. Only a few are here mentioned as examples. Here are some historical facts that may interest the present generation now suffering under the oppressive hand of Satan and his chief instrument Big Business.

NATIONAL BANKING ACT

The National Banking Law of the United States was forced through the Congress of the United States and enacted by Big Business agents. The money lords of the seventh world power, to wit, England and

America, dictated the conditions under which they would finance the Union, because much financing became necessary during the American Civil War, known as the War of the Rebellion. It is practically certain that that war between the North and the South was fomented by the money interests of Britain, the purpose being to divide the states, that the "old mother country" might profit thereby. John Sherman of Ohio was then a member of the United States Congress. In 1855 Mr. Sherman was admitted as a member of Congress.

"In Congress, Mr. Sherman quickly demonstrated his exceptional power as a master of finance. . . . Mr. Sherman was elected [to the Senate] and took his seat 4 March 1861. . . . From 1860 to 1900, there was scarcely a great financial measure with which the name of John Sherman was not connected. Among these were the making of United States treasury notes legal tender, the enacting of the national banking bill, the refunding act of 1870, and the resumption of specie payments. The detailed record of measures by which the legal tender notes of the government reached par, and by which specie resumption became an accomplished fact at the time fixed for it, exhibits the man under whose leadership this was done as a financier of the highest order."—*The Americana,* Volume 24, page 704.

The National Banking Act of the United States provided for the establishment of national banks in the following manner: In a city of more than six thousand population such a bank could be started with a capital of one million dollars. Government bonds were then selling for fifty cents on the dollar, and with five hundred thousand dollars in cash one million dollars of the United States government bonds could be bought. These bonds must be deposited with the government at Washington as security for currency furnished by the government to the bank organized. These bonds deposited with the government belonged, of course, to the bank, and the government paid the bank an annual interest of six percent in gold coin on one million dollars of bonds, which had cost the bank only half a million, and which was therefore equivalent to twelve percent interest on the amount invested by the private interests. In consideration of this deposit of bonds the government then issued currency to the bank up to ninety percent of the par value of the bonds, or nine hundred thousand dollars, which currency must be signed by the president of the bank before it was used and was therefore in fact the money issued by the bank. This was a subterfuge to get around the Constitutional provision for issuing money. This nine hundred thousand dollars so issued in currency, the bank could loan at ten percent interest for thirty or sixty days, the interest payable in advance, of course, which amounted to twelve percent on the nine hundred thousand dollars. The bank, of course, received deposits from the people and was permitted to loan such deposited money for its own private use. The national bank, therefore, was really a gold mine. Rothschild Brothers were then the great money kings of Britain. Those money changers conspired with their allies in the United States in putting through the United States Congress the National Banking Act.

Letters passed between Rothschild Brothers, bankers of London, and Ikleheimer, Morton and Vandergould, of Wall Street, New York, two of which letters, together with a circular appearing with them, and which relate to the National Banking Act, are published below. More than thirty years ago a St. Louis magazine published these letters, and their authenticity has never been disproved. There is still living at this time in the state of New York a man upward of eighty-five years of age who had plates made reproducing these letters as they appeared in the publication above mentioned, and which plates he now has in his possession. He used these letters against the money changers during the Populist movement in the United States. There appears to be only ten days between the dates of the letters, and someone raised the point that in 1863 letters could not pass between London and New York within that time. The same gentleman above mentioned made inquiry of the Information Department of the Post Office Department at Washington concerning this matter. That department replied by letter, and from the letter signed by the Director of the Post Office Department, Division of International Postal Service, the following quotation is taken:

"With reference to your inquiry of September 4th last addressed to Mr. Frederick M. Kirby of the Washington Bureau, this city, requesting information with respect to the shortest time required for a letter to reach New York from London in the year 1863, you are informed that in the year 1863 the SS. "Scotia" crossed the Atlantic in 8 days 3 hours, which

was a record at that time. The average time of mail
steamers was about 9 days.''

The letters between the Rothschild and the Ikleheimer firms, as well as the attached circular, are un-
doubtedly genuine. They are exactly in keeping with
the history of the movements of the bankers and
money powers since 1861 through all of their financial
conspiracies, particularly in reference to the following things, to wit: The EXCEPTION CLAUSE on the
greenbacks; the BANK ACT of 1863; the resumption
of specie payment in 1875; the repeal of the PURCHASE
CLAUSE of the Sherman law of 1878; which acts, of
course, are matters of public record. The above-
mentioned letters and the circular are as follows:

"ROTHSCHILD BROTHERS BANKERS

"London, June 25th. 1863.

"Messrs. Ikleheimer, Morton and Vandergould,
No. 3 Wall Street, New York, U.S.A.

"DEAR SIRS: A Mr. John Sherman has written us
from a town in Ohio, U.S.A., as to the profits that
may be made in the National Banking business under
a recent act of your Congress, a copy of which act
accompanied his letter. Apparently this act has been
drawn upon the plan formulated here last summer by
the British Bankers' Association and by that Association recommended to our American friends as one that

if enacted into law, would prove highly profitable to the banking fraternity throughout the world.

"Mr. Sherman declares that there has never before been such an opportunity for capitalists to accumulate money, as that presented by this act and that the old plan, of State Banks is so unpopular, that the new scheme will, by mere contrast, be most favorably regarded, notwithstanding the fact that it gives the National Banks an almost absolute control of the National finances. "The few who can understand the system," he says, "will either be so interested in its profits, or so dependent on its favors, that there will be no opposition from that class, while on the other hand, *the great body of the people, mentally incapable of comprehending the tremendous advantages that capital derives from the system, will bear its burdens without complaint, and perhaps without even suspecting that the system is inimical to their interests.*"

"Please advise us fully as to this matter, and also, state whether or not you will be of assistance to us, if we conclude to establish a National Bank in the City of New York. If you are acquainted with Mr. Sherman (he appears to have introduced the National Banking act), we will be glad to know something of him. If we avail ourselves of the information he furnished, we will of course make due compensation.

"Awaiting your reply, we are,

　　　　　"Your Respectful Servants,

　　　　　　ROTHSCHILD BROTHERS."

"IKLEHEIMER, MORTON & VANDERGOULD

"Private Bankers, Dealers and Brokers in Stocks and
Bonds and Gold, and American Agents for the
Investment of English Capital.

"Number 3, Wall Street

"New York July 5th. 1863.

"Messrs. Rothschild Brothers,
          London, England.

"DEAR SIRS: We beg leave to acknowledge the
receipt of your letter of June 25th, in which you refer
to a communication received from the Hon. John
Sherman of Ohio, with reference to the advantages
and profits of an American investment, under the
provisions of our National Banking Act.

"The fact that Mr. Sherman speaks well of such
an investment, or of any similar one, is certainly not
without weight, for that gentleman possesses in a
marked degree, the distinguishing characteristics of
the successful modern financier. His temperament is
such that whatever his feelings may be they never
cause him to lose sight of the main chance. He is
young, shrewd and ambitious. He has fixed his eye
upon the presidency of the United States, and is
already a member of Congress. He rightly thinks he
has everything to gain both politically and financially
(he has financial ambitions too), by being friendly

with men and institutions having large financial resources, and which at times, are not too particular in
their methods, either of obtaining governmental aid,
or protecting themselves against unfriendly legislation. We trust him here implicitly. His intellect and
ambition combine to make him exceedingly valuable
to us. Indeed, we predict that if his life be spared, he
will prove to be the best friend the monied interests of
the world have ever had in America.

*"As to the organization of a National Bank here,
and the nature and profits of such an investment, we
beg leave to refer to our printed circular enclosed
herein.* Inquiries by European capitalists, concerning this matter, have been so numerous, that for convenience we have had our views with regard to it
put into printed form.

"Should you determine to organize a bank in this
city, we shall be glad to aid you. We can easily find
financial friends to make a satisfactory directory, and
to fill any official positions not taken by the personal
representatives you will send over.

"Your most obedient servants,

IKLEHEIMER, MORTON & VANDERGOULD"

This latter letter, in the paragraph next to the last,
mentions a circular enclosed, and which circular is
here inserted.

"IKLEHEIMER, MORTON & VANDERGOULD
"Private Bankers, Brokers, Financial Agents, Etc.,

3 Wall Street, New York City

"We have had so many inquiries of late as to the method of organizing national banks under the recent act of congress, and as to the profits that may reasonably be expected from such an investment, that we have thought it best to issue this brief circular as an answer to all questions of our *friends* and *clients:*

"1. Any number of persons, not less than five, may organize a national banking corporation.

"2. Except in cities having 6,000 inhabitants or less, a national bank can not have less than $1,000,000 capital.

"3. They are private corporations organized for private gain, and select their own officers and employes.

"4. They are not subject to the control of the state laws, except as congress may from time to time provide.

"5. They can receive deposits and loan the same for their own benefit.

"6. They can buy and sell bonds, and discount paper and do a general banking business.

"7. To start a national bank on the scale of $1,000,-000 will require the purchase of that amount (par value) of U.S. Government bonds.

"8. U.S. Government bonds can now be purchased at 50 per cent discount, so that a bank of $1,000,000 capital can be started at this time with only $500,000.

"9. These bonds must be deposited with the U.S. Treasurer at Washington, as security for the national bank currency, that on the making of the deposit will be furnished by the government to the bank.

"10. The U.S. Government will pay 6 per cent interest on the bonds, in gold, the interest being paid semi-annually. It will be seen that at the present price of bonds, the interest paid by the government, will of itself amount to 12 per cent in gold, on all the money invested.

"11. The U.S. Government, under the provisions of the national banking act, on having the bonds aforesaid deposited with its treasurer, will on the strength of such security, furnish national currency to the bank depositing the bonds, to the amount of 90 per cent of the face of the bonds, at an annual interest of only ONE per cent per annum. Thus the deposit of $1,000,000 will secure the issue of $900,000 in currency.

"12. This currency is printed by the U.S. Government in a form so like greenback money, that many people do not detect the difference, although the currency is but a promise of the bank to pay—that is, it is the bank's demand note, and must be signed by the bank's president before it can be used.

"13. The demand for money is so great that this currency can be readily loaned to the people across the counter of the bank at a discount at the rate of 10 per cent at 30 to 60 days' time, making about 12 per cent interest on the currency.

"14. The interest on the bonds, plus the interest on the currency which the bonds secure, plus the incidentals of the business ought to make the gross earnings of the bank amount to from 28 to 33 1-3 per cent. The amount of dividends that may be declared will depend largely upon the salaries the officers of the bank vote themselves, and the character and rental charges of the premises occupied by the bank as a place of business. In case it is thought best that the showing of profits should not appear too large, the now common plan of having the directors buy the bank buildings and then raising the rent and the salaries of the president and cashier may be adopted.

"15.   National banks are privileged to either increase or contract their circulation at will and, of course, can grant or withhold loans as they may see fit. As the banks have a national organization, and can easily act together in withholding loans or extending them, it follows that they can by united action in refusing to make loans, cause a stringency in the money market and in a single week or even in a single day cause a decline in all the products of the country. The tremendous possibilities of speculation involved in this control of the money of a country like the United States, will be at once understood by all bankers.

"16.   National banks pay no taxes on their bonds, nor on their capital, nor on their deposits. This exemption from taxation is based on the theory that the capital of these banks is invested in U.S. securities, and is a remarkable permission of the law.

"17.   The secretary may deposit the public money with any bank at will, and to any amount. In the suit of Mr. Branch against the United States, reported in the 12th. volume of the U.S. Court of Claims Reports, at page 287, it was decided that such "Government deposits are rightfully mingled with the other funds of the bank, and are loaned or otherwise employed in the ordinary business of the bank, and the bank becomes the debtor of the United States precisely as it does to other depositors."

"Requesting that you will regard this circular as strictly confidential, and soliciting any favors in our line that you may have to extend, we are,

"Most respectfully yours,

Ikleheimer, Morton & Vandergould."

The reader may draw his own conclusion as to how much aid the selfish bankers had from their political allies in the United States Congress.

"DRAGON IN THE SEAS"

These facts are samples of how a few men have been for many years in the government business and how these financial giants and professional politicians have exploited the people. They claim the right to rule, and did rule, and therefore, as the prophet of God says, Satan likened his offspring to a young lion, the strong or mighty king of his beastly organization. The lamentation that Ezekiel is directed to give against this beastly organization, however, says: "Yet art thou as a dragon in the seas." (*E.R.V.*) Big Business has indirectly been the ruler pictured by a lion, but in so doing it has manifested the monstrous proportions and cruel characteristics of a great crocodile or dragon winding about and hiding itself in the waters, that is, amongst the people, while it has befouled these and exploited the people; and while it has been so doing, the big politicians and big preachers have kept the people's attention turned away from Big Business. This monstrous instrument of the Devil has overflowed the earth and slopped it up and everything around it, and has also tried to drown the Lord's organization: "And the serpent [dragon] cast out of his mouth water as a flood [river, *R.V.*], after the woman, that he might cause her to be carried away of the flood."—Rev. 12:15.

Big Business bears the earmarks of the Devil. Unable to accomplish the desire of self-aggrandizement in an open and clear way Satan and his offspring Big Business 'befoul the waters of the river', that is to say, cloud up and confuse the people in order to prevent detection of the movement and schemes of the wicked thing, and thus the people are deceived and oppressed. Satan and his offspring Big Business have trampled upon every clean thing and clean person with their muddy feet. The offices where the princes of Big Business operate are furnished in elegant and beautiful style and made to appear immaculately clean, but within these walls all manner of crooked schemes and filthy works are carried on by which the people are robbed and made to suffer. Here the products of the land, produced by the hard labor of many honest toilers, are juggled with and gambling schemes are worked out by which the people may be robbed of their honest gains and just dues.

The rich men, the great commercial giants of the world, have lifted themselves up and have taken the religionists, particularly the preachers, by one hand and the conscienceless politicians by the other, and they have walked on together forming a mutual-admiration society. This combination is pictured by the Revelator under the number 666, thus marking it as the beastly thing and offspring of Satan that controls the world. (See Revelation 13:18; *Light*, Book One, page 299.) This beastly monstrosity not only has exploited and robbed the people, but has oppressed and persecuted and killed them, including even those who have committed no greater offense than to boldly speak the truth as witnesses of Jehovah. It must now be apparent to all reasonable persons who give thought to the present unhappy situation, that no earthly power can relieve mankind from the terrible conditions that now exist.

God's time to act has approached. He has heard the cries of the oppressed and his time to give relief as the God of battle is at hand. Therefore he caused his witness to write concerning these modern times of oppression, these last days of Satan's arrogancy manifested by his chiefs in Big Business, big religion and big politics, and who therefore say, "We are rich and have need of nothing," as follows: "Go to now, ye rich men, weep and howl for your miseries that shall come upon you. Your riches are corrupted, and your garments are moth-eaten. Your gold and silver is cankered; and the rust of them shall be a witness against you, and shall eat your flesh as it were fire. Ye have heaped treasure together for the last days. Behold, the hire of the labourers who have reaped down your fields, which is of you kept back by fraud, crieth: and the cries of them which have reaped are entered into the ears of the Lord of Sabaoth. Ye have lived in pleasure on the earth, and been wanton;

ye have nourished your hearts, as in a day of slaughter. Ye have condemned and killed the just; and he doth not resist you.''—Jas. 5:1-6.

In harmony with the foregoing, the Lord God caused Ezekiel to write concerning the monstrous, beastly Big Business: "Thus saith the Lord God, I will therefore spread out my net over thee with a company of many people; and they shall bring thee up in my net." (32:3) Satan's commercial organization is no small fish, and its scales are made great, by which his preachers and professional politicians hang on. It is a powerful thing and in itself is too strong for any other power, except the Lord; but Jehovah's net is strong and will hold it and pull it up and destroy it. Satan and his organization, particularly the commercial element thereof, have fed themselves fat on the small and helpless ones, but their days are numbered and the time of retribution has come.

The ruin of Satan's gigantic organization will bring real satisfaction to honest hearts when they learn its fate: "Then will I leave thee upon the land, I will cast thee forth upon the open field, and will cause all the fowls of the heaven to remain upon thee, and I will fill the beasts of the whole earth with thee. And I will lay thy flesh upon the mountains, and fill the valleys with thy height. I will also water with thy blood the land wherein thou swimmest, even to the mountains; and the rivers shall be full of thee."— 32:4-6.

These words of the prophet of God disclose the vastness of the satanic organization. It now has an international bank that practically controls the money of the world. The overthrow of Big Business, and other parts of Satan's organization hanging on, will be a great slaughter similar to that pictured by the winepress of Revelation 14:19, 20. (See *Light*, Book One, page 342.) Big Business, which is a bloated and a gluttonish thing, and made so by the subtle schemes of robbery and bloodshed, when it is destroyed will be a great spoil. Referring to the wicked thing of the Devil another prophet of God was caused to write: "Their slain also shall be cast out, and their stink shall come up out of their carcases, and the mountains shall be melted with their blood." (Isa. 34:3) Then the righteous will have much cause to rejoice that God has vindicated his name. (Rev. 19:17) Jehovah then indicates his wrath towards Satan and his wicked Big Business organization by sending a gross darkness upon it: "And when I shall put thee out, I will cover the heaven, and make the stars thereof dark; I will cover the sun with a cloud, and the moon shall not give her light. All the bright lights of heaven will I make dark over thee, and set darkness upon thy land, saith the Lord God."—32:7, 8.

When Moses was in Egypt God literally darkened the land so that the Egyptians had no light. (Ex. 10:21-23) Thus God will do to Satan's organization. "I form the light, and create darkness." (Isa. 45:7) At that time in Egypt God's covenant people "had light in their dwellings", while the darkness covered all the Egyptians. Even so now and from now on, Jehovah's witnesses receive the light of the Lord which shines upon them through his Word and through his temple, unfolding to them the meaning of prophecy. This prophecy holds no light or hope for Big Business or for any other part of Satan's organization, but

is dark. Those who are in a covenant with Jehovah
and who now turn away from him will also go immediately into darkness. Jehovah's witnesses now on the
earth by his favor shine forth as the stars that others
may see the light and turn to righteousness. (Dan.
12:3) In doing so, however, these faithful witnesses
of Jehovah do not seek or curry favor of Big Business, nor of any other part of Satan's organization,
but steadfastly continue to proclaim God's message
of truth which speaks vengeance upon every part of
Satan's organization and shows to the people that
their hope of peace and prosperity, life and happiness,
is in Jehovah and his kingdom. At the same time the
clergy, the false prophets of Satan's organization, and
who are hirelings of Big Business, try to brighten the
situation and to create an artificial light for the commercial and political elements; but in this they have
completely failed to accomplish anything. The clergy
take the side of Big Business and big politics in this
time of industrial crisis, and together they deny to
Jehovah's servants the use of the facilities now controlled by Big Business and which might be used to
spread the message of the Lord's kingdom for the encouragement and comfort of the people.

There are many people who still pin their hopes to
the skirts of the commercial wing of Satan's organization. Only the Lord can break the consolidated
power of Big Business, together with other parts of
Satan's organization, and he will do so; and when
that comes to pass Big Business will be amazed and
all who have hung on to it will be amazed: "I will
also vex [margin, provoke to anger, or, grief] the
hearts of many people, when I shall bring thy destruc-

tion among the nations, into the countries which thou hast not known.''—32: 9.

Jehovah will completely destroy Big Business and her methods of exploiting the people: ''Yea, I will make many people amazed at thee, and their kings shall be horribly afraid for thee, when I shall brandish my sword before them: and they shall tremble at every moment, every man for his own life, in the day of thy fall.''—32: 10.

The rulers and the people shall know that the hand of Jehovah God is upon Satan's wicked organization and that Jehovah is the Supreme One. ''For, lo, the kings were assembled, they passed by together. They saw it [Jehovah's sword in the hand of his mighty Officer, Christ Jesus], and so they marvelled; they were troubled, and hasted away. Fear took hold upon them there, and pain, as of a woman in travail. Thou breakest the ships of Tarshish with an east wind.'' (Ps. 48: 4-7) ''He shall judge the poor of the people, he shall save the children of the needy, and shall break in pieces the oppressor.'' (Ps. 72: 4) Big Business has been the chief instrument in the hand of Satan to oppress the people, and both Satan and his instrument shall be completely broken.

Jehovah will use Christ Jesus, his mighty King, to lead his military forces against Satan's organization: ''For thus saith the Lord God, The sword of the king of Babylon shall come upon thee. By the swords of the mighty will I cause thy multitude to fall, the terrible of the nations, all of them; and they shall spoil the pomp of Egypt, and all the multitude thereof shall be destroyed.''—32: 11, 12.

Christ and his army will strike terror to the heart of Egypt and Satan, and his organization shall fall. (Isa. 9:6; Zech. 10:5) Jehovah shows himself in the capacity of a destroyer to his enemies; Abaddon, the mighty One over the army of destruction, is He. (Rev. 9:11) The disturbers and polluters of mankind will be destroyed and, as it is written: "[Thou] shouldest destroy them which destroy the earth." (Rev. 11:18) The hoofs of Satan's war organization shall never again tread down the people. Armageddon will put an end to all militarism.

LASTING PEACE WILL FOLLOW

"Then will I make their waters deep [clear, *R.V.*], and cause their rivers to run like oil, saith the Lord God." (32:14) This certainly pictures perfect peace. Most of the people are shallow-minded and easy to be disturbed by the enemy's propaganda; but the people shall come to know that Jehovah and his Word of truth are right and just, that Jehovah God is their real Friend and Benefactor, and they shall no longer be disturbed. The Lord will bring peace to them. The streams of the people he will cause to flow peaceably to the kingdom, and there will be no more friction, but the people will flow together "like oil". Jerusalem, God's organization, will be their joy. "For thus saith the Lord, Behold, I will extend peace to her like a river, and the glory of the Gentiles like a flowing stream: then shall ye suck, ye shall be borne upon her sides, and be dandled upon her knees." "And it shall come to pass in the last days, that the mountain of the Lord's house shall be established in the top of the mountains, and shall be exalted above the hills; and all nations shall flow unto it."—Isa. 66 : 12; 2 : 2, 3.

The destruction of Satan's oppressive organization must precede the restitution or healing and the prosperity of mankind. Big Business, therefore, God will destroy, and the people shall know that Jehovah is God. The operators of Big Business must be destroyed and multitudes of people on earth, who have been enslaved by this instrument of Satan, must be set free. Jehovah, by his Executive, will accomplish this, and the people shall know that it is Jehovah's hand that did it. "When I shall make the land of Egypt desolate, and the country shall be destitute of that whereof it was full, when I shall smite all them that dwell therein, then shall they know that I am the Lord. This is the lamentation wherewith they shall lament her: the daughters of the nations shall lament her; they shall lament for her, even for Egypt, and for all her multitude, saith the Lord God." (32 : 15, 16) Those who survive and who have relied upon this wing of Satan's organization shall greatly lament.

THE FUNERAL

It would seem presumptuous to say just at what day or hour the Lord will execute his judgment upon Satan's organization at Armageddon, and therefore no attempt is made to comment upon the time that it will take place. Jesus makes it plain that the witness work must be done first and then will come the fight. Just fifteen days after Ezekiel had uttered the foregoing prophecy concerning Egypt the Lord told him to wail for the multitude of Egypt: "It came to pass also in the twelfth year, in the fifteenth day of the month, that the word of the Lord came unto me, saying, Son of man, wail for the multitude of Egypt, and cast them down, even her, and the daughters of the famous nations, unto the nether parts of the earth, with them that go down into the pit. Whom dost thou pass in beauty? go down, and be thou laid with the uncircumcised."—32: 17-19.

This is not to be understood that Ezekiel was to utter a "wail" out of sympathy for Satan's organization, but to deliver in a wailing tone this prophecy. Ezekiel was used not for violence against Egypt, but to prophesy; and in his prophecy he should wail, "and say that it shall go down" (*Leeser*); "and cause it to descend." (*Rotherham*) Satan's representatives have made funerals the occasion for exhibiting a great amount of hypocrisy. It would be appropriate for Jehovah's representative to speak ironically concerning the funeral of Satan's organization and to prophesy that the famous, powerful, 'honorable' and mighty must go down to oblivion. And so the prophet wailed: "Whom dost thou pass in beauty?" "Than whom art thou more precious?" (*Rotherham*) Manifestly these words are spoken ironically, as though the man would say: "You have prided yourself on being more beautiful and precious than others, but you are not, and you must go down and be laid with the unclean." The beauty and grandeur of Satan's crowd cannot save them. "Be thou laid with the (other) uncircumcised."—*Leeser*.

Big Business, militarism and all the hangers-on and preachers of Satan's organization, shall go down just alike. "They shall fall in the midst of them that are slain by the sword; she is delivered to the sword:

draw her and all her multitudes. The strong among the mighty shall speak to him out of the midst of hell with them that help him: they are gone down, they lie uncircumcised, slain by the sword.'' (32: 20, 21) The various parts of Satan's organization will greet each other in hell, doubtless in the same manner that Dives spoke in hell. (Luke 16: 22-24) The various organizations and their power will be destroyed, but some of the erstwhile members thereof will probably survive and wail a while longer before they receive their just deserts. The whole company is mentioned. ''Asshur is there, and all her company: his graves are about him; all of them slain, fallen by the sword: whose graves are set in the sides of the pit, and her company is round about her grave; all of them slain, fallen by the sword, which caused terror in the land of the living.'' (32: 22, 23) Big politics, including the League of Nations, must receive a deadly blow from the sword of the Lord and go down with the other elements of the enemy organization. All parts of the enemy organization have caused terror in the earth and have particularly manifested their wickedness against those of God's people who are in the land of the living.

Verses twenty-four to thirty then describe the various elements of the enemy organization that have perished and gone down to the pit, and are therefore considered in the wail at the funeral. ''There is Elam and all her multitude round about her grave.'' Even as far back as Abraham's day Elam was a prominent power and had imperialistic ambitions and headed a league of kings. Abraham defeated them. (Gen. 14: 1-16; Isa. 21: 2) Thus the Elamites seem well to foreshadow rulers with imperialist designs and in favor of the League of Nations, but opposed to God's kingdom and his Christ, the true seed of Abraham. "There is Meshech, Tubal, and all her multitude." Tubal and Meshech were sons of Japheth, whence comes the white European race. They both did a commercial business with Tyre. (27: 13) They carried on a slave trade. They traded in the persons of men. 'Gog was their prince.' (38: 2) They were eager to take spoil, and carried away silver and gold. In these was made manifest the greedy commercial spirit willing to deal in human flesh, and which was made manifest in the ones engaged therein by capturing the negroes of Africa and selling them in slavery to American plantation owners; and in more modern times by carrying Chinese coolies to the mines of South Africa and there using them as slaves. This shows a hard-hearted company of great rapacity that causes them to invade the land of the peaceful and contented and carry them away and sell them to further the selfish interest of Big Business.

The history of the chief countries of the seventh world power, Britain and the United States, and some of their chief men of these countries, and faithless politicians in particular, are here clearly pictured. In the past these nations have buried their supposed great men with much pomp and honor and glory, and the clergy have harangued the people concerning their greatness; but now they must lie with the uncircumcised and the unclean, and thus Ezekiel wails for their funeral. In the past "the mighty men" of the land of the seventh world power in particular have been buried with "their swords under their heads", that

is to say, with military honors; but Ezekiel now tells
their successors that they and all others of the Devil's
crowd must go down in disgrace and dishonor, and
with no hypocritical preachers to sing their praises
or to eulogize them at the funeral.

Then mention is made of Edom, her mighty men,
and the Zidonians. These were associates with Meshech and Tubal. These well picture the cool, shrewd
financial gamblers and profiteers that have formulated
divers and numerous schemes to exploit and rob the
people. Also, the Zidonians well represent the "strong-
arm squad" and "big navy" crowd that have fraudulently tried to use the Word of God to justify the
building of great naval machines to publicly murder
and destroy. The crooked politicians, the bribe-givers,
and the bribe-takers, the public exploiters and public
thieves, all share in that funeral concerning which
Ezekiel is commanded to ironically wail.

Then, says the Lord: "Pharaoh shall see them, and
shall be comforted over all his multitude, even Pharaoh and all his army slain by the sword, saith the
Lord God." (32:31) This supports the conclusion
that Satan will see his mighty organization fall and
then he will be killed. (See *Light*, Book Two, page
186.) Only the Devil, or one having his spirit, could
be comforted at the fall of others. He probably concludes that he has succeeded in defaming the name
of Jehovah and in taking away this great multitude
from Jehovah, and sees them plunged into destruction, and such brings to Satan some satisfaction. As
Ezekiel was commanded to utter the prophetic wail
for the slaying of Satan and his multitude, even so
now the Ezekiel class utters the wail for the enemy

organization because at the final funeral of Satan and his "big guns" there will be no clergymen present to extol the greatness of those that lie in hades. The witnesses of Jehovah see what God will bring to pass by Christ Jesus, and they tell others about it, even before the actual funeral of Satan's crowd takes place.

WHY PERMITTED

The prophecy of the thirty-second chapter of Ezekiel was delivered by the prophet about two months after his dumbness had ended and his mouth was opened at the coming of the refugee from Jerusalem to inform him that the city had fallen. He concluded this particular prophecy by delivering the message of Jehovah, to wit: "For I have caused my terror in the land of the living; and he shall be laid in the midst of the uncircumcised with them that are slain with the sword, even Pharaoh and all his multitude, saith the Lord God."—32:32.

In this day of great suffering and distress many persons propound the question: "Why is Big Business permitted to exploit and oppress the people? If Jehovah is the God of justice and love, why does he not prevent such oppression?" Also they propound the question: "Why did God permit the Devil to blind the people and to build a massive organization by which he oppresses them? Why has God permitted Satan all these centuries to bring so much wickedness on mankind?"

The correct answer to these questions can be had only when we see the great issue or question that has long existed and which now must be for ever settled. That issue or question involves the word and name of

Jehovah God. Is God true? and is his name worthy of all praise? This question must be settled right. Jehovah has permitted the whole matter to be made to appear so clear to his remnant that they may have no doubt about it, and soon he will make it plain and clear to others that all may know that he is the only true and almighty God, and the one from whom comes life. God has not permitted this wickedness in order to teach men lessons. He could not be a party to any such wicked thing. God created Lucifer a perfect creature and assigned him to his high position. Lucifer rebelled and defied Jehovah to put men on earth who would at all times, and under all circumstances, remain true and faithful to God. Lucifer not only declared God to be a liar, but raised the issue that Jehovah God is not supreme and that his name is not worthy of praise. Lucifer, thereafter called Satan the Devil, became God's opposer, and as Satan the Devil he has gone his length in wickedness; and God has permitted him to go until His own due time arrives to prove that Jehovah is the Almighty God. The prophecy of Ezekiel stresses the point that all shall know that Jehovah is God.

Pharaoh the king of Egypt was without doubt a type of Satan the Devil. Egypt was for a time the abode of God's people, and Pharaoh and other Egyptians oppressed them while there. Pharaoh builded a mighty commercial machine by which he exploited and oppressed the people. He made slaves of the people and profited by their unpaid labor. He also builded a mighty military machine to support his commercial power. In this Pharaoh the king of Egypt, and his multitude, pictured the Devil and his mighty organization that has exploited and oppressed the peoples of earth and particularly those who have been servants of Jehovah God. The Prophet Ezekiel is caused to say: "For I have caused my terror in the land of the living." Other translators rendered these words as follows: "For I have suffered his terror to be in the land of the living." (*Roth.*) This must mean that Pharaoh represented that which God originally had made but which became corrupted because of wickedness in the creature. Lucifer was put in the land of the living, but because of his own wicked covetousness he became Satan the old Serpent, the Dragon and Devil. It was the will of God that men should trade with each other, but on terms of justice and righteousness. One of the primary requirements of men is that they must do justly. (Mic. 6:8) Satan has perverted the whole manner of trade and barter. He began his commerce with the human family. Satan and his agents have made trade or commerce the most wicked and oppressive thing on earth, and that because of a covetous desire to possess what others rightfully had. They have not at all done justly. Pharaoh and his multitude of supporters therefore picture the Devil and his oppressive organization unjustly compelling the people to work for them, robbing them of their just possessions, and oppressing them.

Concerning Pharaoh and his multitude it is written: "For now I will stretch out my hand, that I may smite thee and thy people with pestilence; and thou shalt be cut off from the earth. And in very deed for this cause have I raised thee up, for to shew in thee my power; and that my name may be declared throughout all the earth."—Ex. 9:15, 16.

These words apply with greater force to Satan himself and also to his organization. The primary application of the text is to Satan. The application to Pharaoh is only in a representative capacity as picturing Satan. Mark that the text does not say that God made Satan and approved his wickedness, nor that he made Pharaoh and approved his wickedness. The marginal reading of the text is this: "For this purpose have I let thee remain, for the purpose of showing thee my might, and that my name may be celebrated in all the earth." (Ex. 9: 16, *Roth.*) "But for this cause have I allowed thee to remain, in order to show thee my power; and in order that they may proclaim my name throughout all the earth."—*Leeser.*

JEHOVAH'S NAME

When Lucifer rebelled and defied Jehovah, God could have immediately destroyed him; but, had he done so, there would have been no opportunity afforded to try out before creation the question which Lucifer had raised. God merely changed his name from Lucifer to Satan, meaning opposer of God, and then gave him the additional names of Devil, which means slanderer of God; and Serpent, meaning deceiver of others; and Dragon, the devourer of those who would serve God. This would put all creation on notice that God's opposer is the arch wicked one claiming to be equal to God. The word of God is always right, and he is right and true. The issue was then squarely joined and Satan must go his limit in order that the issue might be settled properly, conclusively, and for all time. God has permitted Satan to take his own wicked course until he has reached the limit.

At the end of the world Satan's organization appears in its most hideous form, with almost all of the peoples of earth turned against God and into Satan's organization. Never was his organization so powerful as now. At this time his people see what the issue is and what is the true answer to the question so often propounded, to wit, Why has God permitted the wicked oppression to be upon the peoples of earth? The correct answer is that God in due time must prove to all creation that Satan is a liar, and a murderer, and that Jehovah is just, righteous and true, and that Jehovah's Word of truth and his name is above all reproach. All creation must see that the Devil is responsible for all the wickedness that has been upon creation. Now God will destroy Satan and his creation to settle the issue that Jehovah is supreme.

The foregoing text of Exodus 9:16 fully and completely corroborates this conclusion. The part of the text that is to be emphasized is THE NAME OF JEHOVAH GOD. The time must come when he would have his name placed where it properly belongs before all creation. His name must be proclaimed throughout the earth, because God says: 'I have permitted thee to remain, that my name may be declared throughout all the earth.' This must be done in God's due time, and that due time has arrived. Who are the people that will have such a privilege of proclaiming God's name? Necessarily those men and women on earth who maintain their integrity and prove their loyalty and faithfulness to God under the test. This must be done, therefore, by the people whom God has taken out of the world as a people for his name. (Acts 15:14, 15) It is his people that he has called out of darkness into his marvelous light that they might show forth his praises. (1 Pet. 2:9, 10) Thus the Scriptures identify the remnant now on earth whom God uses to proclaim his name. These scriptures, including the prophecies, were written for the special benefit of the remnant at this time. —Rom. 15:4.

In harmony with his promise God has now brought to light the meaning of the prophecies which show why God permitted Satan to pursue his wicked course, and that it is that Satan may put forth all his efforts, and then God will demonstrate before all that Satan's efforts are in vain. God's time approaches for him to destroy Satan and his entire organization, both visible and invisible. Before doing so he first informs his remnant as to the meaning of his Word, and then he puts upon these his anointed a new name designating them as Jehovah's witnesses, and sends them forth to proclaim his Word and name to the nations before the destruction that shall come at Armageddon. It is therefore incumbent upon those who are in the covenant for the kingdom, and who truly love God, to make known these truths, that those who will hear may have due notice of God's purposes, and that he is the Supreme One, and the Blesser of those who love righteousness. For this reason Jehovah's witnesses are now going from place to place telling the people the truth and exhibiting to them books that contain the message of truth. Thus they are singing Jehovah's praises, proclaiming his name, making it known throughout the earth, and particularly within the borders of "Christendom", which is modern "Jerusalem", that the people may see who is supreme and whence their blessings must come. What a marvelous privilege the remnant thus enjoy!

God used Pharaoh to make a prophetic record disclosing the Devil and his wicked operations in opposition to God. He sent Moses down to Egypt to appear before Pharaoh that he might make a record under Jehovah's direction, and to the name of Jehovah. Moses mentioned Jehovah's name, and Pharaoh replied: 'Who is Jehovah, that I should obey him?' Pharaoh had builded a great commercial and military power in Egypt. This was a picture of Satan, who has builded the great commercial and military power of the earth. Pharaoh enslaved the Jews and robbed them, as well as oppressing and killing them. Satan, by his commercial and military Big Business, and its allies, has enslaved the people, exploited and robbed them, and unjustly killed the defenseless. It is therefore clearly seen that Pharaoh and his supporters pictured Satan and his organization. Pharaoh and his army were destroyed. Even so God will destroy Satan and his host. Before destroying Pharaoh God caused Moses and Aaron to serve them with notice and warning. Before the destruction of Satan and his organization God sends Jesus Christ, to whom is delivered the testimony, and Christ Jesus now present brings into his temple the remnant and directs the remnant, to whom he has committed the work to bear the testimony, to go throughout the land and serve notice and warning of God's purpose to destroy the enemy and to deliver his people; and this must be done before Armageddon.

Let the people now understand that their sufferings have come upon them through Satan and through his agencies, to wit, false religionists, Big Business, big politics, militarism, and all hangers-on, and that Satan is the invisible and wicked ruler of the world, and that now the time is at hand when God will destroy these wicked ones, and such destruction will result in releasing the people from oppression. This he does for his own righteous name's sake. He will make the people "know", that all may see that he is supreme. This he will make known fully at the great battle of Armageddon, at which time Satan and his crowd shall go down in disgrace. "For I have caused my terror in the land of the living; and he shall be laid in the midst of the uncircumcised with them that are slain with the sword, even Pharaoh and all his multitude, saith the Lord God." (32:32) Those who love righteousness, and who now see the truth, will take their stand on the side of Jehovah God, and will have full faith and confidence in his word: "The Lord preserveth all them that love him: but all the wicked will he destroy."—Ps. 145:20.

CHAPTER VII

RESPONSIBILITY

(EZEKIEL, CHAPTER 33)

JEHOVAH is supreme and above all. He is over his organization, and of every one whom he saves and receives as a member of that organization he requires obedience. His word is law to all who love him, and his approval is given only to those who do obey his law. When he says in his Word that he requires of creatures to 'walk humbly before him' (Mic. 6:8), that means that the one who receives a knowledge of God is in duty bound to do what God commands. Man's responsibility before God is according to his knowledge of God's will. When Jehovah made a covenant with Israel he said: "Now therefore, if ye will obey my voice indeed, and keep my covenant, then ye shall be a peculiar treasure unto me above all people: for all the earth is mine. And ye shall be unto me a kingdom of priests, and an holy nation." (Ex. 19:5,6) That is a statement of the divine rule which determines who shall be in the kingdom of God. Because the Israelites failed to obey him God took away that privilege of his kingdom, and declared he would give it to those who do obey him. (Matt. 21:43) Only those who are diligent to obey the voice of God shall abide in his temple. (Zech. 6:15) One may be pursuing an unlawful way because of ignorance, but upon learning the truth the obligation is upon him to obey the truth. (1 Tim. 1:13;

Eph. 4: 17-21) Those who diligently seek a knowledge and understanding God will reward by having their understanding opened; and then their responsibility increases and they are under obligation to obey. "Then he sheweth them their work, and their transgressions that they have exceeded. He openeth also their ear to discipline, and commandeth that they return from iniquity. If they obey and serve him, they shall spend their days in prosperity, and their years in pleasures: but if they obey not, they shall perish by the sword."—Job 36: 9-12.

The Prophet Ezekiel, being Jehovah's servant, pictures the "servant" class now on the earth, that is to say, those who have agreed to do the will of God and who have been enlightened and made to understand his purposes and who have been anointed to do his service. These are particularly responsible before God to obey his commandments and never to deviate therefrom because of any influence exercised by another. Ezekiel was again commanded by the Lord to speak to the Israelites, after the period of his dumbness toward Jerusalem was broken or ended. Nebuchadnezzar having assaulted the city of Jerusalem and destroyed it, the responsibility upon Ezekiel as watchman toward Israel to warn them against danger would seem to have ended or expired. But now he is commanded to speak a prophecy after the city had fallen. Probably this prophecy (chap. 33: 1-20) came to Ezekiel on the evening before the escaped messenger from Jerusalem reached Ezekiel on the morning following, but on the same day, since the day of the Jews began after six o'clock in the evening. The fact that the prophecy was given at that late day shows that Ezekiel's duty as watchman had not terminated and he was not discharged from such responsibility. He must continue as watchman toward the Israelites now going into captivity. This shows that God's faithful "servant" class now on earth is obligated at all times to watch and to give warning to others against dangers. (Luke 21:36; Rev. 16:15) Says the Prophet Ezekiel: "Again the word of the Lord came unto me, saying, Son of man, speak to the children of thy people, and say unto them, When I bring the sword upon a land, if the people of the land take a man of their coasts, and set him for their watchman."—33: 1, 2.

This shows that God's "servant" class must now proclaim the warning and serve notice upon the people and rulers before the sword of Armageddon smites Satan's organization. The Lord gives the instruction to Ezekiel first to use an illustration that relates to other lands round about Jerusalem, such as Ammon, Moab, Edom, Philistia, Tyre and Zidon, Egypt and Ethiopia, upon which God had declared he would bring the sword of destruction. (Jer. 25:13-36) This illustration shows that the fulfilment or application of this prophecy of the thirty-third chapter of Ezekiel must take place before the battle of Armageddon. "The sword" represents God's judgment being executed, and which sword Jehovah brings down upon the enemy. "If the people of the land take a man of their coasts [from among them, R.V.]," it is his duty, the prophecy says, 'to give warning.' The people of "Christendom" have done that very thing. They have chosen the clergymen of the various denominational systems to scan the spiritual horizon and to read in the sky and to give them warning concerning their eternal welfare; but concerning this the clergymen have been unfaithful.

The clergymen cannot be relieved of responsibility because of being entirely ignorant. They profess to know the Word of God, and they have had the opportunity to know it, and they hold themselves forth as teachers of it. The World War was clearly a fulfilment of prophecy with which they should all have been familiar. Therefore says the prophet: "If, when he seeth the sword come upon the land he blow the trumpet, and warn the people; then whosoever heareth the sound of the trumpet, and taketh not warning; if the sword come, and take him away, his blood shall be upon his own head. He heard the sound of the trumpet, and took not warning, his blood shall be upon him: but he that taketh warning shall deliver his soul."—33:3-5.

When the war was on, a company of preachers in London issued a manifesto which was blown like a big trumpet through Britain and America and a copy sent to each and every preacher. That manifesto called the attention to the words of the great Prophet Christ Jesus concerning the end of the world and the coming of the kingdom. But the clergymen throughout "Christendom", and the principal ones of their flock, failed to give any heed to the men which the people had chosen from amongst themselves and from their organization to be their watchmen, and all the clergymen failed to do their duty. The responsibility therefore rests upon those who spurned the words calling attention to fulfilment of prophecy.

The clergymen claimed to represent God, and Christ, and to be watchmen of their respective flocks.

Therefore says the prophecy: "But if the watchman see the sword come, and blow not the trumpet, and the people be not warned; if the sword come, and take any person from among them, he is taken away in his iniquity; but his blood will I require at the watchman's hand." (33:6) The clergymen have no excuse for not seeing what was coming and what the events of that day portended, and hence it is written of them that "they willingly are ignorant". (2 Pet. 3:5) Willingly going on in darkness does not at all relieve them of their responsibility. They should have known from the Lord's Word that the World War marked the beginning of the sorrows upon the nations, and was evidence of the end of the world, and the second coming of Christ (Matt. 24:3-8), and they should have thus warned the people, but they did not. Even the distinguished gentlemen of the cloth who signed the London manifesto above mentioned have gone back on that manifesto.

But there is another class that is even more reprehensible and therefore more responsible than the clergy of the denominations of "Christendom". Prior to the coming of the Lord to the temple of Jehovah there were a number who had made a covenant to do God's will and who were favored with the truth then due and had received a knowledge of the meaning of "the end of the world". They claimed to be looking for the kingdom and talked about its coming. In 1918, or about that time, they said, however, by their actions and therefore in their hearts: "My Lord delayeth his coming." They then began to oppose their brethren who were telling about the kingdom. They have made no further progress in the truth,

but continue to oppose those who serve God, and
therefore Christ Jesus our Lord designates such as
the "evil servant". They scoff at the statement published that the parable of the "sheep and the goats"
applies at the present time; they deny that the kingdom began in 1914; and they ignore the fact of the
existence of Satan's organization, if they believe it,
and they fail to warn the people of the sword of God's
vengeance that shall come upon the nations and the
people. The Lord will not hold the clergy of "Christendom" blameless, as the prophecy shows, and surely he will not pass the "evil servant" class by without requiring such to come under the terms of his
judgment announced.

WATCHMAN

Having given Ezekiel the foregoing illustration,
then Jehovah points out the responsibility that is upon the watchman, whom the Lord has chosen. "So
thou, O son of man, I have set thee a watchman unto
the house of Israel; therefore thou shalt hear the word
at my mouth, and warn them from me." (33:7) Although Ezekiel was the watchman to only the house
of Israel, yet the Lord used him to pronounce the
judgment of doom upon the seven other nations mentioned in the preceding chapters. This shows that the
watchman of the Lord for his own people must and
will see and recognize the satanic organization and
plainly point it out to the people. Let it be noted that
the "watchman" of the seventh verse above quoted
is Jehovah's watchman appointed by him, and not
appointed by the people, as the clergymen are. Men

have nothing to do with the appointment of God's watchman, even though they may think they have. The remnant class, being the feet members of Christ on earth, constitute the watchman unto their brethren, that is to say, for each other and others who will hear. (Rom. 12:1) The word "watchman" here used means one who leans forward and peers into the distance and observes, awaits developments, and makes known what appears. The watchman recognizes that he has a duty to perform, and performs it as unto the Lord.

The entire remnant collectively is designated "the watchman". Jehovah lets his servants know that God has appointed this watchman; and this "servant" or "remnant" class has a far greater responsibility than if appointed or chosen by the people. The "watchman" would be expected to see clearly, and to him the Lord would make known the meaning of his prophecies to the end that he might have a clear vision and then use it to the glory of the Lord. It would be expected that God would show the "watchman" what is his own organization, and his purposes in his organization, and would also disclose to the "watchman" the enemy organization; furthermore, that God would reveal to the "watchman" the great issue that must now be settled, and why the battle of Armageddon will be fought. That is exactly what the Lord God has given to the temple class during the past few years. Then the "servant" class is told by the Lord: "Thou shalt hear the word at my mouth, and warn them from me." It is not the "servant's" warning, but the Lord's message of warning, that must be given. The "servant" or "watchman" merely hears it and repeats it to others as commanded. There is no excuse for failure so to do.

Jehovah further emphasizes that the warning is his, and not that of some creature, when he directed Ezekiel to say: "When I say unto the wicked, O wicked man, thou shalt surely die; if thou dost not speak to warn the wicked from his way, that wicked man shall die in his iniquity; but his blood will I require at thine hand." (33:8) Therefore when Jehovah's witnesses go forth with the message they should always bear in mind that the message is the Lord's, and not man's, and that it is the privilege and duty of these witnesses to speak only as the Lord dictates. Obedience to organization directions must be observed, and Jehovah is the Head over all of his great organization. Christ Jesus, the executive of Jehovah, is directing the course of the organization. The Hebrew word that is here translated "wicked" is rendered "lawless" by *Rotherham;* which means that one who has received a knowledge of the truth and light and then deliberately goes contrary thereto is lawless or wicked, and such is destroyed in the second death, from which there is no resurrection.

Those who constitute God's "watchman" must use the means God has provided for them with which to give the warning, and a failure so to do would mean death to the "watchman". Evidently this text applies to those who are pursuing a course of lawlessness that leads them into the "evil servant" class, or the "man of sin", "the son of perdition," but who have not yet reached the stage where "it is impossible to renew them again unto repentance". (Heb. 6:6, *R.V.*) When one has reached that stage further warning is

WATCHMAN TO THE HOUSE OF ISRAEL   Page 206

superfluous, and hence the "watchman" would then say: "I will keep my mouth with a bridle, while the wicked is before me." (Ps. 39:1) Jehovah's "watchman" must give the warning, but it is unprofitable for Jehovah's witnesses to engage in a controversy with those who were once enlightened and who now openly oppose the proclamation of the kingdom message and the message against Satan's organization. To such opposers the words of Jehovah apply: "He which is filthy, let him be filthy still." When that stage is reached no further warning would be in order and the "watchman" is relieved of the responsibility for such. "Nevertheless, if thou warn the wicked of his way to turn from it; if he do not turn from his way, he shall die in his iniquity; but thou hast delivered thy soul. Therefore, O thou son of man, speak unto the house of Israel, Thus ye speak, saying, If our transgressions and our sins be upon us, and we pine away in them, how should we then live?" (33:9, 10) This scripture shows that the lawless are beyond the point of recovery, but, if the warning has been given, then the "watchman" has shown faithfulness and is relieved of further responsibility.

Those who have covenanted to do the will of God and who are pursuing an unlawful course may and sometimes do resent the warning and retort substantially in these words: 'According to you, watchman, we are due to die because of a lawless course, so why bother us with your warning? Keep your counsel to yourself.' If there yet seems to be a hope of recovery of those who are warned, then the "servant" class is directed to speak thus: "Say unto them, As I live, saith the Lord God, I have no pleasure in the death

of the wicked; but that the wicked turn from his way
and live; turn ye, turn ye from your evil ways; for
why will ye die, O house of Israel?'' (33:11) In
other words, God says to the ones pursuing a lawless
course: 'This is no idle matter; take my words seriously that are spoken by my watchman. You are on the
road to death, and that will bring me no pleasure.
That is why I have directed my watchman to warn
you, for your own welfare. Do not feel resentful toward my watchman for obeying my instructions.'
Of course, this conclusion as to what Jehovah says is
based upon the words of the prophet: ''He that hath
an ear [to hear], let him hear what the Spirit saith
unto the churches.''—Rev. 3:22.

The fact that one has been made a member of the
temple class, and hence brought under the robe of
righteousness, is no absolute guarantee that he is safe.
He must continue to be faithful in obedience to God's
commandment even unto death. Indifference and
negligence will not be tolerated by the Lord. Hence
the Lord directs his prophet to speak a message to
those of his own organization: ''Therefore, thou son
of man, say unto the children of thy people, The
righteousness of the righteous shall not deliver him in
the day of his transgression: as for the wickedness of
the wicked, he shall not fall thereby in the day that
he turneth from his wickedness; neither shall the
righteous be able to live for his righteousness in the
day that he sinneth.'' (33:12) What righteousness
one has done or the righteous position that he occupies
today will not save him in the day that he sins.
''When I shall say to the righteous, that he shall
surely live; if he trust to his own righteousness, and

commit iniquity, all his righteousnesses shall not be re-membered; but for his iniquity that he hath com-mitted, he shall die for it." (33:13) The Lord does not tell any individual that now he is certain to win regardless of what he does; but the Lord does point out the conditions of righteousness to which such must conform themselves if they receive the life promised. When one examines himself by the standard of right-eousness which God gives, and determines whether or not he is one of the righteous to whom God has prom-ised life, and if he continues in the right way, he will receive life. But if he thinks he has developed a char-acter that is finished, and that henceforth he can do no wrong, he is deceiving himself and is in great danger. 'If he trusts in his own righteousness and commits iniquity' the righteousness that he previous-ly possessed will avail him nothing. Such is in har-mony with the warning: "Let him that thinketh he standeth take heed lest he fall." (1 Cor. 10:12) There is no obligation upon the Lord's part to excuse wrong-doing merely because one has once been righteous. No man can be righteous of himself; but his right-eousness is by reason of what God does for him. If one then willfully sins against the light there is no forgiveness for such.—Matt. 12:32.

When Jehovah pronounces final judgment there is no change of it, because God does not change. "Again, when I say unto the wicked, Thou shalt surely die; if he turn from his sin, and do that which is lawful and right." (33:14) This verse therefore must mean that the Lord's "watchman" is pointing out the course that has the Lord's approval, and that which God states he disapproves, and he gives warning to those who are pursuing an unlawful course that they will die if they continue in that unlawful way; hence God's "watchman" must 'Cry aloud and spare not', and do this in obedience to God's commandment. (Isa. 58:1) The "watchman" is the "faithful servant" class, composed of many but addressed collectively. This class is used as the channel or means which the Lord has provided to give such warning. —See *The Watchtower* 1929, page 131.

If those who are pursuing an unlawful course give heed to the warning and turn about and do right, such shall profit thereby, as the Lord states: "If the wicked restore the pledge, give again that he had robbed, walk in the statutes of life, without committing iniquity; he shall surely live, he shall not die. None of his sins that he hath committed, shall be mentioned unto him; he hath done that which is lawful and right; he shall surely live." (33:15, 16) "Then shall thy light break forth as the morning, and thine health shall spring forth speedily; and thy righteousness shall go before thee: the glory of the Lord shall be thy rereward [rear guard]. Then shalt thou call, and the Lord shall answer; thou shalt cry, and he shall say, Here I am. If thou take away from the midst of thee the yoke, the putting forth of the finger, and speaking vanity."—Isa. 58:8, 9; *The Watchtower*, 1929, pages 134, 135.

God's mercy is extended to those who acknowledge the wrong committed, confess it, and again pursue a lawful course. The Mosaic law provided that the sinner must acknowledge his sin and then offer some sacrifice to God through his priesthood as a basis for God's forgiveness. Likewise in the fulfilment of this

prophecy (vs. 16), the wrongdoer must first acknowledge his sin and ask for the intervening of Christ Jesus in his behalf as his advocate before God forgives
and restores the sinner. "We have an advocate with
the Father, Jesus Christ the righteous." (1 John 2:1)
Such is the rightful course and is pleasing to Jehovah. "And if so be that he find it, verily I say unto
you, he rejoiceth more of that sheep, than of the
ninety and nine which went not astray." (Matt.
18:13) All the heavenly creatures reflect this attitude. "I say unto you, that likewise joy shall be in
heaven over one sinner that repenteth, more than over
ninety and nine just persons, which need no repentance. Likewise, I say unto you, there is joy in the
presence of the angels of God over one sinner that repenteth." (Luke 15: 7, 10) Those who return to the
Lord with a pure heart and in his appointed way he
will receive. "For as the heaven is high above the
earth, so great is his mercy toward them that fear
him. As far as the east is from the west, so far hath he
removed our transgressions from us."—Ps. 103: 11, 12.

Some complain against the Lord and his way of extending mercy to the erring one who repents and re-
turns, like the son who objected to the killing of the
fatted calf at the return of the prodigal. Therefore
says the prophet: "Yet the children of thy people
say, The way of the Lord is not equal; but as for them,
their way is not equal." (33: 17) This complaint may
be made by those who think they have developed a
perfect character, and hence they say that they only
should receive the favors of the Lord. Their com-
plaints are wrongfully made. The ways of the Lord
are equal, equitable and impartial, for he is both

'just, and the justifier of them that believe in Christ Jesus'. (Rom. 3:26) God is no respecter of persons. Neither the righteousness of the righteous nor the wickedness of the wicked results in profit or loss to Jehovah God. It can therefore be easily seen that God could have no occasion to be otherwise than equal in his ways toward all creatures.—Job 35:6-9.

God's law is just and right and his mercy endureth for ever. Therefore reads the prophecy: "When the righteous turneth from his righteousness, and committeth iniquity, he shall even die thereby: but if the wicked turn from his wickedness, and do that which is lawful and right, he shall live thereby. Yet ye say, The way of the Lord is not equal. O ye house of Israel, I will judge you every one after his ways." (33:18-20) Those who have sought to justify themselves rather than God will find that they do not judge themselves aright and equally according to God's standard. "So then every one of us shall give account of himself to God." (Rom. 14:12) "For we must all appear before the judgment seat of Christ; that every one may receive the things done in his body, according to that he hath done, whether it be good or bad."—2 Cor. 5:10.

NO MORE DUMB

A certain man had escaped from the city of Jerusalem, and when it fell he hastened to notify Ezekiel that the city had fallen. "And it came to pass in the twelfth year of our captivity, in the tenth month, in the fifth day of the month, that one that had escaped out of Jerusalem came unto me, saying, The city is smitten." (33:21) This was five days short of being three years after the beginning of Nebuchadnezzar's final siege of Jerusalem and of Ezekiel's dumbness. No part of the prophecy has been yet fulfilled which seems to correspond with the 'escaped one from Jerusalem' and his announcement that the city was smitten, and his coming to the Ezekiel class. The fulfilment of this seems to correspond to the fulfilment of Revelation 17:16, 17.—See *Light,* Book Two, page 108.

Jehovah would vindicate his word by his prophet by proving that the prophecy uttered by Ezekiel was from God and was therefore true. "Now the hand of the Lord was [had been, *R.V.;* had come, *Roth.*] upon me in the evening, afore he that was escaped came, and had opened my mouth, until he came to me in the morning, and my mouth was opened, and I was no more dumb." (33:22) The fall of Jerusalem proved that Ezekiel had spoken according to the will of God and proved that Ezekiel was a true prophet; hence he could now speak with boldness and authority as never before. His dumbness toward Jerusalem until then would well picture this: After Jehovah's witnesses have given their testimony as commanded by the Lord concerning "organized religion" they may leave their case with the Lord until the Lord chooses to confirm the word of his servants. When God confirms their testimony by the fulfilment of the prophecy, such would then be a time to speak with more boldness and authority than ever before. But the Lord does not require his servant to wait until the confirmation (pictured by the escaped one) fully arrives, to open the lips of his "servant" to be his witness, but when the prophecy is in fulfilment or is in course of fulfilment God opens the mouth of his "servant" and commands that speech be made. Ezekiel's mouth was opened before the messenger arrived, and that must have convinced Ezekiel that the messenger confirming his prophecy would arrive that day. He would be certain that the messenger was coming. Even so now, God has opened his prophecies to the class pictured by Ezekiel and thus opened the mouth of his "servant" to declare them, and this is an indicator that the confirmation of the prophecy by the fulfilment thereof is in the very near future.

Jehovah then directed Ezekiel to speak, and he speaks the words that a self-important class utter, to wit: "Son of man, they that inhabit those wastes of the land of Israel speak, saying, Abraham was one, and he inherited the land; but we are many; the land is given us for inheritance." (33:24) To be sure, the Lord knew that the land of Israel was "desolate without an inhabitant"; hence the prophecy must have referred back to the time when the inhabitants occupied the now waste places, as a subsequent part of the prophecy shows, and the prophecy is intended to apply to a self-reliant company of religionists of "Christendom" at the present time. These self-important and puffed-up ones, particularly the clergy amongst the Jews, had said in substance: 'Abraham was one, but we are many, and we are the fulfilment of the promise to Abraham; hence we are the seed that shall inherit the land and possess it for ever, and we don't believe the testimony of this so-called "prophet Ezekiel" that we shall be cast out.' They overlooked the conditions that attached to the inheriting of the land for ever.

This self-important class corresponds to the ones whom Jesus addressed: "And think not to say within yourselves, We have Abraham to our father: for I say unto you, that God is able of these stones to raise up children unto Abraham. And now also the axe is laid unto the root of the trees: therefore every tree which bringeth not forth good fruit, is hewn down, and cast into the fire." (Matt. 3: 9, 10) "They answered and said unto him, Abraham is our father. Jesus saith unto them, If ye were Abraham's children, ye would do the works of Abraham. But now ye seek to kill me, a man that hath told you the truth, which I have heard of God: this did not Abraham." (John 8: 39, 40) In "Christendom" there is that same self-important and self-relying class of religionists who claim to be the first ones entitled to God's favor and hence are cocksure of going to heaven because they have, as they say, such well-developed and perfect characters that God really needs them.

Concerning these that are impressed with their self-importance God then directs his prophet to say: "Wherefore say unto them, Thus saith the Lord God; Ye eat with the blood, and lift up your eyes toward your idols, and shed blood: and shall ye possess the land? Ye stand upon your sword [ye depend upon your sword, *Leeser*], ye work abomination, and ye defile every one his neighbour's wife: and shall ye possess the land?" (33: 25, 26) These are violators of their covenant; and no violator of his covenant with God need think that he can continue as an heir of God's promises and remain in God's organization. He must be faithful to the Lord in order to obtain the promises. Therefore says the Lord: "Say thou thus unto them, Thus saith the Lord God; As I live, surely they that are in the wastes shall fall by the sword, and him that is in the open field will I give to the beasts to be devoured, and they that be in the forts and in the caves shall die of the pestilence. For I will lay the land most desolate [a desolation and an astonishment, *R.V.*], and the pomp of her strength shall cease; and the mountains of Israel shall be desolate, that none shall pass through. Then shall they know that I am the Lord, when I have laid the land most desolate because of all their abominations which they have committed." (33: 27-29) Because of their pride these do not learn by his Word or by experience that Jehovah is God, but by God's judgment executed upon them they do learn and experience that he is the Almighty.

Then the prophet, at the direction of the Lord, describes a class of religionists that hang on to the truth by their eyelashes, so to speak: "Also, thou son of man, the children of thy people still are talking against thee by the walls and in the doors of the houses, and speak one to another, every one to his brother, saying, Come, I pray you, and hear what is the word that cometh forth from the Lord. And they come unto thee as the people cometh, and they sit before thee as my people, and they hear thy words [*margin,* they pretend outwardly to care for what the prophet tells them in God's name, *Leeser*], but they will not do them: for with their mouth they shew much love, but their heart goeth after their covetousness." (33: 30, 31) God has favored some with the truth and begotten them as his children who continue to associate with his faithful people for a time at least because they believe that such is the best religion known to man and that the publications issued of and concerning the truth are the most beautiful, reasonable and harmonious explanations of the Bible. When there is a public meeting held and some well known person is to speak these notify others of their acquaintance to attend with them and hear, and while the speaker speaks they themselves pretend to hear, but when it comes to real service to the glory of the Lord they are not there. They leave that to others. Such are "church-goers", and their love is divided between God and some creature or things, and they hold on to these things that prevent them from rendering a full obedience to God's commandments. "And, lo, thou art unto them as a very lovely song of one that hath a pleasant voice, and can play well on an instrument: for they hear thy words, but they do them not." (33:32) Usually such are loud in their praises of the public speaker or teacher and of the message that has been delivered. They hear the words of the speech explaining the prophecy, and probably read something about it, but they do not give the matter serious consideration, thinking that those who are so zealous in making these prophecies known are somewhat extremists. They make no attempt to do what the Lord has commanded concerning his witnesses and the work that they must do. If there is a convention of God's people in the community they will be found there, often sitting in the front seats, looking wise, but when it comes to giving testimony to the people they are "too tired". They are not wise, and Jesus says concerning them: "And every one that heareth these sayings of mine, and doeth them not, shall be likened

unto a foolish man, which built his house upon the
sand: and the rain descended, and the floods came,
and the winds blew, and beat upon that house; and
it fell: and great was the fall of it." (Matt. 7: 26, 27)
God's purpose is that these shall know that his prophecy has been uttered in their midst. "And when this
cometh to pass, (lo, it will come,) then shall they know
that a prophet hath been among them." (33: 33)
They will not heed now, but they will wake up to the
fact ere long that God has not left himself without
a witness in the land and that they have failed to give
heed to what was said.

FEEDERS
(Ezekiel, Chapter 34)

Jehovah God by and through his organization has
provided certain ones to be shepherds of his flock,
among whom are those who feed themselves, and concerning whom the Lord directed Ezekiel to utter the
prophecy as set forth in the thirty-fourth chapter.
This prophecy is undated; hence it would appear that
its application is at all times during the instruction
of his covenant people and the giving of the testimony of Jesus Christ. "And the word of the Lord
came unto me, saying, Son of man, prophesy against
the shepherds of Israel, prophesy, and say unto them,
Thus saith the Lord God unto the shepherds, Woe be
to the shepherds of Israel that do feed themselves!
should not the shepherds feed the flocks?"—34: 1, 2.

"Shepherd" in the Hebrew means literally "a
tender, a pasturer or a feeder". He therefore stands
as a leader amongst God's people and whose duty it
is to care for God's Word, to feed the flock of God,

not for personal gain, but willingly and of a ready mind. (1 Pet. 5:2) "Feed [them] with knowledge and understanding." (Jer. 3:15) Moses, David and Joshua were shepherds of God's people. (Ps. 77:20; Isa. 63:11; Num. 27:17, 18) The "shepherds" against whom this prophecy is leveled consist of the clergymen of "organized Christianity", who hold multitudes of God's children as prisoners, and also consist of elders of companies of God's people who have been too much impressed with their own importance and who seek to draw others as followers after them rather than to follow the Lord's commandment. Concerning this class the apostle wrote: "Also of your own selves shall men arise, speaking perverse things, to draw away disciples after them." (Acts 20:30) The Lord is against this class of self-important ones, as the prophet wrote: "Woe be unto the pastors that destroy and scatter the sheep of my pasture! saith the Lord. Therefore thus saith the Lord God of Israel against the pastors that feed my people, Ye have scattered my flock, and driven them away, and have not visited them: behold, I will visit upon you the evil of your doings, saith the Lord."—Jer. 23:1, 2.

Such self-important ones are greedy and feed themselves: "For many walk, of whom I have told you often, and now tell you even weeping, that they are the enemies of the cross of Christ; whose end is destruction, whose God is their belly, and whose glory is in their shame, who mind earthly things." (Phil. 3:18, 19) They do not heed the admonition of God's Word to "feed the flock of God". (1 Pet. 5:2-4) They acquire a head knowledge of the Word of God but they do not appreciate Jehovah and his kingdom.

They satisfy a personal ambition in assuming the office of an elder or teacher and they seek self-advantage but fail to feed God's flock upon the meat that he has provided for them. They prefer to serve up the food to the Lord's people in their own way for their own personal aggrandizement. They have no regard for organization directions, regarding such as less important than themselves. They fail to see that the Lord is at the head of his organization and that he gives the directions. To such the Lord says: "Is not this the fast that I have chosen? to loose the bands of wickedness, to undo the heavy burdens, and to let the oppressed go free, and that ye break every yoke? Is it not to deal thy bread to the hungry, and that thou bring the poor that are cast out to thy house? when thou seest the naked, that thou cover him; and that thou hide not thyself from thine own flesh?"— Isa. 58: 6, 7. See *The Watchtower*, 1929, page 133.

These selfish shepherds or feeders use God's flock for their own gain; hence says the Lord: "Ye eat the fat, and ye clothe you with the wool, ye kill them that are fed; but ye feed not the flock." (34:3) Being selfish they hate those who do feed the flock of God, and have and manifest the spirit of murder toward them and do violence to those who feed at the Lord's table. (1 John 3: 15) Companies of God's consecrated and spirit-begotten ones that merely hold meetings amongst themselves, and who fail and refuse to go about with the message of the Lord to others and pass it along to the diseased and needful ones, are feeding themselves and not feeding the people of God. There is a multitude of "prisoners" that need to be fed. The radio may awaken them, and then it is the priv-

YE EAT AND CLOTHE YOU WITH THE WOOL   Page 224

ilege of those who love the Lord to carry more food to such hungry and needy ones. An elder who, then, thinks he is too important to engage in such menial (?) work of feeding the hungry does not appreciate the kingdom of God and is not proving faithful to the Word of God and to the privileges that the Lord gives him.

Jehovah lays upon his anointed the obligation of 'preaching the gospel to the people, to heal the broken-hearted, to preach deliverance to the captives, and recovery of sight to the blind, and to preach the day of the vengeance of our God'. (Isa. 61: 1-3) There are many that need help, and concerning the un-faithful feeders God by his prophet declares: "The diseased have ye not strengthened, neither have ye healed that which was sick, neither have ye bound up that which was broken, neither have ye brought again that which was driven away, neither have ye sought that which was lost; but with force and with cruelty have ye ruled them." This prophecy concerning those that were driven away does not apply to the unfaith-ful whom the Lord by his angels gathers out of his kingdom. (Matt. 13: 41) It applies to those who have by reason of the false doctrines of men been driven away from the Lord and his Word and who have gone away from the systems of "organized Christianity" because they found no truth there. It includes those who have been held back from the truth by reason of the misrepresentations made by the clergy. Those who are elders in the companies of God's people and who oppose the house-to-house service work, and refuse to bring aid and comfort to such needy ones, the Lord also speaks against in this prophecy: "But with force

and with cruelty [rigour, *R.V.*] have ye ruled them."
Without a question of doubt these words of the prophet apply to the clergy of "Christendom" and also to
the "evil servant" class. (Matt. 24:48, 49) When an
elder of the company of God's people hinders the
efforts of the anointed to preach the gospel by engaging in the house-to-house service work he is guilty
of the same offense as that committed by the clergy.

During the World War not one clergyman of "organized Christianity", so called, sought to render aid
to the faithful followers of Christ Jesus. "And they
were scattered because there is no shepherd: and they
became meat to all the beasts of the field when they
were scattered." (34:5) Because the clergy were not
truly shepherds of God's flock, but were mere hirelings
of the savage and warring governments, the faithful
followers of Christ Jesus were scattered during the
World War. When they were scattered Big Business
and its allies took great delight in seeing that these
faithful ones were humiliated and caused to suffer.
Even now, because the clergy make no distinction between Jehovah's organization and the beastly political
governments of this world, the "prisoner" class still
lend themselves to be exploited by conscienceless rulers. These prisoners are still induced to believe that
"the higher powers" are the beastly governments of
the world and that they must be patriotic and therefore must be subject to such "higher powers". There
are some elders amongst the company of God's people
who still hold and teach that "the higher powers"
mentioned by the apostle (Rom. 13:1-4) are the governments or ruling powers of this world. In so holding and teaching they likewise do violence to God's

Word and to his people and they too scatter God's people and make them meat for the beastly governments of Satan's organization.

Today there is a great responsibility resting upon the shoulders of the clergy of "organized Christianity" by reason of the position they have put themselves in, but there is even a greater responsibility resting upon the shoulders of those who hold themselves forth as elders and teachers in companies of God's people to whom is committed the testimony of Jesus Christ. "My sheep wandered through all the mountains, and upon every high hill: yea, my flock was scattered upon all the face of the earth, and none did search or seek after them." (34: 6) Every servant of God should consider seriously the responsibility that rests upon him by reason of his position. In every nation and kingdom ("mountain" or "high hill") of "Christianity" the consecrated people of God who are not of the remnant are in a scattered or divided condition of mind and activity. The clergy of "Christendom" do not seek and heed the truth which is free and open to them, nor do they seek to give the truth to the consecrated of their congregations. On the contrary, they hold back and hinder their congregations from hearing the truth. In many places the clergy go about amongst the people that attend their congregations and deliberately and wickedly induce them to burn the books containing the message of God's kingdom with which the poor people have recently provided themselves. These clergymen are not trying to locate God's people and unite them, but they strive to swell their own congregations for their own personal gain. When they invite them to their buildings they do not tell them about the Scriptures, but talk about anything except the Scriptures. These clergymen are therefore reprehensible before God and must bear their responsibility. The elders in companies of God's covenant people who have separated themselves from "organized Christianity" and who then oppose or refuse to support and participate in the service work of carrying the gospel of the kingdom from house to house are chargeable with a like crime of not seeking after the scattered sheep of the Lord, and because of their favored position they are far more reprehensible and responsible before God than the clergymen.

Against these unfaithful feeders God pronounces his judgment, to wit: "Therefore, ye shepherds, hear the word of the Lord; As I live, saith the Lord God, surely because my flock became a prey, and my flock became meat to every beast of the field, because there was no shepherd, neither did my shepherds search for my flock, but the shepherds fed themselves, and fed not my flock; therefore, O ye shepherds, hear the word of the Lord; Thus saith the Lord God, Behold, I am against the shepherds; and I will require my flock at their hand, and cause them to cease from feeding the flock; neither shall the shepherds feed themselves any more: for I will deliver my flock from their mouth, that they may not be meat for them." (34:7-10) But now God has delivered his remnant from the influence of the wicked, and henceforth the rod of the wicked no longer rests upon their lot. This he has done that they might be entirely free to boldly declare the testimony of Jehovah in this day. Soon the "prisoner" class will be loosed and delivered by the hand of the Lord. (Ps. 146:7) The clergy and unfaithful elders will be compelled to settle their account with the Lord because of their unrighteous conduct toward his consecrated people. If they loved God they would keep his commandments; but they do not love him, and hence his judgment against them. —Ps. 145:20.

GATHERING HIS SHEEP

Jehovah had caused his prophet to write, "Gather my saints together unto me" (Ps. 50:5), and by Ezekiel he now says: "For thus saith the Lord God, Behold I [am here, *Leeser*], even I, will both search my sheep, and seek them out." (34:11, 12) This prophecy must be fulfilled in the day of Jehovah when he is present representatively at his temple. He does not leave to men the work of gathering together his sheep, but he sends his official Representative, his "Messenger of the covenant", to the temple for this very purpose. He causes his "Ruler" to come out of Bethlehem Ephratah to represent him in the search for his flock. (Mic. 5:2-4) It is the day when the shepherd is amongst his people; the 'day of the coming of the Lord Jesus Christ, and of our gathering unto him' who is the Head of Jehovah's organization. (2 Thess. 2:1) The prophet describes the time as "the cloudy and dark day". This day began in 1914 and reached a climax in 1918 at which latter date the Lord Jesus appeared at the temple of Jehovah, concerning which time the prophet of God wrote: "The Lord reigneth, let the earth rejoice; let the multitude of isles be glad thereof. Clouds and darkness are round about him: righteousness and judgment are the habitation of his throne."

(Ps. 97:1, 2) It is the day described by the prophet
when deliverance is come and "at that time thy people shall be delivered, every one that shall be found
written in the book". (Dan. 12:1) The Lord knows
them that are his, and he finds them.

God's people were amongst the uncircumcised, that
is, the unclean. "And I will bring them out from the
people, and gather them from the countries, and will
bring them to their own land, and feed them upon the
mountains of Israel by the rivers, and in all the inhabited places of the country." (34:13) The people
of Satan's organization had God's flock in custody
and the Lord gathered them out and brought them
unto himself. His people did not there have the freedom of worship and service which is now to be found
in God's organization. The Lord gathered his own to
the temple and there he has fed them. The real Feeder
or Shepherd, Christ Jesus, has fed them upon the best
food. "I will feed them in a good pasture, and upon
the high mountains of Israel shall their fold be; there
shall they lie in a good fold, and in a fat pasture shall
they feed upon the mountains of Israel."—34:14.

Christ Jesus is the Ruler that comes out of Bethlehem and he serves also in the capacity of Feeder of
the people of Jehovah. "And he shall stand and feed
in the strength of the Lord, in the majesty of the name
of the Lord his God; and they shall abide; for now
shall he be great unto the ends of the earth." (Mic.
5:4) The faithful ones were watching for the Lord
and they heard and obeyed his commandments.
"Blessed are those servants, whom the lord, when he
cometh, shall find watching; verily I say unto you,
that he shall gird himself, and make them to sit down

to meat, and will come forth and serve them." (Luke 12:37) These faithful ones the Lord forms into his "faithful and wise servant" class.—Matt. 24:45-47.

God's sheep are shielded and protected within the fold of Jehovah's organization which is symbolized by "the high mountains" where they are at complete rest in the Lord and where they are fed upon the best food, that is, food that is convenient and upbuilding for them. The Lord sets them on high from danger. (Ps. 91:14) "For he hath strengthened the bars of thy gates; he hath blessed thy children within thee. He maketh peace in thy borders, and filleth thee with the finest of the wheat." (Ps. 147:13, 14) This is now the happy condition of God's remnant, the faithful flock of God who 'follow the good Shepherd [The Lamb] whithersoever he goeth'. As to the "great multitude", these are still scattered sheep and are prisoners, and upon the faithful the obligation rests to feed them. "They shall not hunger nor thirst; neither shall the heat nor sun smite them: for he that hath mercy on them shall lead them, even by the springs of water shall he guide them. And I will make all my mountains a way, and my highways shall be exalted." (Isa. 49:10, 11) This prophecy of Isaiah must yet be fulfilled toward the "great multitude", and the remnant must continue to carry the message to them.

The great Shepherd marks the unfaithful ones to whom has been given the privilege of feeding God's flock, and he now takes in his own hands the matter of feeding them: "I will feed my flock, and I will cause them to lie down, saith the Lord God. I will seek that which was lost, and bring again that which was driven away, and will bind up that which was broken, and will strengthen that which was sick; but I will destroy the fat and the strong; I [myself] will feed them with judgment." (34:15, 16) This is positive proof that God's remnant people are no longer to be left in doubt as to the food that they are receiving, but they will know, and they do know, that it is coming from the hand of the Lord God. "For I am the Lord; I will speak, and the word that I shall speak shall come to pass; it shall be no more prolonged." (12:25) God's elect Servant, Christ Jesus, is bringing together and strengthening those who have been scattered and in need of food. The faithful remnant, being a part of "the servant" of Jehovah, now have a part in this work. The Lord Jesus, the great Judge at the temple, began his judgment work in 1918, and the latter part of the sixteenth verse shows that because of the condition existing in the house of God judgment was necessary. "The fat and the strong" means the self-satisfied feeders and the self-important ones who use their power to boss and crowd on the side and hold in restraint their weaker brethren. Now the Lord feeds them with the justice that is due them for their improper course. Those who do not respond to the Lord's chastisement or correction will be destroyed. It is certain from the Scriptures that God will not permit amongst his "servant" class any bosses or any who will lord it over his flock and maltreat them. The Lord will see that his people receive justice.

The Lord uses various dumb brutes to illustrate different kinds of people that get into his flock. "And as for you, O my flock, thus saith the Lord God, Behold, I judge between cattle and cattle [small cattle of lambs and kids, *margin*; between one kind of small cattle and another, *Roth*.], between the rams and the he goats." (34:17) The bossy and unkind leaders or feeders are likened unto "he goats". "Even all the chief ones [leaders, or, great goats, *margin*]." (Isa. 14:9) "There be three things which go well, yea, four are comely in going: a lion, which is strongest among beasts, and turneth not away for any; a greyhound; an he goat also; and a king, against whom there is no rising up." (Prov. 30:29-31) The he-goat has a dignified appearance, and walks with his head high and assumes a very superior air, and tries to appear 'stately in his going', and is self-conscious of his importance, and assumes this attitude to impress all others in the flock of God. To the Lord and to those having the spirit of the Lord these "he goats" among God's flock or company have an offensive or bad odor. They are usually such as cause trouble, because of their desire to shine and to appear to be very important. "Mine anger was kindled against the shepherds, and I punished the goats: for the Lord of hosts hath visited his flock the house of Judah, and hath made them as his goodly horse in the battle." (Zech. 10:3) The Lord makes a difference between "he goats" and the "rams", which according to *Leeser* are called "wethers". A wether is a male sheep that has lost his self-importance and arrogance by reason of a surgical operation. A man who is an elder may be like a butting, shoving buck or he-goat, but if he puts away or cuts away his selfishness and then unselfishly serves God's people because of his love for God and his people, he is then likened unto a "wether". Those who indulge in butting or horning others, the Lord will judge them accordingly.

Continuing to address the selfish "he goat" leaders the Lord says: "Seemeth it a small thing unto you to have eaten up the good pasture, but ye must tread down with your feet the residue of your pastures? and to have drunk of the deep waters, but ye must foul the residue with your feet?" (34:18) These high-headed and odoriferous he-goats have waxed fat by eating up everything in sight, while those meek ones of the flock grow lean. They feed themselves upon the best, but, not being satisfied with that, they go further and because of their selfishness they spoil and make unfit the food that is left, so that others may not eat it with relish. This is the spirit of the clergymen who "have taken away the key of knowledge" and who have been brought in contact with the precious truth of God's Word and use such part of it as will satisfy their selfish desires and then spoil it so that others could not enjoy it. This spirit is manifested by those "highbrows" of the clergy who induce the people to burn books containing the message of God's kingdom. There are some who have been, and some who are yet, amongst the Lord's true people who have wanted to get all the good food possible from the Lord's table and munch it and mess it up and then dish it up in their own way and claim credit for all that is given to others to eat. Also, there are those who receive good food from the Lord's hands but who are unwilling or too lazy to pass it on or to bring it to other hungry ones, and they prevent some of God's sheep from getting the food, by opposing the witness work that the faithful ones of the Lord are doing. These selfish ones tread upon the food that the Lord provides and attempt to befoul it with their soiled feet and to prevent all efforts of the organized service to be carried on by God's faithful people and in his name. During the Elijah period of the church these selfish ones ate the best and drank of the flowing waters. During the Elisha period they tried to foul up the present-day pure waters of truth so that they appeared unsightly and uninviting to the flock of God. Their responsibility is to Jehovah, and against such his judgment is written.

Those of the ''great multitude'' are classed as God's flock or sheep; and the clergy in particular attempt to destroy the food, that these hungry ones may not get it. To such false leaders God says: ''And as for my flock, they eat that which ye have trodden with your feet; and they drink that which ye have fouled with your feet.'' (34: 19) The clergymen make claim before the people that they are teaching the Bible, but they are not. On the contrary, they soil and befoul it by their own false ideas and conclusions such as higher criticism, evolution and self-righteousness, and therefore the ''prisoners'' are without food unless God's faithful servants carry the food to them. The ''billy goat'' elders in the companies of God's true people cooperate with the clergy, and by their course of action prevent the ''prisoner'' class from being fed; and this they do by opposing the house-to-house testimony work. The faithful remnant have now turned themselves away from the ''billy goats' '' influence and are going on in the work, giving the testimony as God has commanded it shall be given.

When the Lord appeared at the temple for judgment the "fat" and the "lean" were in the same corral. "Therefore, thus saith the Lord God unto them, Behold I, even I, will judge between the fat cattle and between the lean cattle." (34: 20) The Lord's judgment is a righteous judgment. This rule is announced by one who spoke by authority of the Ruler and in his name. "The Lord maketh poor [the fat cattle], and maketh rich [the lean cattle]: he bringeth low, and lifteth up. He raiseth up the poor out of the dust, and lifteth up the beggar from the dunghill, to set them among princes, and to make them inherit the throne of glory: for the pillars of the earth are the Lord's, and he hath set the world upon them." (1 Sam. 2: 7, 8) "He hath shewed strength with his arm; he hath scattered the proud in the imagination of their hearts. He hath put down the mighty from their seats, and exalted them of low degree. He hath filled the hungry with good things, and the rich he hath sent empty away."–Luke 1: 51-53.

Unfaithfulness on the part of feeders made it necessary for the Lord to take drastic action: "Because ye have thrust with side and with shoulder, and pushed all the diseased with your horns, till ye have scattered them abroad." (34: 21) During the World War the clergy without, and the unfaithful elders within the companies of God's people, resorted to violence and scattered the flock of God, and by reason thereof the "prisoners" still suffer at their hands from the same kind of ill treatment. The Lord preserves those that love him; hence he says: "Therefore will I save my flock, and they shall no more be a prey; and I will judge between cattle and cattle."

(34:22) The Lord has saved and preserved his remnant. The troublous times that came upon God's people he really overruled for the deliverance of the faithful. The "great multitude" is yet to be delivered, and must be delivered, and before that is accomplished there must be some witness work done to them by Jehovah's witnesses. Appreciating this fact the faithful remnant is anxious to participate in this work.

ONE SHEPHERD

According to his promise God brings peace and joy to his faithful ones. "And I will set up one shepherd over them, and he shall feed them, even my servant David; he shall feed them, and he shall be their shepherd. And I the Lord will be their God, and my servant David a prince among them; I the Lord have spoken it." (34:23, 24) There is now no "strange god" among the faithful remnant of the Lord's people. Christ Jesus is at his temple, and he is the feeder and leader of the people of God. To the faithful he has become "the head stone of the corner". These faithful ones are joined with Christ Jesus in his everlasting covenant, even the sure mercies of David. (Isa. 55:3) To the faithful remnant the Lord God has fulfilled the prophecy, to wit: "And I will gather the remnant of my flock out of all countries whither I have driven them, and will bring them again to their folds; and they shall be fruitful and increase. And I will set up shepherds over them which shall feed them; and they shall fear no more, nor be dismayed, neither shall they be lacking, saith the Lord. Behold, the days come, saith the Lord, that I will raise unto David a righteous Branch, and a King shall reign and prosper, and

shall execute judgment and justice in the earth. In
his days Judah shall be saved, and Israel shall dwell
safely; and this is his name whereby he shall be called,
THE LORD OUR RIGHTEOUSNESS."–Jer. 23:3-6.

Jehovah establishes his faithful ones in his organization and gives peace. "And I will make with them a
covenant of peace, and will cause the evil beasts to
cease out of the land; and they shall dwell safely in
the wilderness, and sleep in the woods." (34:25) This
has no reference to the New Covenant. (Jer. 31:31-34)
It refers to God's organization to which he says: "For
the mountains shall depart, and the hills be removed;
but my kindness shall not depart from thee, neither
shall the covenant of my peace be removed, saith the
Lord that hath mercy on thee. And all thy children
shall be taught of the Lord; and great shall be the
peace of thy children. No weapon that is formed
against thee shall prosper; and every tongue that
shall rise against thee in judgment thou shalt condemn. This is the heritage of the servants of the
Lord; and their righteousness is of me, saith the
Lord." (Isa. 54:10, 13, 17; see *The Watchtower*, 1931,
page 329) "Open ye the gates, that the righteous
nation which keepeth the truth may enter in. Thou
wilt keep him in perfect peace, whose mind is stayed
on thee: because he trusteth in thee." (Isa. 26:2, 3)
This does not mean that the faithful remnant is now
free from all assaults of the enemy. On the contrary,
the enemy continues to make war on the remnant because of their faithfulness in giving the testimony of
Jesus Christ. The enemy will continue to assault the
faithful, but those who remain true to the Lord and
within his organization will be saved.

God's faithful people "shall dwell safely in the wilderness, and sleep in the woods". (See also 34:28.) This shows that the Lord cleanses his organization of the vicious beastly ones and that no part of his organization shall be harmed by them, and no matter where they may be, as long as they are in God's organization, and faithful in doing their duty in obedience to the commandments of the Lord, they shall be safe from Satan's agents and his beastly organization. This security is only within God's organization, and is pictured by "the holy land". If any of the remnant get outside of God's organization they may no longer expect such security. 'The Lord preserves the faithful.' (Ps. 31:23) The remnant have forsaken Satan's organization and are now in the "holy land", that is, the condition of righteousness and safety, and their continued safety depends upon their continued faithfulness to the Lord.

Jehovah now comforts his faithful people by the fulfilment to them of the promise, "And I will make them and the places round about my hill a blessing; and I will cause the shower to come down in his season: there shall be showers of blessing." (34:26) Since the Lord has gathered together his people into the temple he has continued to shower them with his blessings. (Zech. 10:1; Joel 2:23; Ps. 147:8) "Thou, O God, didst send a plentiful rain, whereby thou didst confirm thine inheritance, when it was weary [exhausted]." (Ps. 68:9) Jehovah has unfolded his Word and continues thus to do for the benefit of his people, and these precious things drop like dew upon the tender grass. "My doctrine shall drop as the rain, my speech shall distil as the dew, as the small rain

upon the tender herb, and as the showers upon the
grass." (Deut. 32:2) He has brought his faithful
ones into the condition of peace and joy. "As the
dew of Hermon, and as the dew that descended upon
the mountains of Zion: for there the Lord commanded
the blessing, even life for evermore."—Ps. 133:3.

Let those who love God know for a certainty that
he is feeding his own people and that their food is
certain and always satisfying and always will be:
"And the tree of the field shall yield her fruit, and
the earth shall yield her increase, and they shall be
safe in their land, and shall know that I am the Lord,
when I have broken the bands of their yoke, and delivered them out of the hand of those that served
themselves of them." (34:27) No famine for spiritual
food shall afflict the faithful remnant of God's organization; and their activities in God's work, as well
as their faithful performance of that work, shall prosper and be fruitful. Let no one who is now of the
remnant be induced to act foolishly by giving credit
to any man or men for the message of truth that comes
to the people of God. "Who then is Paul, and who
is Apollos, but ministers by whom ye believed, even
as the Lord gave to every man? I have planted,
Apollos watered; but God gave the increase. So then
neither is he that planteth any thing, neither he that
watereth; but God that giveth the increase. Now he
that planteth and he that watereth are one: and every
man shall receive his own reward according to his own
labour. For we are labourers together with God: ye
are God's husbandry [tillage, *margin*; God's farm,
Roth.], ye are God's building." (1 Cor. 3:5-9; Hag.
2:18, 19; see *The Watchtower*, 1931, page 70) God's

people are "safe in their land", that is to say, their proper place or condition in God's organization, and not outside of it.

The promises that follow in this chapter are made to God's anointed people, the remnant. "And I will raise up for them a plant of renown [plantation for a name, *Roth.*, margin], and they shall be no more consumed with hunger in the land, neither bear the shame of the heathen any more." (34: 29) The "plant of renown" or "plantation" is Jehovah's anointed One. The period of waiting came to an end and God sent Christ Jesus forth to vindicate his name. "The Lord shall send the rod of thy strength out of Zion: rule thou in the midst of thine enemies." (Ps. 110: 2) "And in that day there shall be a root of Jesse, which shall stand for an ensign of the people; to it shall the Gentiles seek: and his rest shall be glorious." (Isa. 11: 10) The remnant has also by the grace of God come to see that they are the planting of the Lord, delivered from Satan's organization and brought unto God's organization for his renown or the fame of his name. God has planted his anointed people that his name may be glorified. "To appoint unto them that mourn in Zion, to give unto them beauty for ashes, the oil of joy for mourning, the garment of praise for the spirit of heaviness; that they might be called trees of righteousness, the planting of the Lord, that he might be glorified." (Isa. 61: 3) "Thy sun shall no more go down; neither shall thy moon withdraw itself; for the Lord shall be thine everlasting light, and the days of thy mourning shall be ended. Thy people also shall be all righteous; they shall inherit the land for ever, the branch of my planting, the work of my hands, that I may be glorified. A little one [remnant] shall become a thousand, and a small one a strong nation: I the Lord will hasten it in his time."—Isa. 60:20-22.

Satan and his agents continue to hurl reproaches upon the remnant, but no longer do these faithful ones suffer themselves to be shamed by the enemy or to appear in an apologetic manner before any of the enemy's representatives. On the contrary, they go on and have boldness in this day of judgment and they delight to bear the reproaches that the enemy casts upon them because of their faithfulness to God and to his kingdom. (1 John 4:17) The shame shall be upon the enemy.–Isa. 61:6, 7; 45:16, 17; Mic. 7:9-11.

Jehovah now shows his faithful servants how he has been using them, and they know that the Lord God is with them and that they are on his side and under his protection. "Thus shall they know that I the Lord their God am with them, and that they, even the house of Israel, are my people, saith the Lord God. And ye my flock, the flock of my pasture, are men, and I am your God, saith the Lord God." (34:30, 31) Jehovah has brought his faithful forth and given them a new name which his own mouth has named, and now they know for a certainty that they are Jehovah's witnesses. The precious promises of these last two verses apply to God's remnant now, while they are on the earth faithfully performing the service the Lord has given into their hands. These are members of the "son of man"; therefore they are the Lord's men and know that he is their God. (Ps. 95:7) The faithful do not harden their hearts, but joyfully and unselfishly press on publishing the name of Jehovah and his kingdom.

THE WICKED
(Ezekiel, Chapter 35)

The wicked are those who have received light from the Lord God as revealed by his Word and who then disregard that favor and become opposers of God and his kingdom. Such as willfully and maliciously oppose those who are faithfully endeavoring to serve God by bearing witness to his name and his kingdom are the opposers of Jehovah. Mount Seir, or Edom, pictures such a class of the enemies of God. This class, once enlightened and claiming to be spiritual brothers of the Lord's faithful sons, thereafter prove themselves unfaithful to their covenant and barter away their inheritance in the kingdom, and this they do for a selfish reason. (See Ezekiel 25: 12, and comments thereon.) All the evidence points to the fact that these join in the alliance or conspiracy with the Devil. This prophecy is written without reference to time, and God caused Ezekiel to utter it against these enemies. "Moreover, the word of the Lord came unto me, saying, Son of man, set thy face against mount Seir, and prophesy against it. And say unto it, Thus saith the Lord God, Behold, O mount Seir, I am against thee, and I will stretch out mine hand against thee, and I will make thee most desolate."—35: 1-3.

The faithful servants of God whom Ezekiel foreshadowed are to turn their attention against the enemies of God and count them as their own enemies. Whom God hates, his true sons likewise hate. "Do not I hate them, O Lord, that hate thee? and am not

I grieved with those that rise up against thee? I hate them with perfect hatred; I count them mine enemies.'' (Ps. 139:21, 22) The Edomites (''mount Seir'') were descendants of Esau, and God hated Esau: ''As it is written, Jacob have I loved, but Esau have I hated.'' (Rom. 9:13) ''And I hated Esau, and laid his mountains and his heritage waste for the dragons of the wilderness.'' (Mal. 1:3) The same Hebrew word used and translated ''hate'' in Psalm 139:21, 22 is also used at Malachi 1:3, which latter text the Apostle Paul quotes. It means that the one hated is utterly odious and hateful and is a personal foe or enemy. These scriptures cannot be properly construed to mean that God loved Jacob and loved Esau some but less than he loved Jacob. God hated Esau because he followed after the Devil. All the evidence shows that the ''mount Seir'' or ''Esau'' class wind up in the Devil's organization and in league with him and against God's faithful people whom Jacob pictured. The favor that God bestowed upon Esau he spurned, and sold it to gratify his selfish desire; and this foreshadows a class that have received God's favor and who in order to gratify selfish desires sell their birthright and become the enemies of God and enemies of his faithful people. Such God hates.

It is against this hateful class that Ezekiel was told to prophesy: ''And say unto it, Thus saith the Lord God, Behold, O mount Seir, I am against thee, and I will stretch out mine hand against thee, and I will make thee most desolate. I will make thee perpetual desolations, and thy cities shall not return; and ye shall know that I am the Lord.'' (35:3, 9) This scripture identifies the ''mount Seir'' or ''Esau'' class as the second-death class, which has no restitution hopes. For them the judgment of Jehovah is destruction, and he will make them to know they have committed their wrongs against him. Then Jehovah tells them the reason why they shall be destroyed. "Because thou hast had a perpetual hatred, and hast shed the blood of the children of Israel by the force of the sword in the time of their calamity, in the time that their iniquity had an end." (35:5) Becoming haters of their brethren, and persecutors of them, God designates them as murderers. "He that loveth not his brother abideth in death." (1 John 3:14, 15) According to other translators Ezekiel 35:5, in part, reads: 'Because of enmity thou hast delivered up.' (Roth.) "Because thou hast had an undying hatred, and didst surrender the children of Israel to the power of the sword at the time of their calamity." (Leeser) This is in accord with the prophecy of Jesus concerning the World War time: "And then shall many be offended, and shall betray one another, and shall hate one another. And because iniquity shall abound, the love of many shall wax cold." (Matt. 24:10, 12) The prophecy began to have its fulfilment about 1917, and in the year following a great calamity or misfortune came upon God's people. It was then that the Judas spirit began to be made manifest by some who willingly connived with the agents of Satan's organization to have their brethren punished. Had it been the blood of God's enemies that these sought to have shed there would have been much responsibility, but because it was the Lord's chosen people at whose downfall they connived the matter is far more serious. (Obad. 10-15) "Therefore, as I live, saith the Lord

God, I will prepare thee unto blood, and blood shall pursue thee: sith thou hast not hated blood, even blood shall pursue thee.'' (35: 6) There was, on the part of the Esau class, a complete absence of love for their brethren. The stress of the World War furnished no excuse or extenuating circumstances for their hateful conduct toward their brethren who were in the toils of the law at the hands of Satan's agents.

Because of the exhibition of this malicious hatred Jehovah caused his judgment against such enemies to be written, to wit: ''Thus will I make mount Seir most desolate, and cut off from it him that passeth out, and him that returneth. And I will fill his mountains with his slain men; in thy hills, and in thy valleys, and in all thy rivers, shall they fall that are slain with the sword.'' (35: 7, 8) The fulfilment of this prophecy corresponds with the treading of the wine-press in Edom and its capital city Bozrah. ''And their blood shall be sprinkled upon my garments, and I will stain all my raiment.'' (Isa. 63: 1-4) ''It is a righteous thing with God to recompense tribulation to them that trouble you; . . . when the Lord Jesus shall be revealed from heaven with his mighty angels in flaming fire, taking vengeance on them that know not God, and that obey not the gospel of our Lord Jesus Christ: who shall be punished with everlasting destruction from the presence of the Lord, and from the glory of his power.'' (2 Thess. 1: 6-9) ''Shall I not in that day, saith the Lord, even destroy the wise men out of Edom, and understanding out of the mount of Esau? And thy mighty men, O Teman, shall be dismayed, to the end that every one of the mount of Esau may be cut off by slaughter. For thy violence against thy brother Jacob, shame shall cover thee, and thou shalt be cut off for ever.''—Obad. 8-10.

Making themselves the enemies of God and his organization, they determine to take possession regardless of his will. ''Because thou hast said, These two nations, and these two countries, shall be mine, and we will possess it; whereas the Lord was there.'' (35: 10) The two nations primarily refer to the northern kingdom of the ten tribes and to the southern kingdom of Judah and Benjamin and which seem to picture God's anointed ones, whom he has placed in his organization. The northern kingdom was later characterized by the ''sin of Samaria'', that is, the worship of leaders or heroes. (Amos 8: 14) This shows the malicious covetousness of the class pictured by Mount Seir or Esau. This very spirit of hate or murder found its place in the heart of Esau: ''And Esau said in his heart, The days of mourning for my father are at hand, then will I slay my brother Jacob.'' (Gen. 27: 41, 42) Esau was thereby a ''profane person'', whom the Lord hates; and so are those whom Esau foreshadowed. (Heb. 12: 16) These therefore fight against God by fighting against his people, and of which he says: ''He that toucheth you toucheth the apple of his eye.''—Zech. 2: 8.

Jehovah declares his purpose to administer just retribution upon those who have persecuted his anointed. ''Therefore, as I live, saith the Lord God, I will even do according to thine anger, and according to thine envy, which thou hast used out of thy hatred against them; and I will make myself known among them, when I have judged thee.'' (35: 11) In the fulfilment of this prophecy God permits the psalmist to write his judgment upon these enemies: "Thou hast known my reproach, and my shame, and my dishonour; mine adversaries are all before thee. Reproach hath broken my heart, and I am full of heaviness: and I looked for some to take pity, but there was none; and for comforters, but I found none. They gave me also gall for my meat; and in my thirst they gave me vinegar to drink. Let their table become a snare before them: and that which should have been for their welfare, let it become a trap. Let their eyes be darkened, that they see not; and make their loins continually to shake. Pour out thine indignation upon them, and let thy wrathful anger take hold of them. Let their habitation be desolate; and let none dwell in their tents. For they persecute him whom thou hast smitten; and they talk to the grief of those whom thou hast wounded. Add iniquity unto their iniquity; and let them not come into thy righteousness. Let them be blotted out of the book of the living, and not be written with the righteous. The humble shall see this, and be glad; and your heart shall live that seek God." (Ps. 69: 19-28, 32) The Apostle Peter records the partial fulfilment of this prophecy upon Judas, the betrayer of Jesus, and the greater fulfilment will be upon "the son of perdition" whom Judas foreshadowed.

Jehovah's purpose is that all shall know that he is the Almighty God. "And thou shalt know that I am the Lord, and that I have heard all thy blasphemies which thou hast spoken against the mountains of Israel, saying, They are laid desolate, they are given us to consume. Thus with your mouth ye have boasted against me, and have multiplied your words against me: I have heard them." (35:12, 13) "Yet they say, The Lord shall not see, neither shall the God of Jacob regard it. Understand, ye brutish among the people; and, ye fools, when will ye be wise? He that planted the ear, shall he not hear? he that formed the eye, shall he not see? He that chastiseth the heathen, shall not he correct? he that teacheth man knowledge, shall not he know? And he shall bring upon them their own iniquity, and shall cut them off in their own wickedness; yea, the Lord our God shall cut them off." (Ps. 94:7-10, 23) "And they say, How doth God know? and is there knowledge in the Most High? Behold, these are the ungodly, who prosper in the world; they increase in riches." (Ps. 73:11, 12) "Woe unto them that seek deep to hide their counsel from the Lord, and their works are in the dark, and they say, Who seeth us? and who knoweth us?"— Isa. 29:15.

Desolation shall be the portion of the Esau class, while all the peoples of earth who seek righteousness shall rejoice. "Thus saith the Lord God, When the whole earth rejoiceth, I will make thee desolate. As thou didst rejoice at the inheritance of the house of Israel, because it was desolate, so will I do unto thee; thou shalt be desolate, O mount Seir, and all Idumea, even all of it; and they shall know that I am the Lord." (35:14, 15) This rejoicing shall follow the battle of Armageddon. "All the earth shall worship thee, and shall sing unto thee; they shall sing to thy name." (Ps. 66:4, 5) These scriptures prove that there will be no restored antitypical Mount Seir or Edom class.

CHAPTER VIII

CONSOLATION

(EZEKIEL, CHAPTER 36)

JEHOVAH is the Father of mercies and God of all comfort and he now gives many comforting assurances to his anointed people and thereby strengthens them to press on in his service. The remnant know that Jehovah is the only true and almighty God, and they have an abiding confidence in his Word. God has spoken it, and he will also do it. Nothing can set aside or prevent the carrying out of his purposes. Jehovah's witnesses continue to suffer abuse and reproach at the hands of God's enemies, but they are neither discouraged nor dismayed. When they go from house to house to bear the testimony concerning the goodness of God and his kingdom these faithful witnesses are often reproached and Satan's agents frequently cause their arrest and persecution and imprisonment. In all this they rejoice because God has given his word that in his due time he will destroy the enemies and lift up those who love him. Jehovah will vindicate his witnesses before his enemies, and this will vindicate his name and let it be known that he loves and preserves those who love and faithfully serve him.

The thirty-sixth chapter of Ezekiel's prophecy contains many words of consolation to the faithful people of God. To Ezekiel Jehovah said: "Also, thou son of man, prophesy unto the mountains of Israel, and

say, Ye mountains of Israel, hear the word of the
Lord.'' (36:1) This is in direct contrast to the pro-
nouncement of doom against Mount Seir appearing in
the thirty-fifth chapter of the prophecy. Mount Seir
is given a spiritual significance which cannot be applied to the literal land of Edom, and this proves that
''the mountains of Israel'' must also have a spiritual
application and that the prophecy concerning the same
is fulfilled upon Jehovah's faithful people and not
upon the land of Palestine. It is also of interest to
compare the thirty-sixth chapter of Ezekiel with the
sixth chapter of that prophecy. In the sixth chapter
the prophecy is directed against those who have falsely
claimed to be God's people. The rulers, and their supporters in ''Christendom'', have used the name of
God and Christ in order to carry out their work of
hypocrisy, and for this God pronounces his judgment
of condemnation against them. In the thirty-sixth
chapter of this prophecy ''the mountains of Israel''
refer to the faithful anointed ones of God's people,
that is to say, to the entire family of God of which
Christ Jesus is the Head and which includes the
faithful remnant on earth. Hence the prophecy says:
''Ye mountains of Israel [the faithful ones who com-
pose the true followers], hear the word of the Lord.''

This conclusion is further supported by the fact
that God speaks words of consolation to them and
declares his purpose to bless them because his enemies
have maltreated them. ''Thus saith the Lord God, Because the enemy hath said against you, Aha, even the
ancient high places are ours in possession.'' (36:2)
The enemies of God have said, in substance: 'We are
the ones who have and are entitled to all the favors

and we occupy the place of the kingdom of the Lord; hence we are the favored ones on the earth.' When the enemies of God recognized the Head of the house of sons they sought to kill him. (Matt. 21:38, 39) During the World War they slew the Elijah–John-the-Baptist work and caused those doing the work to appear as dead. The Devil's organization, and particularly the nations composing ''Christendom'', have greatly envied the true kingdom of God and have desired the power, honor, domain and name which are due God's kingdom people, without rendering unto God true devotion and service. ''Christendom'' has ignored the duty and responsibility that attaches to those who would be of the kingdom of God. When the time came for Jehovah to lay in his foundation the chief corner Stone, Christ Jesus the King, ''Christendom'' was willing to assume the name of the kingdom of God on earth but refused to acknowledge Christ Jesus as the Head thereof. On the contrary, ''Christendom'' set up in the place and stead of God's kingdom that abominable thing, the creation of the Devil, to wit, the League of Nations, and called it ''the political expression of God's kingdom on earth''.

''Organized Christianity,'' with other parts of Satan's organization, has made God's true people desolate on every side, but the time approaches when God will make a change in the situation: ''Therefore prophesy and say, Thus saith the Lord God, Because they have made you desolate, and swallowed you up on every side, that ye might be a possession unto the residue of the heathen, and ye are taken up in the lips of talkers, and are an infamy of the people.'' (36:3) Such action on the part of the enemy has been a reproach to God and to Christ, including his faithful witnesses on the earth. Therefore Jesus said: "Ye shall be hated of all nations for my name's sake." (Matt. 24:9) "But all these things will they do unto you for my name's sake, because they know not him that sent me."—John 15:21.

During the World War, except for the intervention of the Lord on behalf of his people, the enemy would have buried them alive. "If it had not been the Lord who was on our side, when men rose up against us; then they had swallowed us up quick, when their wrath was kindled against us: then the waters had overwhelmed us, the stream had gone over our soul. Then the proud waters had gone over our soul." (Ps. 124:2-5) Such state of persecution continued until the courts of the United States, according to their own law, were compelled to relieve those who were held in prison and in custody because they had preached the gospel of the truth. Such was finally done on May 5, 1920.

These words of consolation manifestly are intended for those faithful ones yet on the earth, that they might take comfort and hope and be strong in the Lord and in the power of his might. "Therefore, ye mountains of Israel, hear the word of the Lord God; Thus saith the Lord God to the mountains and to the hills, to the rivers and to the valleys, to the desolate wastes and to the cities that are forsaken, which became a prey and derision to the residue of the heathen that are round about." (36:4) This is a message of comfort not only to the "mountains", that is, the faithful remnant, but to all of those on earth who are begotten of the spirit of God. The "mountains" and "hills" refer to the kingdom class, and the 'desolate' places refer particularly to the great multitude, which is like "the desolate heritages". (Isa. 49: 8) For some time even God's faithful ones were like "cities [organizations] that are forsaken" of the Lord and they were "a prey". They have been held in derision, and are still thus held, especially by the ruling powers of "Christendom" and their allies the heathen that are round about.

God's people may have need of some chastisement, but that is not for anyone to administer except the Lord. He will determine what is needed and administer it. The enemy used God's people despitefully, and this is true especially with reference to Idumea and the Esau class. "Therefore thus saith the Lord God, Surely in the fire of my jealousy have I spoken against the residue of the heathen, and against all Idumea, which have appointed my land into their possession with the joy of all their heart, with despiteful minds, to cast it out for a prey." (36: 5) God's faithful people have been the objects of reproach and have been a shame at the hands of Satan and his agents. "Prophesy, therefore, concerning the land of Israel, and say unto the mountains and to the hills, to the rivers and to the valleys, Thus saith the Lord God, Behold, I have spoken in my jealousy and in my fury, because ye have borne the shame of the heathen."—36: 6.

There was a partial fulfilment of this prophecy upon Palestine in the days of Ezekiel and Nehemiah. The complete fulfilment could not apply to the literal land of Palestine. The Jews were evicted from Palestine and 'their house left unto them desolate' because they rejected Christ Jesus, the beloved and anointed King of Jehovah. To this day the Jews have not repented of this wrongful act committed by their forefathers. Many of them have been returned to the land of Palestine, but they have been induced to go there because of selfishness and for sentimental reasons. During the long period elapsing from the time of their expulsion to the present day the Jews have not "borne the shame of the heathen" for Jehovah's sake, nor for the name of Christ. During all this period of time, and particularly during the World War, the true followers of Christ Jesus devoted to God, and to his kingdom, have been bearing the shame of the heathen and have been hated by all the nations for Christ's sake and for the sake of Jehovah's name. (Matt. 24: 9; Mark 13: 13) In contrast to this, during the World War the Jews received recognition of the heathen nations. In 1917 the Balfour Declaration, sponsored by the heathen governments of Satan's organization, came forth, recognized the Jews, and bestowed upon them great favors. In this the seventh world power took the lead. Now Big Business and other wings of Satan's organization place the Jews alongside of and in the same category as the Gentiles. Heretofore even God's people have overlooked the fact that the affairs of God's kingdom with reference to the things of earth are of far greater importance than the rehabilitation of that little strip of land on the eastern side of the Mediterranean sea. The Jews have received more attention at their hands than they have really deserved. Therefore this prophecy must have its chief fulfilment upon the true people of God's kingdom which are now on the earth.

Jehovah declares his purpose to cause the heathen nations to bear their shame. By "heathen" nations here are meant those who are against his kingdom, all that are anti-God and anti-kingdom. "Therefore, thus saith the Lord God, I have lifted up mine hand, Surely the heathen that are about you, they shall bear their shame." (36:7) But for what reason does God thus declare? Surely not because of what the natural Jews, the non-believers in and the persecutors and slayers of Christ Jesus do or have done, but because of the shame and reproach these nations have heaped upon the true believers in and the true followers of Christ Jesus. These are the people of God which he has taken out from amongst the Gentiles that they might be used by him as a people for his own holy name. (Acts 15:14) Even in this day God has brought a measure of shame upon "Christendom" by the wide circulation of the message of truth printed and put in the hands of the people, including the statements in the 'seven vials of wrath' (Rev. 16:1-21) foreshadowed by the plagues that came upon Egypt. The greatest shame upon these, however, will come at Armageddon, when God's great sword desolates the nations.

PROSPERITY

Jehovah will prosper his people while some of them are on the earth, that the enemy may see that they have his favor. "But ye, O mountains of Israel, ye shall shoot forth your branches, and yield your fruit to my people of Israel; for they are at hand to come. For, behold, I am for you, and I will turn unto you, and ye shall be tilled and sown. And I will multiply men upon you, all the house of Israel, even all of it: and the cities shall be inhabited, and the wastes shall be builded.'' (36:8-10) This prophecy could not be applied properly to natural Israel, but does apply to God's faithful people now on earth. The prosperity of his people must therefore begin before the heathen nations are dashed to pieces at Armageddon, in order that these heathen nations may know that the hand of Jehovah God is doing these things.

God's sanctuary has been trodden down by the enemy, and the kingdom interests committed to his servants were scattered and desolated. (Dan. 8:11-13) The words in the foregoing verses of Ezekiel's prophecy constitute a promise of Jehovah that he will revive and reorganize his people and set them in their native condition, that is to say, in the condition of being occupied in the service of his kingdom interests, and that the kingdom interests thus brought forward by him might flourish and prosper. The facts show the fulfilment of this prophecy upon the spiritual Israel, that is, the anointed people of God now on the earth. Since the World War God has caused his King at his temple to revive his work and his people relating to the interests of his kingdom. Companies of the faithful have been formed and organized for active service and have been and are serving the kingdom interests. New ''plantations'' in the nature of offices, factories and organizations in many parts of the earth have been formed and established to carry forward (and are carrying forward) the kingdom work. God's people have pushed forward, and each year he has blessed their efforts by a wider publication of his name and of his kingdom. The work in behalf of ''desolate places", the "prisoner" or "great multitude" class, is progressing and the name of Jehovah is being made known to the "prisoner" class. This is far more noteworthy and of far greater importance and is a more wonderful work than the bringing of the Jews back to the land of Palestine. Why should God give any attention to the Jews who continue to defame his name?

Jehovah promised that his kingdom interests shall be enhanced. "And I will multiply upon you man and beast; and they shall increase and bring fruit [increase and be fruitful, R.V.]; and I will settle you after your old estates [cause you to be inhabited after your former estate, R.V.], and will do better unto you than at your beginnings; and ye shall know that I am the Lord."—36:11.

Domesticated animals are beasts of burden for the aid of man in doing his work, and hence used here as an illustration. "Beast" therefore here represents the increased equipment the Lord has provided for carrying forward the work of his kingdom. The number of pioneer witnesses has been far greater during the years that followed 1924 than ever before. The public speakers have been succeeded by regional service directors, and these, together with local service directors, have strengthened the organization and have carried forward the house-to-house work of bearing testimony. This work has progressed as never before. To aid God's people in doing this work, and to relieve them of many physical burdens, the Lord has provided for the use of his people the radio, the best equipped book factories, machines, and printing presses, trucks and automobiles, service or house cars, supply depots, and a far greater efficiency in the organization for carrying on the kingdom work. His organized work, therefore, is fruitful, bringing forth fruit of the kingdom, to the glory of God. Beyond all question of doubt the kingdom is here and the Lord's people on earth have entered into the heritage thereof and the kingdom is more productive than at the beginning of the work of the church on earth. This is in harmony with the words of Jesus: "Verily, verily, I say unto you, He that believeth on me, the works that I do shall he do also; and greater works than these shall he do; because I go unto my Father." (John 14:12) God's remnant people now restored to their "former estate" are now accomplishing more in the interests of the kingdom than heretofore, and this is in exact harmony with the foregoing prophecy uttered by Ezekiel.

Jehovah is using and will continue to use his faithful remnant as instruments to aid and comfort the "great multitude". "Yea, I will cause men to walk upon you [mountains], even my people Israel; and they shall possess thee, and thou shalt be their inheritance, and thou shalt no more henceforth bereave them of men [thou shalt not any more henceforth cast them out, *Leeser*]." (36:12) God has made his remnant "like a sharp sword" used to cut away falsehoods and to make known the truth. The "prisoner" class must be served by the faithful remnant with the food from the Lord's table. "They shall feed in the ways, and their pastures shall be in all high places. And I will make all my mountains [the faithful kingdom class] a way [to walk], and my highways shall be exalted." (Isa. 49:9,11) The "great multitude", and even those of good will, must take their stand on the side of the Lord before Armageddon and learn to walk in the way where the Lord has placed his faithful people now. (Isa. 62: 10; 35: 8; *The Watchtower*, 1931, page 307) The "great multitude" and peoples of good will seek the truth at the hands of God's faithful remnant.

"Organized Christianity," so called, falsely takes the name of Christ and then devours up men and oppresses mankind. Others who are enemies of God see its wicked work, and they say of God's true people: 'They are just like all others who call themselves Christians.' (25: 8) "Thus saith the Lord Jehovah: Because they say unto you, Thou land art a devourer of men, and hast been a bereaver of thy nation; therefore thou shalt devour men no more, neither bereave thy nation any more, saith the Lord Jehovah."— 36: 13, 14, *A.R.V.*

The people will come to know God and to know that God has a people in the land that are faithful to him, and therefore the enemy will have no more occasion to say that those who bear the name of Christ are devourers of men. The vindication of Jehovah's witnesses will be a vindication of his own great name. "Neither will I let thee hear any more the shame of the heathen, neither shalt thou bear the reproach of the peoples any more, neither shalt thou cause thy nation to stumble any more, saith the Lord God."— 36: 15, *R.V.*

God's true people have been put to shame amongst all the nations, but that condition must come to an end before all of his anointed people finish their earthly course. "Behold, at that time I will undo all that afflict thee; and I will save her that halteth, and gath-

er her that was driven out: and I will get them praise
and fame in every land where they have been put to
shame. At that time will I bring you again, even in
the time that I gather you: for I will make you a name
and a praise among all people of the earth, when I
turn back your captivity before your eyes, saith the
Lord.'' (Zeph. 3: 19, 20) Those who have reproached
God's people will have no more reason or excuse to
lay reproaches upon them. Furthermore, there will be
no occasion for a falling away or stumbling in God's
organization. Thus the Lord pictures his people as
cleansed and made a whole nation and devoted entirely to his service and to his praise. Fullness of
bread and prosperity caused the people of Palestine
to forget God; and that has been true of all so-called
''organized Christian'' nations. (Deut. 8: 10-14) But
we are in that day which the Lord God has made for
his people and for the vindication of his own holy
name. God now sends prosperity upon his people and
upon the work which he has assigned to their hands
and they rejoice to do it, and those who have his
spirit will never again have occasion to stumble.

FOR HIS NAME'S SAKE

When the Jews dwelt in Palestine they defiled the
land, and this foreshadowed what would come upon
''organized Christianity''. Ezekiel therefore prophe-
sies: ''Moreover the word of the Lord came upon me,
saying, Son of man, when the house of Israel dwelt in
their own land, they defiled it by their own way, and
by their doings: their way was before me as the uncleanness of a removed woman.'' (36: 16, 17) In the
day of the early church false prophets in the church

led God's spirit-begotten ones into uncleanness. (2 Pet. 2:1, 3) This uncleanness was pictured in the provision by the ceremonial law concerning a menstruous woman. (Lev. 15:19-27) Uncleanness amongst the professed people of God has been manifested at all stages of the selection of the church of God. Now the time has come when God has separated the false from the true worshipers, and it is by and through the truth, and his true and faithful ones, that he makes others to know his great and holy name.

Because of the wickedness of the Jews in Palestine God poured out his fury upon them. Because of the wickedness of "Christendom" God has poured out his fury upon that part of Satan's organization. "Wherefore I poured my fury upon them for the blood that they had shed upon the land, and for their idols wherewith they had polluted it; and I scattered them among the heathen, and they were dispersed through the countries; according to their way, and according to their doings, I judged them." (36:18, 19) Their greater scattering and the execution of the judgment upon them are in the near future.

When the World War came "Christendom", including many spirit-begotten ones, followed the guide and leadership of men and shed much blood upon the land. The scattering that had been in progress in "Christendom" for many years culminated in the exile and captivity of "organized Christianity" to the Devil's organization, particularly in the World War period. Many professed Christians went into the World War claiming to be the representatives of God and Christ, and thereby defamed his holy name. "And when they entered unto the heathen, whither they

went, they profaned my holy name, when they said
to them, These are the people of the Lord, and are
gone forth out of his land." (36:20) The nations of
earth that had taken the name of God and his Christ
prosecuted the World War, and by so doing greatly
profaned God's name. There was a great multitude of
professed Christians that engaged in that war. There
were a few who took advantage of the law of Satan's
organization and became conscientious objectors. These
who objected to the taking of human life were persecuted and forcibly led into involuntary captivity to
the enemy organization. Thus the God of these faithful witnesses seemed to be weak and powerless, and
hence their captivity by the enemy was a reproach
upon the great name of Jehovah. The enemies of God
and his kingdom said: "Where is their God?"—Ps.
79:8-10.

It is the name of Jehovah God that must be vindicated. That is the important issue. However, even the
faithful Christians for many years thought that the
chief purpose of Jehovah was and is to get men saved
and into heaven. Many have thought that God fights
their battles for them merely to get them saved. God's
name has long been profaned; and this has been done
voluntarily by many who claim to be Christians, and
it has been involuntarily done by others by the course
of action which they have taken. The Lord now makes
it plain that he will take drastic action against his
enemies, not for the mere purpose of saving some that
are consecrated to him, but because of his own holy
name. "But I had pity for mine holy name, which the
house of Israel had profaned among the heathen,
whither they went. Therefore say unto the house of

Israel, Thus saith the Lord God, I do not this for
your sakes, O house of Israel, but for mine holy name's
sake, which ye have profaned among the heathen,
whither ye went." (36: 21, 22) The paramount issue
is, Who is God? Does the name of Jehovah stand for
a supreme and intelligent power who can defend himself? Who shall rule the universe? This issue now
must be settled and the name of God made known to
all creation. Therefore says the Lord God: "I do not
this for your sakes, . . . but for mine holy name's
sake." Do what for his holy name's sake? may be
asked. Does the returning of the natural descendants
of Israel to the land of Palestine vindicate the name
of Jehovah God? It certainly does not; especially
since they have returned there in unbelief. On the
other hand, the restoring of his faithful remnant people to their proper position as his true and bold witnesses, and causing them to declare his name fear-
lessly and boldly, is for his own holy name's sake and
is for the vindication of his name. It is not for the
benefit of the remnant, but it is that the name of
Jehovah God may be made known and be put in its
proper place in the minds of creatures that they might
know that he is the Supreme One. This prophecy,
therefore, has its fulfilment chiefly in this present day,
in which we are now, and its purpose is the vindication of Jehovah's name.

Let us bear in mind that God's professed people,
and including many who were sincere, have profaned
his name amongst the nations. Also let us keep in
mind that Jehovah's chief purpose is to sanctify his
great name. Therefore says the prophet of Jehovah:
"And I will sanctify my great name, which was pro-

faned among the heathen, which ye have profaned in the midst of them; and the heathen shall know that I am the Lord, saith the Lord God, when I shall be sanctified in you before their eyes.'' (36:23) The fact that many Jews are now back in Palestine does not sanctify the name of Jehovah. On the other hand, God has brought forth his people and given them a new name and made them his witnesses, and it is for his own name's sake and is the work of sanctifying his great name amongst the people. ''When I will be sanctified through you before your eyes.'' (*Leeser*) God's anointed people now have the testimony from Jehovah that they are his, called forth to his work, for the purpose of making known his great name, and thus he is sanctified before the eyes of his people, and other people are being made to know that Jehovah is God. The facts therefore prove that the prophecy has its fulfilment upon spiritual Israel, God's true people now on the earth.

The ''land'' or country is symbolic of the condition in which God's people are put. This prophecy was written for the comfort of God's anointed people, and not for the benefit of unbelieving Jews. The seventh world power and the League of Nations composing parts of Satan's organization signed the mandate over Palestine to Britain, and ungodly men take all the credit for the present condition of the Jews being established in Palestine; whereas this prophecy, addressed to God's anointed people, gives credit to Jehovah for its fulfilment because it says: ''I [Jehovah] will bring you into your own land.'' This clearly means, into the proper condition whereby this people represent Jehovah on the earth at the present time, and hence Jehovah alone must be given credit for this, and therefore it shows the prophecy has its fulfilment upon God's remnant. When the Jews are actually restored to Palestine and then obey God and fully accept Christ as their Redeemer, and then walk in the way of righteousness, then these texts would have an application to natural Israel, but the primary application of these texts clearly is to God's anointed people which people were foreshadowed by Israel or Jacob. The great multitude of ''prisoners'' must yet be loosed and brought forth and placed in the condition pictured by the land, that is, in God's organization, where they properly belong; hence the prophecy has an application to that class also.

The gathering of the Lord's true people began after the coming of Christ Jesus to the temple. (2 Thess. 2:1) Then and there the cleansing work began, and which was foreshadowed by the following prophecy: ''Then will I sprinkle clean water upon you, and ye shall be clean: from all your filthiness, and from all your idols, will I cleanse you.'' (36:25) This prophecy could not be fulfilled upon fleshly Israel, at least until the resurrection of the faithful patriarchs, and by that time such prophecy will be of no comfort to Jehovah's remnant people according to the spirit. The Scriptures were written for the comfort of God's remnant. The prophecy therefore manifestly has its primary application now and before the battle of Armageddon, and while there are heathen nations to observe what is going on. The gathering of his people to the temple, that is to say, the proper condition of those who are in line for the kingdom, must of necessity be followed by the cleansing work according to the prophecy of Malachi 3:3,4. The Lord has made clear to his people his truth since the coming to the temple, and they have been cleansed from their idols of man-worship, and from every part of Satan's organization. They are now able to clearly see and do see that the "higher powers" are not anyone of Satan's organization, as they have formerly believed, but that these "higher powers" are the ruling ones in God's organization. His true people have been separated from the false by the Lord's pure water of truth and are clean, and are not contaminated by mixing further with Satan's organization. They now appreciate the name of Jehovah and his organization and are witnesses to his great and holy name. They could not offer an offering to the Lord in righteousness until this cleansing work took place, but now Jehovah's witnesses do offer unto the Lord an offering in righteousness; hence they 'offer the sacrifices of praise to God continually [not occasionally], that is to say, the fruit of their lips; giving thanks to his name'. (Heb. 13:15) The Lord himself does the separating or cleansing work upon coming to the temple, and he uses his angels in this connection.—Matt. 13:41.

Addressing his faithful ones he says: "A new heart also will I give you, and a new spirit will I put within you; and I will take away the stony heart out of your flesh, and I will give you an heart of flesh." (36:26) Amongst the consecrated and called ones to the kingdom some have had hearts like stone and did not bring forth the fruit of the kingdom, but they brought their own fruit, and because thereof they were cleared out from God's organization. (Matt. 13:5, 20, 21, 41) "So then because thou art lukewarm, and neither cold

nor hot, I will spue thee out of my mouth." (Rev.
3:16) Those whose hearts are warm and wholly devoted to Jehovah God are brought into his organization. Since the revelation to his people of the true
meaning of God's name, and of his purposes and of
his organization, and since the exhibition to them of
Satan's organization, God has truly given his anointed
ones "a new heart", wholly and completely devoted
to him. These are no longer deceived by idols, such as
"the sin of Samaria", or self-development, or any
other foolish doctrines or things.

In the temple there is a unity of God's people and
all are of one spirit. This was foreshadowed by the
prophecy: "And I will put my spirit within you, and
cause you to walk in my statutes, and ye shall keep
my judgments, and do them." (36:27) The spirit
of Christ Jesus, the vindication of Jehovah's name,
is the spirit that moves God's remnant; and this God
has put upon them after they were brought into the
temple and received the robe of righteousness. (Joel
2:28, 29) Therefore these faithful ones of the remnant "keep the commandments of God ['my statutes'
and 'my judgments'], and have the testimony of Jesus Christ". Seeing the application of the prophecy
is to them, his faithful remnant are now comforted
and their hope is made bright. The "great multitude"
must be brought into this condition for the vindication of Jehovah's name in his due time. Later the
faithful patriarchs and all obedient ones that come
into God's great organization will be a vindication to
his Word and to his name.

The Lord made the twelve apostles of the Lamb the
foundation of his organization here on earth, "Jesus

Christ himself being the chief corner stone.'' (Eph. 2:20) This corresponds to the twelve tribes of Israel. John designated himself one of the fathers when he wrote, 'To my dear children,' and he addressed part of his epistle to the ''fathers, because ye have known him [Christ Jesus] that is from the beginning [of the church]''. (1 John 2:13) In harmony with this the prophecy says: ''And ye shall dwell in the land that I gave to your fathers; and ye shall be my people, and I will be your God.'' (36:28) This prophecy could not now apply to fleshly Israel, but it does clearly apply to God's remnant. To the twelve apostles the kingdom interests and privileges on earth were originally committed, and now these kingdom interests and privileges are committed to the ''faithful and wise servant'', which is the remnant of spiritual Israel. These are the people of God, and to his name they bear witness. These have obeyed the commandments of the Lord and have become his people. ''Wherefore come out from among them, and be ye separate, saith the Lord, and touch not the unclean thing; and I will receive you, and will be a Father unto you, and ye shall be my sons and daughters, saith the Lord Almighty.'' (2 Cor. 6:17, 18) These are the people of God whom he has made his witnesses and named them such. (Isa. 43:10-12) They are the last members of Christ on earth, hence ''the feet of him'', and they say to each other in Zion: ''Thy God reigneth!'' (Isa. 52:7) Jehovah has committed a work to them, putting his words in their mouth, and to them says: ''Thou art my people.''—Isa. 51:16.

Prior to the coming of the Lord to the temple his people were mixed up with others and were therefore unclean. "I will also save you from all your uncleanness; and I will call for the corn, and will increase it, and lay no famine upon you." (36:29) The Lord brought them into the temple and under the robe of righteousness, and gave them the garments of salvation, thereby approving them and identifying them as his people, and thus he took away their uncleanness. "Be ye clean that bear the vessels of the Lord." (Isa. 52:11; 2 Cor. 7:1) Jehovah's witnesses now enjoy the increase of corn (wheat) which in the language of the prophecy means an abundant supply of spiritual nourishment from the Word of God. There is no famine amongst his people and they can boldly testify to others concerning the truth.

In the past the heathen had some reason to reproach God's people because they held to many things of "organized Christianity", and did not have an abundant supply of pure spiritual food. "And I will multiply the fruit of the tree, and the increase of the field, that ye shall receive no more reproach of famine among the heathen." (36:30) Now the heathen have no more occasion to reproach God's people the remnant, because these are now ready always to give a reason for their hope with meekness and fear. (1 Pet. 3:15) For instance, in times past the faithful people of God ignorantly thought with others that Jehovah had permitted the Devil to carry on his gross wickedness in order to teach men lessons. That teaching defamed God's name; but now the remnant, by the grace of the Lord, have the truth upon this question and have declared the truth concerning the permission of wickedness, and they tell the people that in due time Jehovah will fully vindicate his great and holy

name. The remnant now brings forth fruit of the
kingdom to others that they might know that Jehovah
is the only true God, and God continues to increase
the quantity of fruit.

Since the coming of Christ to the temple the faithful have seen that in times past they have done unlawful things in the name of Christ and hence these were
evil ways. "Then shall ye remember your own evil
ways, and your doings that were not good, and shall
loathe yourselves in your own sight, for your iniquities, and for your abominations." (36:31) Among
these things were ecclesiasticism; self-perfection by
what was understood to be "character development";
human leadership; hero worship; flattering titles;
apologetic and sanctimonious attitude before the "big
guns" of the world; bowing to the "higher powers"
of Satan's organization; and many like things. These
things the true and faithful remnant now loathe, and
are exceedingly sorry that they ever thus reproached
Jehovah's holy name.

Now let the self-righteous who have concluded that
God was doing everything in his power for them, in
order that they might be taken to heaven, learn a lesson from these words of the prophet: "Not for your
sakes do I this, saith the Lord God, be it known unto
you: be ashamed and confounded for your own ways,
O house of Israel." (36:32) The remnant now sin-
cerely acknowledge that they are truly ashamed that
they ever thought themselves or any other creature on
earth of such great importance that God was doing
these things for their sakes. No longer do they magnify men, but they diligently try to seek the honor
of Jehovah's name and to inform others about God

and his kingdom. When the "great multitude" or "prisoners" are loosed they also will be ashamed of their hero-worship practices and all foolish things done by them. The restored of the earth will learn similar lessons, that there is no such thing as a great man.

"LIKE THE GARDEN OF EDEN"

The comments upon verses ten and eleven are appropriate upon verse thirty-three. "Thus saith the Lord God, In the day that I shall have cleansed you from all your iniquities, I will also cause you to dwell in the cities, and the wastes shall be builded." God's faithful people shall abide in his organization. During the World War period they were in a desolate condition. The enemy thought that God's people were done for; but now those of the enemy organization see the people of God more bold and earnest than ever before in declaring the kingdom. "And the desolate land shall be tilled, whereas it lay desolate in the sight of all that passed by. And they shall say, This land that was desolate is become like the garden of Eden; and the waste, and desolate, and ruined cities, are become fenced, and are inhabited." (36: 34, 35) The work of God's people will continue to increase and flourish even as it has since 1919. It is likened unto the garden of Eden; for the hand of the Lord is upon it. For this reason the Lord's faithful appreciate the words of the prophet: 'O the blessedness of him that waiteth and cometh unto the thirteen hundred and thirty-five days.' (Dan. 12: 12; see *The Watchtower*, 1929, page 375) The Lord's people in his organization on earth, as the prophecy says, are become a 'fenced and inhabited city'. This is true because of

Jehovah's protection. The prophecy is an encouragement to the remnant. Zion is God's organization, a part of which is now on the earth; and in support of this conclusion that the prophecy of Ezekiel thirty-six applies to God's remnant now on the earth, mark the words of Isaiah 51: 2-4: "Look unto Abraham your father, and unto Sarah that bare you: for I called him alone, and blessed him, and increased him. For the Lord shall comfort Zion: he will comfort all her waste places, and he will make her wilderness like Eden, and her desert like the garden of the Lord; joy and gladness shall be found therein, thanksgiving, and the voice of melody. Hearken unto me, my people, and give ear unto me, O my nation; for a law shall proceed from me, and I will make my judgment to rest for a light of the people." "And all thy children shall be taught of the Lord; and great shall be the peace of thy children. In righteousness shalt thou be established: thou shalt be far from oppression; for thou shalt not fear: and from terror; for it shall not come near thee." (Isa. 54: 13, 14) "And the Gentiles shall see thy righteousness, and all kings thy glory: and thou shalt be called by a new name, which the mouth of the Lord shall name. Thou shalt no more be termed Forsaken; neither shall thy land any more be termed Desolate; but thou shalt be called Hephzi-bah, and thy land Beulah: for the Lord delighteth in thee, and thy land shall be married."— Isa. 62: 2, 4.

What is the purpose of Jehovah's bestowing such blessings upon his faithful remnant? Is it for the benefit of the remnant? It is not; but that Jehovah's name may be vindicated. "Then the heathen, that are

left round about you, shall know that I the Lord build
the ruined places, and plant that that was desolate:
I the Lord have spoken it, and I will do it.'' (36:36)
The enemy cannot give credit to any part of Satan's
organization for the publishing and increase of God's
message of the kingdom, because no support is received or desired from any part of Satan's organization. We once thought that probably the Lord would
touch the heart of some worldly rich man who would
contribute a lot of money and thus greatly increase
the financial power for the spreading of his message
of truth. Now God's people see that this is wrong and
they would not accept a penny of the ill-got gains of
Big Business men, because their money is tainted and
corrupted. Enemies of the truth have maliciously
lied, stating that God's work is supported by Bolshe-
vik Jews. Not only is such a malicious lie, but the
Lord's faithful people receive nothing from the Devil's organization. Jehovah God is rebuilding that
which the enemy sought to tear down; and in his due
time he will destroy the enemy and his organization,
to the vindication of his name.

In this day God's true people are more anxious to
learn than ever, and to see that the message of his
kingdom is heralded throughout the earth. ''Thus
saith the Lord God, I will yet for this be inquired
[prevailed upon, *Roth.*; entreated, *Leeser*] of by the
house of Israel, to do it for them; I will increase them
with men like a flock.'' (36:37) Jehovah has been inquired of, entreated and besought by his faithful remnant in that they have prayed and continue to pray:
''Save now, I beseech thee, O Lord; O Lord, I beseech thee, send now prosperity.'' (Ps. 118:25) And

'send more laborers into the field'. (Matt. 9:38) The Lord continues to cause his service organization to increase, enlarge and multiply, and now, in 1932, there are more earnest souls actively engaged in delivering the testimony of the kingdom than at any time past. The companies are small in number, but the individual workers in the field have increased in numbers and their zeal has greatly increased.

Jehovah's people now on earth are joyful, as one blessed with great prosperity. "As the holy flock, as the flock of Jerusalem in her solemn feasts, so shall the waste cities be filled with flocks of men; and they shall know that I am the Lord." (36:38) God's service organization in the earth is thrilled with joy. It is a time of feasting for them. They are feasting upon prophetic truths which the Lord has given to his people, and the remnant delight to have the privilege of singing the praises of Jehovah's name. Thus they follow as a flock Christ Jesus their Leader and they know that Jehovah is their God. (Rev. 14:4; 19:14) The faithful are "come unto mount Sion, and unto the city of the living God", unto God's organization, and their joy is great. (Heb. 12:22) Now they offer unto the Lord an offering in righteousness and to his praise. Jehovah's chariot is moving majestically forward to the vindication of his name. These truths are a great consolation to God's people.

DRY BONES
(Ezekiel, Chapter 37)

The increased light which Jehovah sheds upon his Word brings ever increasing joy to the temple class which is privileged to receive that light. In this the thirty-seventh chapter of Ezekiel's prophecy, verses one to fourteen, a description is given of dry bones. Heretofore this prophecy has been made to apply exclusively to the people of fleshly Israel brought into the land of Palestine. It now seems quite certain that such application, if correct, is but a secondary fulfilment of the prophecy. The chief fulfilment of this prophecy must be upon spiritual Israel, that is, the spirit-begotten ones including the remnant and the "great multitude". There can be no deviation from the divinely announced rule, to wit, that "all scripture is given . . . that the man of God may be . . . throughly furnished unto all good works" (2 Tim. 3:16, 17) ; that "all these things happened unto them [natural Israel] for ensamples [types], and they are written [to foreshadow things] for our admonition, upon whom the ends of the world are come" (1 Cor. 10:11) ; and that "whatsoever things were written aforetime were written for our learning, that we through patience and comfort of the scriptures might have hope". (Rom. 15:4) It is impossible to get away from the truth that Jehovah caused these prophecies to be written for the benefit of those who shall be engaged in the work of publishing his name and his kingdom on earth, when the Devil is making his desperate and final effort to destroy them, and that one of the purposes in giving the remnant such understanding and appreciation of prophecy is that they might be encouraged and increased in patience and comfort of receiving the things which the Lord has provided for the faithful. In view of these indisputable and divine rules we must look for a fulfilment of these prophecies, in their primary significance, while the remnant is still on the earth serving Jehovah God.

To make Ezekiel see this prophetic vision the hand of the Lord came upon him, as he says. Likewise the power of the Lord God must be upon his faithful people in these last days in order that these may discern the importance of the fulfilment of that vision. "The hand of the Lord was upon me, and carried me out in the spirit of the Lord, and set me down in the midst of the valley [plain, *Roth.*] which was full of bones." (37:1) This was not in the valley (*emek*, a vale or broad depression) of Jehoshaphat, but a plain (*biqah*, a split, that is to say, a wide, level valley, plain, between mountains) in the land of Shinar, the site of Babylon, to which the Jews were carried away from their homeland and where they pined away. "By the rivers of Babylon, there we sat down; yea, we wept, when we remembered Zion."—Ps. 137:1.

Prior to 1918 God's faithful witnesses on earth were engaged in doing the Elijah work of the church. From 1917 to 1919 they were carried away and compelled to suffer restraint and confinement in prison and, by suppressive measures accompanying the World War, were hindered from proceeding with the Lord's work. These faithful ones were thus carried away by the forces of Babylon, the Devil's organization, and between the governments of Satan's organization. This was foreshadowed by the carrying away of Israel to Babylon. Ezekiel states that the place of the valley where the spirit of the Lord set him down was full of bones. He does not say 'one skeleton', but enough of bones to make the skeletons of "an exceeding great army". (37:10) "And caused me to pass by them round about: and, behold, there were very many in the open valley; and, lo, they were very dry.''—37: 2.

Ezekiel was told that these bones are ''the whole house of Israel'', and not merely the house of Judah, the royal tribe. The delinquency on the part of the spirit-begotten ones in the churches led to their being carried captive into the World War. These conditions also took the faithful ones involuntarily into a state of inactivity; thus the entire spirit-begotten ones of ''Christendom'' are pictured. These bones in the valley therefore pictured the entire company of spirit-begotten ones, including the anointed and the great multitude of ''prisoners'', and show the condition of such in respect to the work of the Lord during the period of the World War. The bones do not picture those who are literally dead and in the grave, because the prophecy states that they speak and say: 'Our bones are dry and our hopes are lost.' (37: 11) They do, however, picture those who are near literal death and also in a dead condition as regards the Lord's work, this condition being the result of the faithful's being restrained by the enemy organization. Such were therefore unclean to the Lord, just as bones of the dead were unclean according to the law. (Num. 19: 16, 18; Matt. 23: 27) The Prophet Isaiah, representing God's people, saw that the people of God were in an unclean condition, when he cried out, ''Woe is me! for I am undone; because I am a man of unclean lips.'' (Isa. 6: 5) This was at the time when the Lord appeared at Jehovah's temple. In 1918 the Lord's faithful people were truly interested in his work and endeavored to carry it on, but in that year God's organization, the Society, was disrupted. Many of God's people were confined behind prison walls. The publications of the Society were banned, martial law was enforced, and activity in the Lord's service stopped. Activity is a manifestation of life, and inactivity is well pictured by dry bones. The outlook for the work of the Lord during that World War period was as cheerful as a pile of dry bones, and about as hopeful. No doubt Ezekiel was much depressed at the sight he beheld. The facts show that the Ezekiel class was greatly depressed by the conditions that obtained during the World War period. God's people were a hopeless-appearing company.

According to *Rotherham* 'there were many bones upon the face of the valley and "they were very dry"'. The bodies had not been gathered and buried, but had been left to the fowls of the air and the ravenous beasts of the field. This condition is described by the psalmist: "O God, the heathen are come into thine inheritance; thy holy temple have they defiled; they have laid Jerusalem on heaps. The dead bodies of thy servants have they given to be meat unto the fowls of the heaven, the flesh of thy saints unto the beasts of the earth. Their blood have they shed like water round about Jerusalem; and there was none to bury them. We are become a reproach to our neighbours, a scorn and derision to them that are round about us."—Ps. 79:1-4.

"Christendom," Ammon, Moab and others of the enemy view God's people as "the filth of the world, . . . the offscouring of all things". (1 Cor. 4:13) "And their dead bodies shall lie in the street of the great city, which spiritually is called Sodom and

Egypt, where also our Lord was crucified. And they
of the people, and kindreds, and tongues, and nations,
shall see their dead bodies three days and an half,
and shall not suffer their dead bodies to be put in
graves." (Rev. 11: 8, 9; see *Light*, Book One, page
205) Such is a description of the condition of God's
faithful people on earth during the World War period. All their bones were disjointed. "I am poured
out like water, and all my bones are out of joint: my
heart is like wax; it is melted in the midst of my
bowels. My strength is dried up like a potsherd; and
my tongue cleaveth to my jaws; and thou hast
brought me into the dust of death." (Ps. 22: 14, 15)
This pictures the broken hopes of God's people and
the world-wide disorganized company thereof.

The prophet further says the bones were "very
dry". They were truly bleached. That was exactly
the condition of God's people in the period above
mentioned. That was a fine prospect for return of
life and activity to the service of the Lord. How well
this pictures the outlook of God's people in 1918. Behind prison bars some of them were heard often to
say: "Our work is done. We shall be left here to
rot." The heat of Satan's organization had made them
very dry and the spirit of God's people was broken.
"A broken spirit drieth the bones." (Prov. 17: 22)
Compelled to remain within prison walls with vile
creatures, and kept away from the work of the Lord
which they loved better than their lives, many tears
of bitterness were shed because of their hopes dried
up. Cursed, abused and reviled by vicious prison
guards, hated and reproached because they had stood
for the truth, some of the faithful ones of the Lord

were almost consumed with grief. The condition of
many who were outside of prison walls but restrained
of their liberty and in full sympathy with their brethren inside was exactly as above stated. Well has the
psalmist described the condition of such: "For my
life is spent with grief, and my years with sighing:
my strength faileth because of mine iniquity, and my
bones are consumed. I was a reproach among all mine
enemies, but especially among my neighbours, and a
fear to mine acquaintance: they that did see me without fled from me. I am forgotten as a dead man out
of mind: I am like a broken vessel. For I have heard
the slander of many: fear was on every side: while
they took counsel together against me, they devised to
take away my life." (Ps. 31: 10-13) It was the religionists of "Christendom" or "organized Christianity" that mocked these witnesses of the Lord and
heaped upon them the greatest amount of cruel reproach; hence they were pierced and broken with
reproach and cried: "I will say unto God my rock,
Why hast thou forgotten me? why go I mourning because of the oppression of the enemy? As with a sword
in my bones, mine enemies reproach me; while they
say daily unto me, Where is thy God?"—Ps. 42: 9, 10.

Throughout the borders of "Christendom" God's
people were restrained of all activity in the service
of the Lord, and therefore they were not in health.
In their hearts they cried out as the psalmist says:
"There is no soundness in my flesh, because of thine
anger; neither is there any rest in my bones, because
of my sin." (Ps. 38: 3) Would there ever be a possibility of again engaging in the service of the Lord?
This question was often propounded. Some days a

hope would arise for a time, only to be shortly dashed to the ground. Some of God's children behind prison bars, pacing the floor of their cells, would be heard in the night to cry out and weep with great bitterness and with indignation at the insult and infamy heaped upon God and upon his work.

The Lord propounded the question to Ezekiel: "Son of man, can these bones live?" (37:3) That same question the Lord put into the mind of his consecrated ones during that period of restraint. Even after the World War ended and the war prisoners were let out of cells, the question was put by the Lord to his people: "Are you going to remain as a dead and disorganized company, or will you get busy and show signs of life in my work?" This question emphasizes in the minds of his servants the miracle that the Lord was about to perform. Ezekiel did not manifest a stubborn unbelief or doubt about what the Lord could do, but trusting in the Lord he said: "O Lord God, thou knowest." In September 1919 a large company of God's people assembled in convention at Cedar Point, Ohio, and the question there was: Would the work be revived? Those who put their trust in the Lord did not say, It cannot be done. There were some present, however, who said it could not be done. But the faithful and zealous were ready for action. Immediately upon being released from prison steps were taken by some of the Lord's people to reorganize his work; and now at this convention the Lord revealed to his people that the work of the church done up to that time had been foreshadowed by Elijah and was now dead, and that Elisha foreshadowed a work yet to be done. The hope of God's people began to revive.

"YE SHALL LIVE"

Ezekiel must become active, and the Lord directed what he should do; therefore he was directed to prophesy: "Again he said unto me, Prophesy upon [over, *R.V.*] these bones, and say unto them, O ye dry bones, hear the word of the Lord." (37:4) The Ezekiel class fulfilled this part of the prophecy by preaching to each other during the 1,260-day period that 'the woman was nourished in the wilderness from the face of the beast'. (Rev. 12:14) A great deal of prophesying was required to drum it into the minds of the consecrated that they must organize for service and carry forward the work foreshadowed by Elisha. Some of the "lazybones" never did wake up and busy themselves, for the reason that they doubted that the construction placed upon the Elijah and Elisha pictures by *The Watchtower* was from the Lord. It was in 1919 that this prophecy began to have fulfilment. Those who really trusted in and loved the Lord God did hear and did obey his admonitions to get busy. "Zion heard, and was glad; and the daughters of Judah rejoiced, because of thy judgments, O Lord." —Ps. 97:8.

The Ezekiel class continued to prophesy or preach the message of the Lord. "Thus saith the Lord God unto these bones, Behold, I will cause breath to enter into you, and ye shall live: and I will lay sinews upon you, and will bring up flesh upon you, and cover you with skin, and put breath in you, and ye shall live; and ye shall know that I am the Lord." (37:5,6) *The Watchtower* continued to urge upon God's people the necessity of organization for service, and faithful speakers addressing companies joined in the prophecy, bringing forth many scriptures to prove that the Lord would give new life to his work on earth, as pictured and foreshadowed by Elisha, and that he would strengthen his people to do it, giving to them a double portion of the spirit of Elijah for that purpose. The Elijah and Elisha pictures, understood for the first time in 1919, were really the opening of the work that has increased from that day until the present time. Those who failed to understand the picture never got into the work, and many of them became opposers.

The Ezekiel class from 1919 on continued to search the Scriptures to ascertain the will of God. "So I prophesied as I was commanded: and as I prophesied there was a noise, and, behold, a shaking, and the bones came together, bone to his bone."—37: 7.

From March 1919 to September 1922 this prophesying continued, not according to the obsolete interpretation of the Scriptures, but according to the Lord's will and commandments, such as Matthew 24: 14 and Isaiah 61: 1, 2. As this preaching or prophesying continued there was a noise of dissension amongst the various companies of consecrated people, such as is indicated by the seventh verse of the prophecy. Regardless of this noise of dissension the faithful continued to send forth organization instructions and to lay out the work to be done and to push the work forward. Then came a shaking, or as the *Revised Version* puts it, "an earthquake," and many were shaken out and turned back to their own selfish views and ways, while the faithful ones shook themselves and aroused themselves to greater activity. (Rev. 11: 13) "Awake, awake; put on thy strength, O

Zion: put on thy beautiful garments, O Jerusalem, the holy city: for henceforth there shall no more come into thee the uncircumcised and the unclean. Shake thyself from the dust; arise, and sit down, O Jerusalem: loose thyself from the bands of thy neck, O captive daughter of Zion." (Isa. 52:1,2) As this shaking continued 'the faithful bones came together, bone to bone'. The dead hopes of the war-harassed saints were revived. They began to get the vision properly adjusted. They realized that they were not "clean cut off" or "quite cut off" from the Lord and his service.—Vs. 11, *R.V.*

It was then that the people of God began in earnest to form an active, operating organization, even as the prophecy indicates by the following: "And when I beheld, lo, the sinews and the flesh came up upon them, and the skin covered them above; but there was no breath in them." (37:8) "Thou hast clothed me with skin and flesh, and hast fenced [hedged, *margin*] me with bones and sinews. Thou hast granted me life and favour, and thy visitation hath preserved my spirit." (Job 10:11,12) "A sound heart is the life of the flesh." (Prov. 14:30) Those whose hearts were really devoted to the Lord began to arise from their unclean and dead appearance to a live body of joyful activity in the Lord's service. (Nah. 1:15; Col. 2:19) Thus the Lord's people got into unity and in love in Christ and ceased to be tossed about by the opinions of men. "But, speaking the truth in love, may grow up into him in all things, which is the head, even Christ; from whom the whole body fitly joined together, and compacted by that which every joint supplieth, according to the effectual working in the measure of every part, maketh increase of the body unto the edifying of itself in love."—Eph. 4:15, 16.

The faithful whom Ezekiel foreshadowed in this prophecy comforted their brethren in Zion according to the will of God, that they might be "trees of righteousness, the planting of the Lord, that [his name] might be glorified". (Isa. 61:3) These reorganized companies of God's faithful people had to tarry until they were "endued with power from on high", even as did the apostles. (Luke 24:49) "It is the spirit [power] that quickeneth." (John 6:63) God's people continued to present this matter before the Lord in prayer, secretly and in their assembled companies, and this is pictured by the words of the prophet. "Then said he unto me, Prophesy unto the wind [breath, *margin*], prophesy, son of man, and say to the wind [breath], Thus saith the Lord God, Come from the four winds, O breath [wind, or spirit], and breathe upon these slain, that they may live." (37:9) God's faithful people kept in mind that the work must be accomplished, if at all, not by their own might, but by the spirit of the Lord of hosts. (Zech. 4:6) *The Watchtower* continued to prophesy and to instill the spirit of the Lord's work into the saints, and the prayer of God's people everywhere was that they might accomplish his purposes. This prophesying or preaching reached a climax on September 8, 1922, at a convention of God's people, at which time they were awakened by the power of the Lord as never before.

"So I prophesied as he commanded me, and the breath came into them, and they lived, and stood up upon their feet, an exceeding great army." (37:10) Every faithful witness of God who was present at that convention will never forget that hour of great blessing. It was like a second Pentecost. "And it shall come to pass in the last days, saith God, I will pour out of my spirit upon all flesh: and your sons and your daughters shall prophesy, and your young men shall see visions, and your old men shall dream dreams: and on my servants and on my handmaidens I will pour out, in those days, of my spirit; and they shall prophesy." (Acts 2: 17, 18) It was surely the time of fulfilment of these prophetic words. And those that loved the Lord "stood upon their feet". It was indeed like a great army ready for war. "And after three days and an half the spirit of life from God entered into them, and they stood upon their feet; and great fear fell upon them which saw them. And they heard a great voice from heaven saying unto them, Come up hither. And they ascended up to heaven in a cloud; and their enemies beheld them." (Rev. 11: 11, 12; Dan. 12: 1, 2) "Behold my servant, whom I uphold, mine elect, in whom my soul delighteth; I have put my spirit upon him; he shall bring forth judgment to the Gentiles." (Isa. 42: 1) It was at that time that the faithful saw the Lord in the temple and realized that they had, as Isaiah stated, been 'unclean of lips', and they prayed unto the Lord and he heard and cleansed them and they began to greatly rejoice. (Isa. 6: 1-9; 12: 1-3) Those who then came to the front were no mere skeletons, by any means, but, as the prophet said, like "an exceeding great army" in the service, moved by His spirit and His strength, and ready to do His will. This organization that stands up, as indicated by the prophecy and as also shown by the facts, is not a peace-time force, but it is a real military or militant company under the command of Christ Jesus. "And the Lord shall utter his voice before his army; for his camp is very great: for he is strong that executeth his word: for the day of the Lord is great and very terrible; and who can abide it?" (Joel 2:11) Thus are pictured those whom the Lord brought into his temple and commanded to go forth as his witnesses to do his service.

Under the direction of the Lord, Ezekiel in the prophecy now identifies the bones thus: "Then he said unto me, Son of man, these bones are the whole house of Israel; behold they say, Our bones are dried, and our hope is lost; we are cut off for our parts." (37:11) It is manifest, then, from this prophecy that both the remnant and the "great multitude" class are included in the prophecy of the dry bones. The faithful remnant class is now fully alive and brought together and constitutes a well organized and working machine. The "prisoners" must yet become awakened and to a full realization that they have been negligent and that they must do something. The faithful ones are also well illustrated by the expression of the Prophet Jeremiah, who for a time remained quiet and inactive but who later was fired for service and went forward in obedience to God's commandments. "Then I said, I will not make mention of him, nor speak any more in his name. But his word was in mine heart as a burning fire shut up in my bones, and I was weary with forbearing, and I could not stay."—Jer. 20:9.

There was an attempt made to bury the faithful ones alive, and for a time it seemed or looked as though they were in fact in their graves, not literally in graves in the earth, but confined, and hence in a dead condition concerning the witness work of the Lord in the earth. The Lord must bring them out of their graves; therefore the prophecy reads: "Therefore prophesy, and say unto them, Thus saith the Lord God, Behold, O my people, I will open your graves, and cause you to come up out of your graves, and bring you into the land of Israel." (37:12) "Wherefore he saith, Awake thou that sleepest, and arise from the dead, and Christ shall give thee light." (Eph. 5:14) God did awaken them out of this condition and brought them "into [their] own land", that is to say, into their proper condition and place of freedom to serve him as his witnesses that his name might be made known in the earth. This he did for his own great name's sake, as stated in Ezekiel 36:22-24.

Now addressing the faithful class whom Ezekiel foreshadowed, the Lord said: "And ye shall know that I am the Lord, when I have opened your graves, O my people, and brought you up out of your graves, and shall put my spirit in you, and ye shall live; and I shall place you in your own land; then shall ye know that I the Lord have spoken it, and performed it, saith the Lord." (37:13, 14) Today Jehovah's faithful witnesses know to a certainty that he has spoken to them and that he has given them a new name and that he has restored them to their "own land". Every bone among them is now filled with the spirit of the Lord and these delight to do his service. "And when ye see this, your heart shall rejoice, and your bones shall flourish like an herb: and the hand of the Lord shall be known toward his servants, and his indignation toward his enemies. For, behold, the Lord will come with fire, and with his chariots like a whirlwind, to render his anger with fury, and his rebuke with flames of fire.'' (Isa. 66:14, 15) Jehovah has given to his people a new name. This he did when he brought them into the temple and anointed them, and later he brings his people to a realization of the fact that he has bestowed upon them his name; and they rejoice. To know that the Lord has thus dealt with his people, by showing them the fulfilment of prophecy in which they have been privileged to have some part, has been and is a great consolation to them. The primary purpose of the prophecy is to vindicate Jehovah's name, and the primary purpose of giving the remnant an understanding thereof now is for their comfort and strength. Truly now the remnant say: "Bless the Lord, O my soul, and forget not all his benefits [unto me]." The prophecy of the valley of dry bones has had its primary fulfilment upon God's faithful remnant, and it appears clear how its further fulfilment will be brought about.

U N I T Y

Jehovah's organization is now clearly discerned by the remnant. These see that Christ Jesus, the Head of God's organization, is in the temple and that the risen faithful ones and the faithful remnant on earth constitute a part of that organization, and that Jehovah God is above all, and like a mighty war chariot that organization is moving onward to the vindication of his holy name. There must be complete unity in the organization of Jehovah. The apostle was caused to officially write concerning this very time showing that God would place the members in the body as it pleases him, that the organization must be perfected, and that those on earth must be brought into a unity of knowledge and faith, and "unto a perfect man, unto the measure of the stature of the fulness of Christ". (Eph. 4: 3, 13) The purpose of this unity is that all might together speak the truth to the vindication of Jehovah's name. Thanks be to God that the church has come to that point, and which the Lord God illustrated in the prophecy of Ezekiel beginning with the fifteenth verse of the thirty-seventh chapter: "The word of the Lord came again unto me, saying."—37: 15.

This, another prophecy spoken by Ezekiel, who represents the twelve tribes in captivity, logically follows the vision of the valley of dry bones, which vision, as we have seen, primarily applies to spiritual Israel. The prophecy beginning with the sixteenth verse pictures or illustrates the unity, harmony and cooperation of God's remnant following their experiences pictured by the dry bones. "Moreover, thou son of man, take thee one stick, and write upon it, For Judah, and for the children of Israel his companions; then take another stick, and write upon it, For Joseph, the stick of Ephraim, and for all the house of Israel his companions: and join them one to another into one stick; and they shall become one in thine hand."—37: 16, 17.

In miniature this prophecy was fulfilled upon fleshly Israel in the year 536 B.C. and thereafter. Only fifty thousand Jews, the remnant of the nation, left Babylon under Zerubbabel and Joshua the high priest. These representative members of all the twelve tribes became settled again as one people in the land of Palestine. In harmony with this Peter addressed them at Pentecost and said: "Therefore let all the house of

Israel know.'' (Acts 2: 36) Here likewise Paul speaks
of ''our twelve tribes, instantly serving God day and
night''. (Acts 26: 7) There seems to be no reasonable
ground for applying the prophecy of Ezekiel 37: 15-28
to the Jews now in Palestine. Whether there will be
some application thereof to the Jews and others during
the time of restitution of mankind, we do not know.
It seems quite certain that the prophecy applies at
the present day to the spiritual people of God now
on earth, who are representatives of the twelve tribes
mentioned in Revelation 7: 4-8. To discern the prophecy now thus applying is a great comfort and strength
to God's remnant yet on the earth. The primary purpose of the prophecy is to make known the name of
Jehovah, and the remnant after the spirit are the ones
to now make publication of his name and of his kingdom.

The two sticks upon which Ezekiel was commanded
to write were an illustration of something pictured in
verse eighteen, to wit: ''And when the children of thy
people shall speak unto thee, saying, Wilt thou not
shew us what thou meanest by these?'' The leadership in Israel under Joseph's son Ephraim gave way
to Judah, and the Jews did not understand the meaning thereof. God used two prophets, Elijah and Elisha,
to do parts of the same work, and the question arose
amongst the consecrated, ''What is the meaning of
this?'' Jehovah gave to his people in the year 1919
the first understanding of the meaning of this prophecy. (See *The Watchtower*, 1919, page 243.) It was
then seen that Elijah pictured a certain work of the
church and that Elisha pictured the completion of
that work which Elijah had begun; that there is no

variance of one with the other, but that one logically
follows the other, Elisha being anointed in the
"room", place or stead of Elijah to finish the work
which Elijah had begun. It is the Elisha work of the
church that is done by the united people of God, organized and unified in the spirit of Christ, and is
carried forward by those who have the zeal peculiar
to the house of the Lord. Those of the consecrated who
did not see the end of the Elijah work have never
appreciated the Elisha work and have never had the
spirit or zeal of Elisha. Those who did discern the
end of the Elijah and the beginning of the Elisha work
are the ones that have appreciated the unfolding of
the prophecies, and that have joyfully engaged in the
work of making known the name of Jehovah and his
kingdom.

Leadership is represented by the "the stick". "Say
unto them, Thus saith the Lord God, Behold, I will
take the stick of Joseph, which is in the hand of
Ephraim, and the tribes of Israel his fellows, and will
put them with him, even with the stick of Judah, and
make them one stick, and they shall be one in mine
hand. And the sticks whereon thou writest shall be
in thine hand before their eyes." (37: 19, 20) "Joseph" means "increaser; he shall add". "Ephraim"
means "doubly fruitful; double fruit". Though he
was the second son of Joseph, yet Ephraim received
the birthright from his grandfather. (Gen. 48: 14,
18-20) But the tribe of Ephraim did not demonstrate
the proper faithfulness; hence his leadership of the
twelve tribes devolved upon Judah. (Ps. 78: 9, 10;
Judg. 1: 1, 2; 1 Chron. 5: 1, 2) After the split in the
twelve tribes occurred, however, Ephraim assumed the

leadership of the revolting tribes and his name was
frequently used to stand for the ten tribes of Israel.
Ephraim wielded the stick for Joseph; there being
no tribe of Joseph, but merely the half tribes of
Manasseh and Ephraim. The ten tribes were the first
to go into captivity. (2 Ki. 17:4-7) They therefore
seem to picture those spirit-begotten ones who got
free from the religious systems during the period of
the Elijah work of the church, during which period
the Lord Jesus 'was preparing the way before Jehovah'. (Mal. 3:1) When the World War came these
were brought into captivity to serve the ends of the
fighters. Since then the Lord has brought some of
them into his organization. For instance, some who
loved the Lord to a degree and who were consecrated
went into the war and afterwards got a vision of God's
purposes and came fully into God's organization.

In the sixteenth verse appears this statement:
"Take thee one stick, and write upon it, For Judah,
and for the children of Israel his companions," that
is to say, the tribes of Benjamin and the Levites.
Judah and the tribes of Benjamin and Levi here seem
to picture those last to go into captivity. They had
been brought out of the church systems and had been
carrying on the Elijah work, but were unwillingly
taken captive by Babylon's forces, being overwhelmed
by the enemy organization during the World War.
The illustration shows that there must be one organization, one organized people, "and they shall be one
in mine hand." When the captivity of the Lord's
people ended in 1919 the Elisha work began shortly
thereafter. That work was not and has not been confined exclusively to those who had done the Elijah

work and who were pictured by Judah and his companions. Many persons not previously knowing about or connected with the Lord's work came to a knowledge of the truth after the World War ended, left the Babylonish systems and engaged in the service of the Lord. Some of these were really engaged in actual warfare during the World War. These were pictured by Ephraim and his nine brothers. Thereafter all the faithful became united in the service organization and have gone forward with the work which was foreshadowed by the Prophet Elisha. This is in exact harmony with the prayer of the Lord Jesus: ''Neither pray I for these alone, but for them also which shall believe on me through their word; that they all may be one; as thou, Father, art in me, and I in thee, that they also may be one in us: that the world may believe that thou hast sent me.'' (John 17: 20, 21) There is now no division amongst those who are really doing the Lord's work; but there is one entire and harmonious organization and this is working under the leadership of one, Christ Jesus the Head. ''Jerusalem is builded as a city that is compact together: whither the tribes go up, the tribes of the Lord, unto the testimony of Israel, to give thanks unto the name of the Lord. For my brethren and companions' sakes, I will now say, Peace be within thee.''—Ps. 122: 3, 4, 8.

There is an opposing class which was once engaged in the Elijah work, but the members of this class refuse to be ''one [with the anointed] in mine hand'', as stated in verse nineteen of the prophecy. Such are gathered out from the kingdom class by the Lord and are not shown in the picture. The faithful ones become 'one stick in the hand of the Lord' for the use of the Lord's service. Thus the remnant on earth have the token or illustration and proof in this prophetic word of God of their present unity, and this they have in their hand and, by the Lord's grace, set in proof before the eyes of those who desire to know and to do the will of God.

Satan's organization had taken all of God's people into captivity during the World War, but God had something for them to do after the war. "And say unto them, Thus saith the Lord God, Behold, I will take the children of Israel from among the heathen, whither they be gone, and will gather them on every side, and bring them into their own land: and I will make them one nation in the land upon the mountains of Israel; and one king shall be king to them all; and they shall be no more two nations, neither shall they be divided into two kingdoms, any more at all."— 37: 21, 22.

The physical facts prove the fulfilment of this prophecy beyond any question of doubt. At several large conventions a poll was taken showing that the major portion of those now engaged in the Elisha work of the church came out from Babylon and into the Lord's organization after 1919, and many even after 1922. Today there are no Wesleyans, Lutherans, Campbellites, or Russellites in the truth, nor are there any who are the followers of any other man; and they refuse to take the name of any man. This has been fully demonstrated by the resolution adopted by the Columbus (Ohio) convention in 1931 and by all the faithful companies since that day. The reason for this is that the Lord has plainly revealed his truth to those who give honor and glory to the great Creator and not to creatures.—See *The Watchtower*, 1930, page 116.

The faithful are made "one nation in the land upon the mountains"; that is to say, they are made God's royal nation now upon the mountain heights of his organization in the land of the living, in the temple, and for the publication of the good news of Jehovah and his kingdom. (Isa. 52:7) These recognize the fact that God has made his beloved Son "the Head of the corner" and has placed him upon his throne, in his holy hill, and he is to them a "sanctuary". (Isa. 8:14) "Neither shall they be divided"; which shows a unity of faith. They all hold fast their allegiance to Christ Jesus the King, and, being Jehovah's witnesses under the leadership of Christ Jesus, together with him they advertise the King and his kingdom. It is those that try to maintain the "two nations" who are the ones that stumble over the Stone, God's beloved King. (Isa. 8:15) The exaltation of men is defiling, and is an abomination in the sight of Jehovah God. (Luke 16:15) "Neither shall they defile themselves any more with their idols, nor with their detestable things, nor with any of their transgressions: but I will save them out of all their dwellingplaces wherein they have sinned, and will cleanse them: so shall they be my people, and I will be their God." (37:23) The faithful servants of God have gotten away from the "sin of Samaria", hero worship and adoration of men, and from self-righteousness, and all such things that defile. Their worship and devotion is to God and to his kingdom. In times past they made the great mistake, and thus sinned, but now Jehovah graciously puts behind him their past delinquencies

and sets them to doing the Elisha work, having
cleansed them and given them the robe of righteousness, and the garments of salvation, and they, by his
grace, offer unto the Lord an offering in righteousness.
(Mal. 3 : 2, 3) The remnant are not ashamed of making an open confession of this, but they declare themselves the willing and joyful servants of God and his
King, Christ.—Rev. 3 : 5, 12.

D A V I D

"David" means "beloved"; and David, being God's
anointed king over Israel, was a type of Christ Jesus
the beloved King of the whole earth. "And David my
servant shall be king over them: and they all shall
have one shepherd; they shall also walk in my judgments, and observe my statutes, and do them."
(37:24) Christ Jesus is now the King over the remnant, and they are one, and he is their one and only
Shepherd, and he stands and feeds them; and because
they joyfully submit themselves to God's beloved King
they are permitted by his grace to fulfil the prophecy
of Psalm 110 : 3 : "Thy people shall be willing in the
day of thy power, in the beauties of holiness from the
womb of the morning; thou hast the dew of thy
youth." They having responded to the Lord's call
and devoted themselves wholly to his cause, he makes
with them "an everlasting covenant . . . , even the
sure mercies of David". (Isa. 55 : 3) By the grace of
God these become members of The Christ and a part
of Jehovah's "Servant". (Isa. 42 : 1) They walk on
the highway of the Lord and do his commandments,
giving the testimony of Jesus Christ. (Rev. 12 : 17)

The Lord Jesus Christ, the antitypical David, is their Leader and they are united in him.

Jacob foreshadowed God's faithful people on the earth; hence the promise to such faithful company is, to wit: "And they shall dwell in the land that I have given unto Jacob my servant, wherein your fathers have dwelt; and they shall dwell therein, even they, and their children, and their children's children, for ever; and my servant David shall be their prince for ever." (37: 25) The word "children" signifies perpetuation of the family name that it shall not be cut off. (Deut. 25: 5, 6) This figure of speech here used says that the name of the remnant shall not be cut off from or out of God's organization, but that the fruit of the kingdom that they bring shall perpetuate their name in his organization. "My servant David" means God's antitypical 'elect servant', Christ Jesus, who will always be the Head and Leader of the body members, he who is the Lord of lords and King of kings. "And the armies which were in heaven followed him upon white horses, clothed in fine linen, white and clean. And he hath on his vesture and on his thigh a name written, KING OF KINGS, AND LORD OF LORDS."—Rev. 19: 14, 16.

Jehovah will for ever give prosperity to his kingdom class and they will be at peace in Christ and in God's organization. "Moreover, I will make a covenant of peace [prosperity, *Roth.*] with them; it shall be an everlasting covenant with them: and I will place them, and multiply them, and will set my sanctuary in the midst of them for evermore." (37: 26) This is the same covenant as that mentioned in Ezekiel 34: 24, 25. According to that covenant the Lord now 'sends prosperity' to his people in their work and protects them and safeguards them from the old Dragon. This covenant of prosperity is identified with the "everlasting covenant . . . , even the sure mercies of David". (Isa. 55: 3) It includes the extraordinary goodness of God. Furthermore this verse of the prophecy says in effect: 'There shall be no more captivity or exile of God's people.' These shall "neither be barren nor unfruitful in the knowledge of our Lord Jesus Christ". Thrilled with these comforting words of the Lord the faithful remnant now give all diligence to do the work which the Lord has graciously committed into their hands. "Wherefore the rather, brethren, give diligence to make your calling and election sure: for if ye do these things, ye shall never fall: for so an entrance shall be ministered unto you abundantly into the everlasting kingdom of our Lord and Savior Jesus Christ." (2 Pet. 1: 10, 11) This prophecy of Ezekiel also indicates that God's sanctuary "trodden under foot" during the World War shall be vindicated. The remnant is brought into it, and the Lord says: "I will fill this house with glory." —Hag. 2: 7.

Jehovah's dwelling place is Zion, and it is the spiritual class made members of the body of Christ, the Head of the capital organization of Jehovah, that is in Zion. "My tabernacle also shall be with them; yea, I will be their God, and they shall be my people." (37: 27) The word "tabernacle" here does not mean the tabernacle in the wilderness, but it means the dwelling place of the Lord, showing his presence and the intimate relationship between him and his people who do his service. He dwells with no other people.

"Thou hast ascended on high, thou hast led captivity captive; thou hast received gifts for men; yea, for the rebellious also, that the Lord God might dwell among them." (Ps. 68:18) "Blessed be the Lord out of Zion, which dwelleth at Jerusalem. Praise ye the Lord."—Ps. 135:21.

The vindication of Jehovah's name will cause all to know that he is the great Jehovah God. It is the "faithful servant" class that the Lord God uses to make known his name in the earth at this time and who, continuing faithful, shall be in Zion for ever. "And the heathen shall know that I the Lord do sanctify Israel, when my sanctuary shall be in the midst of them for evermore." (37:28) These are the spiritual Israelites. This means that Jehovah will sanctify his faithful "servant" class unto himself and to his service; and that the "servant" class, including the remnant, which are the people of God for his name, will sanctify the name of Jehovah for ever. "Sanctify the Lord of hosts himself; and let him be your fear, and let him be your dread." (Isa. 8:13) "But sanctify the Lord God in your hearts; and be ready always to give an answer to every man that asketh you a reason of the hope that is in you with meekness and fear." (1 Pet. 3:15) "And the very God of peace sanctify you wholly; and I pray God your whole spirit and soul and body be preserved blameless unto the coming of our Lord Jesus Christ." —1 Thess. 5:23.

It must become apparent to the peoples of earth that Jehovah has a people in the earth who do not apologize for being on his side, and are not ashamed or even backward to own and confess his name, and

THEY ALL SHALL HAVE ONE SHEPHERD   Page 301

the name of his beloved King, but who delight always to maintain their integrity toward God and to constantly proclaim his praises. It is likely that in the midst of the battle of Armageddon God will make it very manifest that he is for his remnant people upon whom his name is placed and who are his witnesses. The nations and peoples of earth, including all those who are God's enemies, will be made to realize that Jehovah is God, and that he has set apart this people for himself. Seeing the battle of the great day of God Almighty drawing near, and seeing that he is using his remnant people to make publication of his name and his kingdom, this brings great consolation to the faithful remnant. These now know that Jehovah God is with them and that by his grace they are strong in the Lord and in the power of his might. Therefore they delight to sing unto him: "Thou hast also given me the shield of thy salvation: and thy right hand hath holden me up, and thy gentleness hath made me great." (Ps. 18:35) "How precious also are thy thoughts unto me, O God! how great is the sum of them!"—Ps. 139:17.

the name of his beloved King, but who delight always to maintain their integrity toward God and to constantly proclaim his praises. It is likely that in the midst of the battle of Armageddon God will make it very manifest that he is for his remnant people upon whom his name is placed and who are his witnesses. The nations and peoples of earth, including all those who are God's enemies, will be made to realize that Jehovah is God, and that he has set apart this people for himself. Seeing the battle of the great day of God Almighty drawing near, and seeing that he is using his remnant people to make publication of his name and his kingdom, this brings great consolation to the faithful remnant. These now know that Jehovah God is with them and that by his grace they are strong in the Lord and in the power of his might. Therefore they delight to sing unto him: "Thou hast also given me the shield of thy salvation: and thy right hand hath holden me up, and thy gentleness hath made me great." (Ps. 18:35) "How precious also are thy thoughts unto me, O God! how great is the sum of them!"—Ps. 139:17.

CHAPTER IX

HIS FAME

(EZEKIEL, CHAPTER 38)

JEHOVAH has been slandered, reproached, and his name defamed for many centuries by Satan and his agents. Soon Jehovah's name shall take its proper place in the minds of every creature that lives. His name shall be exalted above the heavens. Jehovah is above all, and cannot therefore be exalted; but his name has been brought low by the enemy, and his name he will exalt. "That men may know that thou, whose name alone is JEHOVAH, art the Most High over all the earth." (Ps. 83:18) "And the loftiness of man shall be bowed down, and the haughtiness of men shall be made low: and the Lord alone shall be exalted in that day." (Isa. 2:17) His fame, good name and reputation must extend to every part of the universe. In times past even the consecrated ones on earth have exalted the name of Jesus above that of Jehovah, but now we are in 'that day of the Lord' and see that the time has come when the great name and fame of Jehovah must be above all; hence the commandment to "make mention that his name is exalted". (Isa. 12:4) "Let them praise the name of the Lord: for his name alone is excellent; his glory is above the earth and heaven." (Ps. 148:13) The destruction of Jehovah's enemies is necessary that his

309

name may be vindicated and find the right place in the hearts of all creation and that his name and fame may be great everywhere.

Following the downfall of the enemy organization all creation shall be brought to an accurate knowledge of the truth. The greatest truth is that Jehovah is the only true God; and the next great truth is that Christ Jesus is God's King, the rightful Ruler of the earth by virtue of the authority conferred upon him by Jehovah, and that his kingdom will afford the opportunity for all men to be reconciled and restored to God. (1 Tim. 2: 3-6) The sacrifice of Christ Jesus was absolutely necessary that man might be redeemed. The kingdom is necessary that men may know Jehovah and Christ Jesus and may be restored. The great name, fame and good reputation of Jehovah is therefore the most important of all questions. The people must know that Jehovah is God and Christ is King, in order to find life. (John 17: 3) Jehovah does not leave his anointed ones in ignorance concerning Satan and the agencies Satan is using and will use in his attempt to destroy them. Jehovah informs his faithful sons of the enemy's tactics and then directs that they shall prophesy against the enemies before God proceeds to destroy them. The thirty-eighth and thirty-ninth chapters of Ezekiel's prophecy is another prophecy the date of which is not indicated. Logically it follows the restoration of Jehovah's covenant people and before the battle of Armageddon. The prophecy, therefore, would find its fulfilment from and after the year 1919.

GOG AND MAGOG

Jehovah tells his prophet Ezekiel to turn his face toward Gog, the land of Magog, and to prophesy against him. This must mean that the Ezekiel class, under the direction of the Lord, prophesy against that which Gog represents. "And the word of the Lord came unto me, saying, Son of man, set thy face toward Gog, of the land of Magog, the prince of Rosh, Meshech, and Tubal, and prophesy against him."— 38: 1, 2, R.V.

A dogmatic statement as to what Gog and the land of Magog represent would hardly be proper. Since Jehovah has promised to show his remnant "new things . . . before they spring forth", we may expect therefore that he will give his people an understanding of this prophecy. (Isa. 42: 9) Based upon the certain truths that are revealed by the Scriptures the following conclusion as to the meaning of Gog and Magog is here set forth, to wit: Gog is one of the princes in Satan's organization, invisible, of course, to human eyes, with a possibility of the power to materialize in human form. The land of Magog pictures the spiritual or invisible realm of Satan, and includes Gog and all the wicked angels within his division of Satan's organization, and which "bear rule over all the earth". It appears that Gog forms and organizes a conspiracy against God's anointed people, into which conspiracy are drawn many other creatures, both men and angels, and including Big Business, the practitioners of and leaders in satanic religion, and the chief rulers of the earth; and that all these conspire and come against Jehovah's organization, including the remnant on the earth; that such conspiracy is carried out by the commission of overt acts; and this is done after the Lord comes to the temple and restores Jehovah's faithful people to himself. The argument in support of this conclusion follows.

Up to this point Ezekiel has prophesied against the religious, commercial and political elements of Satan's organization, and against Satan himself, but aside from Satan himself there is no specific prophecy against the invisible part of Satan's organization, the wicked angels, and officers in his invisible realm. These have had much to do with debauching the human race and have had much to do with the ruling of the nations of the earth, and it is certain that they will be destroyed with Satan because they are enemies of Jehovah God. It is therefore reasonable to expect to find some prophecy setting forth Jehovah's judgment and the execution thereof against these wicked angels or invisible powers. The Apostle Paul calls attention to the fact that in these latter days God's people will be warred against by these invisible powers and principalities.—Eph. 6: 10-12.

The Prophet Daniel describes the organization of Satan, both the invisible realm and the visible part thereof, under the symbol of 'a terrible image' (Dan. 2: 30-34); that the image had a head of gold, his breast and arms were of silver, and his belly of copper (mistranslated in the *Authorized Version* ''brass''). This shows Satan as the supreme ruler of his wicked organization with other parts of his mighty organization under him. A part of that prophecy of Daniel reads: ''And after thee shall arise another kingdom inferior to thee, and another third kingdom of brass,

GOG OF THE LAND OF MAGOG   Page 311

which shall bear rule over all the earth." (Dan. 2: 39)
Special attention is here called to the words "shall
bear rule over all the earth". Satan is the "prince"
(or chief) ruler of the entire world and is the chief
of devils. (John 14: 30; Matt. 9: 34; 12: 24) This
supports the conclusion that Satan has other sub-
rulers in his realm, which are invisible to men, and
that one division thereof is especially assigned to give
attention to the things of the earth. We are informed
that these wicked angels have a special grudge against
God's anointed people. (Eph. 6: 10-12) There is a
direct relationship between wicked angels, represented
by the copper in the image of Daniel's prophecy, and
the visible rulers of the earth. (See *Light,* Book Two,
pages 289-319.) In Revelation 20: 7, 8 the distinction
is made between Satan and Gog and Magog, which
shows that the particular prophecy of Ezekiel, chapters thirty-eight and thirty-nine, is not directly applicable to Satan, but that it does specifically apply
to one of Satan's chiefs, and those gathered under him
in a division of Satan's organization. The Scriptures
show that Satan and all his princes go into death at
Armageddon and are awakened out of death at the
end of the thousand-year reign of the Messiah, and
The Revelation specifically mentions Gog and Magog
in connection therewith, which would mean the prince
Gog and all the wicked ones that have operated in his
division. (See *Light,* Book Two, page 206.) The
prophecy of Daniel specifically mentions the prince of
the kingdom of Persia and the prince of Grecia, members of Satan's wicked organization that oppose God's
people. It appears there are ranks of rulers in Satan's
organization.

CONSPIRACY

According to another translation verse two of the thirty-eighth chapter of Ezekiel reads: "Son of man, direct thy face against Gog, of the land of Magog, the prince of Rosh, Meshech, and Thubal, and prophesy against him." (*Leeser*) "Rosh" means "head"; Meshech and Tubal were Japhetic people. (Gen. 10: 2) They were engaged in digging copper and trading in it, and also in the slavery trade. They were dealers in precious metals and in human flesh and did business with Tyre. (Ezek. 27: 13) "Rosh," meaning "head", would therefore well picture Satan himself and also the head ruling power on earth in Satan's organization. The most powerful part of earth's satanic organization is Big Business. The prophecy therefore seems to relate to the satanic organization of the earth, the chief part of which is Big Business, and also to other parts of that organization under the supervision of Gog, the prince of the Devil's organization and that part thereof having to do with things of the earth. These all enter into a conspiracy against the people of Jehovah, and Gog has charge of the execution of the overt acts of the conspiracy. The conspirators embrace both wicked angels and wicked men. The prophecy shows that Gog controls a great military force which is covetous, preys upon and robs the helpless, and persecutes the apparently defenseless. (38: 4, 11, 12) The fact that Ezekiel was directed to prophesy against Gog proves that the remnant, whom Ezekiel pictures, would not be left in ignorance concerning this conspiracy and the coming assault upon God's organization which would be in their time, and that the remnant would testify against the

conspirators. It should be expected, therefore, that
the Lord would make known to his remnant what is
meant by 'Gog in the land of Magog'.

Since Big Business has its principal location in the
seventh world power, "Rosh," meaning "head",
would well apply to the seventh world power, to wit,
Britain, which lies north of the holy land and which
dominates the nations of the earth. It may be expected, therefore, that the conspiracy against God's
people, hatched in the mind of Satan and prosecuted
by his prince Gog, would start by the commission of
overt acts within the realms of the seventh world
power and spread to all parts of the earth where
God's people are located. It is certain from the Scriptures that Gog represents wicked forces which are
anti-God and anti-kingdom in assaulting and moving
against God's kingdom organization, including the
remnant on earth, and which forces reach a climax at
Armageddon. This is further and conclusively supported by the statement of the prophecy in which the
Lord says: "I am against thee, O Gog."

Because of the wicked conspiracy against his
anointed people Jehovah declares that Gog and his
army shall be destroyed. "And say, Thus saith the
Lord God, Behold, I am against thee, O Gog, the chief
prince [prince of Rosh] of Meshech and Tubal: and
I will turn thee back [derange thee, *Leeser*], and put
hooks into thy jaws, and I will bring thee forth, and
all thine army, horses and horsemen, all of them
clothed with all sorts of armour, even a great company, with bucklers and shields, all of them handling
swords. Persia, Ethiopia [Cush, *Leeser*], and Libya
[Put, *Leeser*], with them; all of them with shield and

helmet; Gomer, and all his bands; the house of Togar-
mah of the north quarters [the remote men of the
North and all his hordes, *Roth.*], and all his bands;
and many people with thee.''—38: 3-6.

Daniel's prophecy specifically shows that in the invisible realm of Satan these princes operate and that
the prince of Persia was so powerful that only Michael
could overcome him. This prince doubtless will again
fight under the leadership of Gog, who is the chief
prince of those who have had to do with the things of
the earth. Gog's great military organization operates
under the direction of the Dragon and makes war
upon God's remnant. (Rev. 12: 17) Gog gathers his
forces from all directions and surrounds the people
of God, thus showing an organized attack upon Jehovah's organization.

Jehovah God is supreme and he has anointed Christ
Jesus as his Chief Officer, who will lead the fight of
his forces at Armageddon. Since Satan has attempted
to mimic God in everything else, and since Satan
claims to be the supreme one or equal to God, it is
reasonable to conclude that Satan has appointed a
special officer on his side to lead the fight at Armageddon; and since Gog is called ''the chief prince''
of Rosh, it is reasonable that Gog is the one that leads
the fight at Armageddon, while Satan as the general
sits in the rear and directs it, even as Jehovah directs
Christ Jesus.

In the army of Gog and under his command will
be all the allies mentioned in the foregoing verses of
the prophecy, including angels and men, and all pitted
against God's organization. This corresponds with
Revelation 17: 12-14: ''And the ten horns which thou

sawest are ten kings, which have received no kingdom
as yet; but receive power as kings one hour with the
beast. These have one mind, and shall give their power and strength unto the beast. These shall make war
with the Lamb, and the Lamb shall overcome them:
for he is Lord of lords, and King of kings; and they
that are with him are called, and chosen, and faithful.'' (See *Light*, Book Two, page 106.) This mixed
multitude that Gog brings against Jehovah's organization, so far as the earthly division thereof is concerned, reminds one of the heterogeneous crowd that
now composes the League of Nations, with the British
empire located in the literal north and being the
chief part thereof, and leading the League of Nations.
This organization of the League of Nations is a subterfuge and a substitute for Christ's kingdom; and
since there are fifty-seven nations in the League, and
since God's remnant people on earth represent his
kingdom, these enemies of the Lord do now surround
God's people and they are literally hemmed in by the
enemy. According to the prophecy Gog himself is
located in the north. (38: 15) Satan declared he
would establish his seat of government on the sides of
the north. (Isa. 14: 13) This further supports the
conclusion that Gog is the wicked angel prince in the
organization of Satan leading the fight and that the
British empire of the north is the chief instrument in
the visible army that takes the lead in the execution
of the conspiracy against God's organization.

The statement of the prophecy against Gog (vs. 4)
is: ''I will . . . put hooks into thy jaws''; meaning
that the Lord will lead him and his organization as
''prisoners'' to destruction. (Isa. 37: 29; Ezek. 29: 4;

Job 41:1) "He [the enemy] hath also prepared for him the instruments of death; he maketh his arrows fiery shafts. He hath made a pit, and digged it, and is fallen into the ditch which he made." (Ps. 7:13, 15, *R.V.*) "The heathen are sunk down in the pit that they made; in the net which they hid is their own foot taken. The Lord is known by the judgment which he executeth: the wicked is snared in the work of his own hands. Higgaion. Selah."—Ps. 9:15, 16.

Before the fight comes off the Lord gives the Devil's crowd fair warning and says to them: "Be thou prepared, and prepare for thyself, thou, and all thy company that are assembled unto thee, and be thou a guard unto them." (38:7) This applies to the entire army of Gog. The League of Nations is supposed to be the special guard of the safety and territorial integrity of the member nations of the League, and Britain is the chief guard over the League of Nations. Jehovah by his prophet declares his purpose to visit this wicked organization, and when he visits them it means their destruction. "After many days thou shalt be visited; in the latter years thou shalt come into the land that is brought back from the sword, and is gathered out of many people, against the mountains of Israel, which have been always waste: but it is brought forth out of the nations, and they shall dwell safely all of them." (38:8) It is "in the latter days" that Gog comes "into the land of the remnant brought back from the sword". (*Roth.*) This definitely fixes the time for the application of the prophecy, which is after God's remnant people have been recovered from their being scattered during the World War, after they have been restored and made a part of and dwell in Jehovah's organization. "For, behold, in those days, and in that time, when I shall bring again the captivity of Judah and Jerusalem, I will also gather all nations, and will bring them down into the valley of Jehoshaphat, and will plead with them there for my people and for my heritage Israel, whom they have scattered among the nations, and parted my land." (Joel 3:1, 2; Ezek. 34:25; 37:25, 26; Ps. 125:2) Until the time of the restoration of God's remnant people following the World War his people are described in the prophecy as "the mountains of Israel, which have been always waste" and against which now Gog leads the fight.

It appears that the enemy will expect to greatly frighten the people of God and also to easily overcome them. "Thou shalt ascend [come up, *Roth.*] and come like a storm; thou shalt be like a cloud to cover the land, thou and all thy bands, and many people with thee." (38:9) The forces of the enemy will be like the Midianites when "they came as grasshoppers for multitude; for both they and their camels were without number; and they entered into the land to destroy it". (Judg. 6:5) This part of the prophecy evidently is given for a forewarning to God's people. To be forewarned by the Lord is to be forearmed.

A conspiracy is a wicked device formed to do injury to others. This prophecy indicates that the conspiracy is formed against God's anointed people for the purpose of destroying them. "Thus saith the Lord God, It shall also come to pass, that at the same time shall things come into thy mind, and thou shalt think an evil thought." (38:10) This is further evidence that the conspiracy formed against the people of God is directed by Satan through Gog. This conclusion is supported by Psalm 83:2-5: "For, lo, thine enemies make a tumult; and they that hate thee have lifted up the head. They have taken crafty counsel against thy people, and consulted against thy hidden ones. They have said, Come, and let us cut them off from being a nation; that the name of Israel may be no more in remembrance. For they have consulted together with one consent: they are confederate against thee." The Lord shows that the conspiracy shall fail: "The Lord bringeth the counsel of the heathen to nought; he maketh the devices of the people of none effect." (Ps. 33:10) It is stated that the evil spirits like frogs shall gather the forces to Armageddon. The croaking of the frogs, no doubt, has much to do with the conspiracy. After the wicked device is hatched, the frogs do the propaganda work amongst the people, and help set the stage for the fight.—Rev. 16:13; see *Light,* Book Two, page 42.

Then the prophet declares what that wicked thought of the enemy is, but evidently the enemy does not give any heed to it: "And thou shalt say, I will go up to the land of unwalled villages; I will go to them that are at rest, that dwell safely, all of them dwelling without walls, and having neither bars nor gates." (38:11) This shows that the prophecy applies to God's remnant following the World War, and not to the Jews back in Palestine. God's remnant, as these appear to the enemy, are now without anyone to protect them; hence they 'dwell without walls, and have neither bars nor gates'. The organization of Satan, and particularly his chief instrument, does not give any heed to the words of God. They do not believe that God furnishes any protection for his people, and hence do not appreciate his words directed to Zion, to wit: "Praise the Lord, O Jerusalem; praise thy God, O Zion. For he hath strengthened the bars of thy gates; he hath blessed thy children within thee. He maketh peace in thy borders, and filleth thee with the finest of the wheat. He sendeth forth his commandment upon earth: his word runneth very swiftly." (Ps. 147:12-15) God's remnant trust implicity in him, well knowing that "except the Lord build the house, they labour in vain that build it; except the Lord keep the city, the watchman waketh but in vain."— Ps. 127:1.

Jehovah has greatly blessed and prospered his people in doing the kingdom work since 1922, which is evidenced and pictured by the chattel goods they possess; so the enemy led by Gog conspires to desolate God's people. "To take a spoil, and to take a prey; to turn thine hand upon the desolate places that are now inhabited, and upon the people that are gathered out of the nations, which have gotten cattle and goods, that dwell in the midst of the land." (38:12) As to the wealth of the remnant at the present day see Ezekiel 36:10, 11 and comments. The witness work of the people of God, taking on a wider scope, and being done with an ever increasing enthusiasm, comes to the attention even of Meshech and Tubal, over which Gog is the prince or immediate ruler. "And I will set a sign among them, and I will send those that escape [faithful remnant] of them unto the nations, to Tarshish, Pul, and Lud, that draw the bow, to Tubal and Javan, to the isles afar off, that have not heard my fame, neither have seen my glory; and they shall declare my glory among the Gentiles." (Isa. 66:19) Big Business is that crowd that is always looking after self, regardless of the interests of others. Beginning with 1931 the message of God's kingdom as the only hope of the world has gone forth to nations never heretofore reached and the testimony has been given very thoroughly throughout "Christendom", and particularly in the realms of the seventh world power. This prosperity and blessing on the part of God's people raises the ire of the enemy and causes him to act. Gog fears for the League of Nations. Gog and his allies become aware of the message of the kingdom by radio, which is reaching many countries and many peoples, and also of the house-to-house testimony work which the remnant is doing, and no doubt the leading nations will become like the Pharisees when the fame of Jesus began to spread, and who then said: "Ye know nothing at all, nor consider that it is expedient for us, that one man should die for the people, and that the whole nation perish not."— John 11:49, 50.

For some time the kingdom message was confined to the religious element. Now it goes to the commercial wing of Satan's organization, which claims to be and, in fact, is the real ruler. "Sheba, and Dedan, and the merchants of Tarshish, with all the young lions thereof, shall say unto thee, Art thou come to take a spoil? hast thou gathered thy company to take a prey? to carry away silver and gold, to take away cattle, and goods, to take a great spoil?" (38:13) These nations here mentioned were the ones that did commercial business with Tyre which represents Big Business. (Ezek. 27:12-25) No doubt in that commercial center they rubbed up against Meshech, Tubal and Javan and did business in the same market. A marginal note on this verse by *Leeser* reads: These are "active merchants, who are in the habit of going out and roaming all countries like young lions, and know where riches can be obtained". We may be sure that Big Business is fully aware of the assault that is to be made against God's organization. The Devil and his chief prince Gog will see to it that every part of Satan's organization is brought into action. The commercial barons, however, by conniving and conspiring to injure and destroy God's remnant will bring them no advantage. If they ever live at all they must become subjects of earth's glorious King. The picture of the prophecy now shows Gog's army coming up to destroy God's organization.

It is made to appear certain that God will not permit the enemy to say that they had no knowledge that the remnant was advertising his righteous kingdom; hence he directs his prophet to say: "Therefore, son of man, prophesy and say unto Gog, Thus saith the Lord God, In that day when my people of Israel dwelleth safely, shalt thou not know it?" (38:14) Jehovah does nothing in the corner nor in secret, and the forces of Gog will have their chance to know that he is causing the kingdom to be advertised and the testimony given concerning the expression of Jehovah's vengeance upon Satan's organization. Jehovah specifically commands the remnant of his organization to declare the day of his vengeance and to proclaim his works in the earth and to say that his kingdom is at hand. (Isa. 61:1, 2; 12:6) "Say among the heathen, that the Lord reigneth: the world also shall be established that it shall not be moved: he shall judge the people righteously."—Ps. 96:10.

The prosperity of the remnant and their zeal for the cause of the kingdom of God will be enough to rouse up Gog and cause the hastening of his army to the battle. God sees to it that the enemy will receive notice thereof; hence the remnant must now busy themselves in giving notice according to God's commandment.

JACOB'S TROUBLE

In the Scriptures Jacob stands for God's chosen people and particularly represents the regathered remnant after the scattering of 1918. It seems quite clear that "Jacob's trouble" means the attempt made by Satan's instruments to destroy the remnant and at which time the remnant will be delivered by the hand of the Lord. (Jer. 30:3-11) By the prophecy of Ezekiel God also shows the conspiracy and the overt act of the enemy to destroy his faithful remnant which is now engaged in proclaiming the message of the kingdom; hence he caused Ezekiel to prophesy: "And thou shalt come from thy place out of the north parts [the uttermost parts of the north, R.V.], thou, and many people with thee, all of them riding upon horses, a great company, and a mighty army: and thou shalt come up against my people of Israel, as a cloud to cover the land; it shall be in the latter days, and I will bring thee against my land, that the heathen may know me, when I shall be sanctified in thee, O Gog, before their eyes." (38:15, 16) This same conspiracy and the carrying of it out is pictured in the following scriptures: "And he [they,

Sinaitic MS.] gathered them together into a place called in the Hebrew tongue Armageddon.'' (Rev. 16:16) ''And I saw the beast, and the kings of the earth, and their armies, gathered together to make war against him that sat on the horse, and against his army.'' (Rev. 19:19) In recent years the remnant have conducted an aggressive campaign of witness work in the name of the Lord, telling the people about Satan's wicked organization and God's purpose to destroy it. The remnant have not taken and will not take up carnal weapons against the Devil's organization, but they do and will continue to boldly declare the message against it. Therefore the prophecy concerning violence must refer to Gog that comes with great fury against God's people. The remnant of God's people have been working hard since the World War to 'build up the land' which represents their part of the kingdom work. It is the ''holy land'', or holy condition of God's people now on earth who have been toiling earnestly to improve and make fruitful these kingdom interests. They have not meddled with politics or with commercial affairs of the world. They have been only telling the truth concerning Satan's entire organization and of God's organization. This is the witness to the nations and is a more complete witness than the beautifying of the literal land of Palestine could possibly be as a testimony to the heathen nations. The prophecy shows, therefore, that the coming of the enemy against God's people in the ''latter day'' is when the Lord is present giving prosperity to his people and when God will cause them to know that he is the Lord supreme. Gog and his allies will not repent and turn to Jeho-

vah, but, as the Scriptures show, the Lord God will
make an example of that crowd, such as will vindicate
his name before all creation. Jehovah is the protector
of his remnant, and hence Gog's moving against the
remnant forces God right into the fight, because God
and the remnant are inseparable. The enemy is
'touching the apple of His eye', and hence the fight
follows. Gog and his coconspirators do not believe that
Jehovah God is the Supreme One, and that the remnant have his protection, and hence conclude to rid
the earth of this 'pestiferous company' called "the
remnant". The occasion of assault by this mighty
army of Gog will be the occasion for God to sanctify
his name and to vindicate it, which he will do.

In olden times God caused these prophecies to be
written, and the faithful remnant can now identify
the Devil's organization and know that God does speak
against that organization by his prophets. Now Jehovah says: "Thus saith the Lord God, Art thou he
of whom I have spoken in old time by my servants the
prophets of Israel, which prophesied in those days
many years that I would bring thee against them?"
(38:17) It seems certain that the Devil will attempt
to spring a surprise attack upon God's remnant people; but, being fully warned, and trusting in Jehovah, the remnant need not be at all alarmed. The
victory will be with Jehovah and he will vindicate his
name and preserve those who love him.

Let the people of the remnant, Jehovah's witnesses,
be very courageous and bold in the proclamation of
the kingdom message, knowing that God will smite
the enemy in due time. "And it shall come to pass
at the same time [in that day, *Roth.*], when Gog shall

come against the land of Israel, saith the Lord God,
that my fury shall come up in my face [nostrils,
Roth.]." (38:18) This is a warning to the enemy and
a message of comfort to the remnant, giving them
strength, and they will not back down or slack their
hand. There will be a tendency on the part of some
to become fearful and suffer distress; but bear in mind
that Jehovah is at the helm, that his chief officer
Christ Jesus is in command of his forces and will win
the victory. Jehovah has caused his Word to be written for the encouragement and comfort of his anointed people, and one of the appropriate promises to
such is: "In my distress I called upon the Lord, and
cried unto my God; he heard my voice out of his
temple, and my cry came before him, even into his
ears. Then the earth shook and trembled; the foundations also of the hills moved and were shaken, because he was wroth. There went up a smoke out of
his nostrils, and fire out of his mouth devoured: coals
were kindled by it. He bowed the heavens also, and
came down: and darkness was under his feet. And
he rode upon a cherub, and did fly; yea, he did fly
upon the wings of the wind. He made darkness his
secret place; his pavilion round about him were dark
waters and thick clouds of the skies."—Ps. 18:6-11.

THE VICTORY

The time having arrived for Jehovah God to vindicate his name, he causes his mighty field marshal
Christ Jesus to lead on in the fight. Victory for Jehovah is absolutely certain, and he causes his fame to
spread throughout the universe. Jehovah has been
long-suffering and has permitted Satan and his crowd

to pursue wickedness to the last degree, and at Armageddon he will express his just wrath against the forces of wickedness. Therefore says the prophet: "For in my jealousy and in the fire of my wrath, have I spoken, Surely in that day there shall be a great shaking in the land of Israel; so that the fishes of the sea, and the fowls of the heaven, and the beasts of the field, and all creeping things that creep upon the earth, and all the men that are upon the face of the earth, shall shake at my presence, and the mountains shall be thrown down, and the steep places shall fall, and every wall shall fall to the ground." (38:19, 20) As the armies move into action there will be the most terrible shaking ever known. At Sinai "so terrible was the sight that Moses said, I exceedingly fear and quake"; but Armageddon will be far more terrible than Sinai. (Heb. 12:21, 22) The Scriptures indicate that some of the remnant at least will be on the earth and witness that fight; and, beholding the demonstration of Jehovah's great power, they will no doubt fear and quake and shake with awe. That will be the most marvelous demonstration of power, destructive of the wickedness of the world. Let the remnant fully trust in Jehovah and abide in safety under his wings.

Birds, fowls and wild animals sense an approaching unusual phenomenon and manifest uneasiness, fear and dread. At Armageddon so terrible will be the shaking that all creatures on the earth, and in the sea, will display fear, and that will add fearfulness to the entire spectacular scene. When Christ Jesus died upon the cross the earth did quake, and the chief purpose of his death was the vindication of Jehovah's name.

When the final battle is fought for the vindication of Jehovah's name, which battle will be led by Christ Jesus, the shaking of the entire earth and heaven shall occur. (Matt. 27:50, 51) The purpose of the shaking is not to terrify the remnant, but to strike terror into the invading army of the enemy and to make known to all creation the name and fame of Jehovah God. God's footstool has been greatly defiled by the enemy, and with the approach of, and during the battle of Armageddon, the very ground will revolt against the presence of the wicked horde and will cry out for the blood that has been unrighteously spilled upon the earth, and it will heave up and shake itself against the enemy, as the prophet of God declares.

Christ Jesus and all of his mighty host will fight against the enemy. "And I will call for a sword against him throughout all my mountains, saith the Lord God: every man's sword shall be against his brother." (38:21) Gog and his horde will realize that they have met a foe that knows no defeat. According to *Rotherham* this verse reads: "Then will I call against him [the enemy] every terror, declareth my Lord Jehovah." The enemy goes forth to make war against Christ Jesus and his army, but the enemy shall fail. (Rev. 17:14) "Speak to Zerubbabel, governor of Judah, saying, I will shake the heavens and the earth; and I will overthrow the throne of kingdoms, and I will destroy the strength of the kingdoms of the heathen: and I will overthrow the chariots, and those that ride in them; and the horses and their riders shall come down, every one by the sword of his brother."—Hag. 2:21, 22.

Gog leads his forces against the people of Jehovah God that he might take a spoil in their midst. He has surrounded the remnant and expects to destroy them and put to flight the entire organization of Jehovah. God permits this fight to come on that he might vindicate his name. He does not call upon his faithful remnant, however, to do any of the actual fighting. He tells them to stand still and "see the salvation of the Lord with you". (2 Chron. 20: 15-17) In that fight the remnant will be protected as God declared: "Behold the day of the Lord cometh, and thy spoil shall be divided in the midst of thee. For I will gather all nations against Jerusalem to battle; and the city shall be taken, and the houses rifled, and the women ravished; and half of the city shall go forth into captivity, and the residue of the people shall not be cut off from the city. Then shall the Lord go forth, and fight against those nations, as when he fought in the day of battle."—Zech. 14: 1-3.

The enemy forces, although of one mind to destroy the Lord's people, allied together in their wicked conspiracy and acting in full harmony, in the beginning can and will be confused by the power of Jehovah and every one be caused to fight the other by his side. In a similar way God caused confusion at the tower of Babel; and he caused the enemy to destroy one another when Gideon engaged them in battle.—Gen. 11: 7, 8; Judg. 7: 22; 2 Chron. 20: 22, 23.

All creation will have reason to know that the Almighty God is manifesting his power against the enemy. "And I will hold judgment over him with pestilence and with blood(-shedding); and an overflowing rain, and great hailstones, fire, and sulphur

will I let rain over him and his armies, and over the
many people that are with him.''—38: 22, *Leeser.*

This is the expression of Jehovah's judgment upon
Gog and upon all of his forces. (Joel 3: 12) "And
this shall be the plague wherewith the Lord will smite
all the people that have fought against Jerusalem:
Their flesh shall consume away while they stand upon
their feet, and their eyes shall consume away in their
holes, and their tongue shall consume away in their
mouth. And it shall come to pass in that day, that a
great tumult from the Lord shall be among them;
and they shall lay hold every one on the hand of his
neighbour, and his hand shall rise up against the
hand of his neighbour. And so shall be the plague of
the horse, of the mule, of the camel, and of the ass,
and of all the beasts that shall be in these tents, as
this plague.''—Zech. 14: 12, 13, 15.

Jehovah will rain down upon the enemy destructive missiles from heaven as he did upon Sisera by
the waters of Megiddo. (Judg. 4: 15; 5: 4, 20, 21)
"Do unto them as unto the Midianites; as to Sisera,
as to Jabin, at the brook of Kison." (Ps. 83: 9) And
also as God did at the first battle of Perazim. (2 Sam.
5: 20, 21) Also at the battle of Gibeon. (Josh.
10: 10-14) And as upon Sodom and Gomorrah. (Gen.
19: 24) The enemy has had knowledge of these examples foreshadowing Armageddon but has taken no
heed thereto. The final fight will come and the Lord
will make a complete work of it. (Ps. 11: 5, 6; Hab.
3: 5) Satan will see his forces completely whipped
before he is chained, and then he will go into the pit.
—Rev. 19: 19, 20.

Jehovah is now defamed. Soon his fame shall be great and all the nations shall come to know that he is the Supreme One. "Thus will I magnify myself, and sanctify myself; and I will be known in the eyes of many nations; and they shall know that I am the Lord." (38:23) All the enemies of Jehovah shall be confounded and brought to naught, that all survivors may know that Jehovah is the Almighty God. "Let them be confounded and troubled for ever; yea, let them be put to shame, and perish: that men may know that thou, whose name alone is JEHOVAH, art the Most High over all the earth."—Ps. 83:17, 18.

SIXTH PART LEFT
(Ezekiel, Chapter 39)

The conclusion is strongly supported by the thirty-ninth chapter of Ezekiel's prophecy that God will leave Satan a small portion of his broken crowd to view the ruins before Satan himself is taken and killed. The wicked ones must be destroyed first, and the universe cleaned, that righteousness established in the earth may continue forever. The class whom Ezekiel represented, to wit, God's anointed remnant, must be witnesses both unto angels and unto men. (1 Cor. 4:9) This they must do by declaring the name and works of Jehovah God and in faithfully giving testimony against the wicked forces of Gog, both angelic and human. "Therefore, thou son of man, prophesy against Gog, and say, Thus saith the Lord God, Behold, I am against thee, O Gog, the chief prince of Meshech and Tubal; and I will turn thee back, and leave but the sixth part of thee, and will cause thee

to come up from the north parts, and will bring thee
upon the mountains of Israel.''—39 : 1, 2.

Thus the Lord attaches the symbol of ''six'' to Gog
and his war organization, which further suggests that
the organization is made up of wicked angels and
wicked men, the latter forming the beast of Revelation 13 : 18. To be sure, the Lord could have easily
wiped out Gog's entire force, but he leaves a portion
of the broken army almost frightened to death and
trembling, and probably these will consider together
the question as to who is supreme, Satan or Jehovah.
It will be a very humiliating time for Satan when he
looks upon his defeated and broken army and con-
siders that he is the next one to be taken. Of course
the enemy conspired to come up against God's organization, and Jehovah permitted him to do so, and His
permitting the remnant to witness the fight will cause
them to more fully appreciate Jehovah's great victory,
the vindication of his name, and their own deliverance. When the enemy comes up God's people are
apparently unprotected; and if this were not so it is
not likely that the enemy would have been so eager
to make the attack, nor would the anointed of God's
people have had such a great opportunity of fully
trusting him.

Jehovah encourages his faithful anointed with the
assurance that he will completely defeat the enemy :
''And I will smite thy bow out of thy left hand, and
will cause thine arrows to fall out of thy right hand.''
(39 : 3) This is in full harmony with the precious
promise given to his anointed sons born of his ''woman'' and taught by him. ''No weapon that is formed
against thee shall prosper ; and every tongue that shall

rise against thee in judgment thou shalt condemn.
This is the heritage of the servants of the Lord; and
their righteousness is of me, saith the Lord.'' (Isa.
54:17; Ps. 46:9) The enemy Gog comes against
God's organization, symbolized by the mountains of
Israel, and shall fall there: ''Thou shalt fall upon the
mountains of Israel, thou, and all thy bands, and the
people that is with thee: I will give thee unto the
ravenous birds of every sort, and to the beasts of the
field, to be devoured.'' (39:4) This is an open and
visible testimony to his restored and faithful remnant.
The ''great dragon'', after being drawn out of his
river, meets exactly the same fate as here described
concerning Gog's army. This further supports the
conclusion that Gog's crowd consists of spirit as well
as human creatures and that all are anti-God and
all are of Satan's organization. (See Revelation
19:20, 21 and comments, *Light,* Book Two.) Jehovah
does not hinder the formation of the conspiracy, nor
the carrying out thereof, but he permits the enemy to
come out and to fight. ''Thou shalt fall upon the open
field; for I have spoken it, saith the Lord God.''
(39:5) Jehovah awaits the attack, and thus he permits wickedness to come to the full and openly manifest itself. There upon the open field he makes an
example of the enemy.

It seems that some of the wicked angels are left
behind in reserve and apparently in security. This
supports the conclusion that ''the land of Magog'' is
the realm of the invisible wicked hordes: ''And I will
send a fire on Magog, and among them that dwell care-
lessly [securely, *R.V.*] in the isles; and they shall
know that I am the Lord.'' (39:6) It was there in

the land of Magog that the conspiracy was formed, and now the Lord attacks the enemy's base of operations, which would mean both the invisible and the visible base for the carrying on of the wicked warfare against God's organization. This is further supported by the apostle's statement: "But the heavens and the earth which are now, by the same word are kept in store, reserved unto fire against the day of judgment and perdition of ungodly men . . . in the which the heavens shall pass away with a great noise, and the elements shall melt with fervent heat; the earth also, and the works that are therein, shall be burned up." —2 Pet. 3: 7, 10.

Jehovah will put an end to wickedness, that his holy name shall never again be profaned: "So will I make my holy name known in the midst of my people Israel; and I will not let them pollute my holy name any more; and the heathen shall know that I am the Lord, the Holy One in Israel." (39: 7) No more will Jehovah permit his people to be taken in captivity to the humiliation of his own name. No more will he permit his holy name to be profaned by the enemy in any manner. This implies faithfulness on the part of all who get life and remain alive. Seeing that the battle of Armageddon completes the victory of Jehovah, and the preservation of those who love him, will cause the people of God to more fully appreciate him than ever. The non-followers of Christ, the heathen, have been repeatedly told the truth but have given no heed to it. Armageddon will cause all of them to know that Jehovah is the Most High.

The understanding of this prophecy will surely bring great joy to the hearts of his anointed and cause them to walk on in the "highway" with fear and trembling: "Behold, it is come, and it is done, saith the Lord God; this is the day whereof I have spoken." (39:8) This scripture suggests that when the prophecy is understood the fulfilment thereof is near at hand. "This is the day," and this time is made very prominent in the Scriptures. The "day" or period referred to by all the holy prophets marks a great epoch in the universe because it is the time in which Jehovah vindicates his name. It means much to the entire universe, and not merely to the earth. Lovers of righteousness delight to know that we have come to that day, and which is the day that Jehovah has made for the vindication of his name.

CLEANSING THE EARTH

Jehovah by and through Christ will clean away the debris and purify the earth, that the judgment of the individuals of the people may proceed in righteousness and without hindrance. (Acts 17: 31) There is nothing that purifies like fire; hence it is used as a symbol of destruction and of cleansing the land of that which defiles. "He maketh wars to cease unto the end of the earth; he breaketh the bow, and cutteth the spear in sunder; he burneth the chariot in the fire. Be still, and know that I am God; I will be exalted among the heathen, I will be exalted in the earth." (Ps. 46: 9, 10) After the battle of Armageddon, as the Scriptures show, there will be some faithful people of God yet on the earth, and these will have something to do with the cleaning-up work: "And they that dwell in the cities of Israel shall go forth, and shall set on fire and burn the weapons, both the shields and the bucklers, the bows and the arrows, and the handstaves and the spears, and they shall burn them with fire seven years." (39:9) These servants of God will not be surrounded by walls, nor will they have navies or armies. Satan's organization at that time will have been overthrown, and the debris which encumbers the earth must now be removed. God's faithful people will not have a desire to preserve the relics of the war machinery of the Devil. The people will want to put all such things out of mind. The Lord directs that they shall "burn them with fire [for] seven years". Doubtless this is a figure of speech as to time and represents the complete destruction of all such war equipment. But even if they should burn literally that long, such would not be unreasonable. History states that after the Spaniards had overthrown the Saracens, in the year 1212, there was left on the battlefields such a vast quantity of lances, javelins and other war equipment as served them for fuel for four years. The time required for the burning draws attention to the immensity of Satan's war organization. It magnifies Jehovah's power and his complete victory. It shows why God has provided such a great "winepress" to crush Satan's machinery. —Rev. 14:19, 20.

This would not necessarily mean that God's faithful remnant will be on earth for seven years after Armageddon, but until there is a complete cleaning up. Doubtless the faithful men of ancient times, the "princes", will be back on earth then to assist in this work: "So that they shall take no wood out of the field, neither cut down any out of the forests; for they shall burn the weapons with fire:

and they shall spoil those that spoiled them, and rob
those that robbed them, saith the Lord God." (39: 10)
The peoples of good will and pure hearts will rejoice
as they see all the evidences of wickedness disappear-
ing from the earth: "Thou hast multiplied the nation, thou hast increased their joy; they joy before
thee according to the joy in harvest, as men rejoice
when they divide the spoil. For all the armor of the
armed man in the tumult, and the garments rolled in
blood, shall be for burning, for fuel of fire." (Isa.
9: 3, 5, *R.V.*) The entire matter will be under the
supervision of Christ Jesus the great King. "He shall
divide the spoil with the strong." (Isa. 53: 12) This
spoil will not be used for selfish purposes.—Mic. 4: 13.

The dead bodies that encumber the ground will have
to be disposed of. Hence the Lord directs the prophet
to say: "And it shall come to pass in that day, that
I will give unto Gog a place there of graves in Israel,
the valley of the passengers on the east of the sea;
and it shall stop the noses of the passengers; and there
shall they bury Gog, and all his multitude; and they
shall call it, The valley of Hamon-gog." (39: 11)
This clearly means that the enemy's army, both the
invisible and the visible parts thereof, that is to say,
the conspirators, except the "sixth part" which shall
be given attention later, must be disposed of. Gog
will not go away alive, nor will the dead have a military burial with high honors, but they will be buried
like brute beasts. The destruction of Gog's army will
be inglorious and odious and will be a vile stench in
the noses of those who pass by, both literally and symbolically. "Their slain also shall be cast out, and
their stink shall come up out of their carcases." (Isa.

34 : 3) There will not be any of Gog and his multitude left to do the burying, as stated by Jeremiah 25 : 33. This shows that the bodies of the dead will be lying around on the ground. After the wild beasts, dogs and carrion birds have stripped their bones, then these bones will be gathered up and buried, and for this the Lord has provided.

The burying ground is called "The valley of Hamon-gog", that is to say, "The valley of the multitude of Gog" (*margin*). This burial ground is not a place of wailing for "Adamic death", but a testimony to God's vindicated name and to the death of the enemy. This is very different from the valley of dry bones described in the thirty-seventh chapter of Ezekiel. From that valley of dry bones the Lord's people are recovered; but there will be no recovery of Gog's host. These will be brought up out of the grave, however, with the Devil, and at the end of the millennial reign of Christ, and then will be wiped out for ever.

It will be a real pleasure for the remnant to have a part in cleaning up the earth before starting the surviving peoples of good will on the right way. This work shall be completely done as indicated by the following: "And seven months shall the house of Israel be burying of them, that they may cleanse the land. Yea, all the people of the land shall bury them; and it shall be to them a renown, the day that I shall be glorified, saith the Lord God." (39 : 12, 13) All the people will then see their privileges of taking a part in this cleaning-up work. It will be a happy day. Jehovah's victory will bring him renown amongst the people such as never before known. It will be a great

privilege then to be known as the people of God.
When Moses and the Israelites under his leadership
had been taken safely across the Red sea, and when the
enemy went down beneath the waves of the sea, a
song of praise to Jehovah was raised by Moses, in
which the others joined: "Then sang Moses and the
children of Israel this song unto the Lord, and spake,
saying, I will sing unto the Lord, for he hath triumphed
gloriously: the horse and his rider hath he thrown
into the sea. The Lord is my strength and song, and
he is become my salvation: he is my God, and I will
prepare him an habitation; my father's God, and I
will exalt him." (Ex. 15:1, 2) This foreshadowed
the song of praise that will be sung shortly following
Armageddon which will mark the victory of Jehovah
and the deliverance of the people from Satan's wicked
organization.

The cleaning-up work will be carried on systemati-
cally: "And men constantly devoted to this shall they
set apart to pass through the land, to bury with those
that pass through those that remain upon the face
of the earth, to cleanse it: at the end of seven months
shall they make a search." (39:14, *Leeser*) This will
mean an organized and orderly procedure. It seems
probable that the remnant and the faithful prophets
of olden times then raised up will together organize
and carry forward this work of cleaning up the earth.
Even the passers-by shall join in the cleaning-up work.
At the end of seven months search shall be made to
see if everything has been cleaned up. This is in
fulfilment of the Scriptures, to wit: "The memory of
the just is blessed: but the name of the wicked shall
rot." (Prov. 10:7) "For yet a little while, and the

wicked shall not be; yea, thou shalt diligently consider his place, and it shall not be.''—Ps. 37:10.

The battle of Armageddon will not be confined to
the small country of Palestine, but will extend
throughout many countries: ''And the passengers that
pass through the land, when any seeth a man's bone,
then shall he set up a sign by it, till the buriers have
buried it in the valley of Hamon-gog.'' (39:15) This
verse shows that the enemy's organization was scattered throughout the land and fell everywhere ''from
one end of the earth even unto the other end of the
earth'', hence passers-by at any time and anywhere
come upon bones of the dead. Touching a bone was
defilement under the law, and was a symbol of death.
Hence the defilement of the land must be removed.
(Num. 19:11) It seems quite certain that any who
pass through the land will be required to mark the
place of the bones where they are found, and these
shall cooperate in the work of cleaning the land: ''And
also the name of the city shall be Hamonah. Thus
shall they cleanse the land.'' (39:16) According to
Rotherham, ''Hamonah'' means ''To the multitude''.
This probably describes the temporary housing place
for the organized workers engaged in burying the
multitude of the dead in the valley of Hamon-gog.
Not one vestige of the enemy or the enemy organization shall be left to defile God's holy place, the earth.

F E A S T

Jehovah God will square the account with the
enemy: ''And, thou son of man, thus saith the Lord
God, Speak unto every feathered fowl, and to every
beast of the field, Assemble yourselves, and come;

gather yourselves on every side to my sacrifice that I do sacrifice for you, even a great sacrifice upon the mountains of Israel, that ye may eat flesh, and drink blood.'' (39: 17) The beasts of the field and the birds and fowls of the air have been woefully mistreated and their blood wrongfully spilled by numerous human creatures in the earth, such, for instance, as those who willfully pursue them to kill them, when there is no necessity nor excuse therefor. God provided that man should have the flesh of these when needed for food, but not merely for sport and willful destruction: ''And surely your blood of your lives will I require; at the hand of every beast will I require it, and at the hand of man; at the hand of every man's brother will I require the life of man.'' (Gen. 9: 5) This prophecy may have a twofold fulfilment: first, with reference to the wild beasts, birds and fowls that are called upon to feed upon the fallen foe; and second, symbolically with reference to the remnant of God's people.—See Revelation 19: 17-21; *Light,* Book Two, pages 171-183.

Furthermore Jehovah's prophet says to these called to the feast: ''Ye shall eat the flesh of the mighty, and drink the blood of the princes of the earth, of rams, of lambs, and of goats, of bullocks, all of them fatlings of Bashan. And ye shall eat fat till ye be full, and drink blood till ye be drunken, of my sacrifice which I have sacrificed for you. Thus ye shall be filled at my table with horses and chariots, with mighty men, and with all men of war, saith the Lord God.'' (39: 18-20) God's remnant will feast upon the great truths and fact that they are privileged to see the holy name of Jehovah God completely vindicated by the wiping out of the enemy and the cleansing of the world. The peoples of the nations that survive Armageddon will quickly learn of Jehovah; for his fame shall spread throughout the entire earth: "And I will set my glory among the heathen, and all the heathen shall see my judgment that I have executed, and my hand that I have laid upon them." (39: 21) "The Lord hath made bare his holy arm in the eyes of all the nations; and all the ends of the earth shall see the salvation of our God."—Isa. 52: 10.

All must be given opportunity to come to an accurate knowledge of the truth, because such is the will of God. (1 Tim. 2: 3, 4) Up to this point the Lord has shown the complete vindication of his own name, and his approval and therefore the vindication of his remnant people on the earth. It appears, then, that God will not leave any room for doubt in the minds of any creature concerning those who have made a covenant with him. Hence the Lord says: "So the house of Israel shall know that I am the Lord their God from that day and forward. And the heathen shall know that the house of Israel went into captivity for their iniquity: because they trespassed against me, therefore hid I my face from them, and gave them into the hand of their enemies; so fell they all by the sword." (39: 22, 23) The Lord's people themselves will first have a full understanding and then all round about shall see the glory of the Lord.

During the World War God's professed people became subject to the enemy organization, not because their God was a myth or was too weak to cope with the enemy, but particularly because those going to make up the "great multitude" did not take a firm stand on the side of Jehovah. For this reason they must be compelled to go through tribulation and fall and go into captivity as stated by the prophet: "And half of the city shall go forth into captivity, and the residue [remnant] of the people shall not be cut off from the city." (Zech. 14:2) The "great multitude" class went into captivity during the World War, and the real reason for their captivity must be made known. Had they stood firm for God and been unwillingly taken into captivity, as the remnant was, they would have been released; but because they held on to Satan's organization they must suffer tribulation, as stated in the seventh chapter of Revelation. All those who have made a covenant with God and who remain in captivity until Armageddon will suffer much tribulation. "According to their uncleanness, and according to their transgressions, have I done unto them, and hid my face from them." (39:24) The "great multitude", having come up out of great tribulation and been cleansed and approved by being brought into God's organization (Rev. 7:14-16), are spoken of as of the "house of Jacob", the name Jacob applying to those approved by the Lord. "Therefore, thus saith the Lord God, Now will I bring again the captivity of Jacob, and have mercy upon the whole house of Israel, and will be jealous for my holy name." (39:25) Justice requires the vindication of Jehovah's holy name. It is not justice, but mercy, that restores the captivity of God's covenant people.—Ezek. 36:21, 22.

For his own name's sake Jehovah will not suffer the enemy to triumph over those who have made a covenant with him, nor over those who because of fear have fallen away to the captivity of the enemy. The tribulation that will come upon the "great multitude" will afford them an opportunity to prove their loyalty to God, and then he will wipe away their tears. (Rev. 7:17) "After that they have borne their shame, and all their trespasses, whereby they have trespassed against me, when they dwelt safely in their land, and none made them afraid. When I have brought them again from the people, and gathered them out of their enemies' lands, and am sanctified in them in the sight of many nations; then shall they know that I am the Lord their God, which caused them to be led into captivity among the heathen; but I have gathered them unto their own land, and have left none of them any more there." (39:26-28) They shall then fully know that Jehovah is the great God, their true and everlasting Friend, and that he has done all this work for his own holy name's sake.

All must come to the knowledge that God permitted the great multitude to go into captivity and then delivered them for his own name's sake. They will also know that the treading down of the sanctuary class during the World War, and their subsequent deliverance, was by God's permission that his name might be made known and vindicated.

The concluding verse of this prophecy shows that the prophecy does not apply to the natural descendants of Abraham, even though there are now some of them back in Palestine. Note the prophecy says: 'I have poured out my spirit upon Israel.' That will not be true as to natural Jews, as such. "Neither will I hide my face any more from them: for I have poured out my spirit upon the house of Israel, saith the Lord

God.'' (39:29) This verse shows a very definite time at which God poured forth his spirit upon the whole house of Israel, and that time is stated by the prophecy of Joel 2:28, 29. This gushing forth of the holy spirit precedes Gog's invasion of the land, to the end that Jehovah's witnesses might, by God's grace, give the warning and the testimony before the great battle is fought. God's face for the time was apparently hidden from his true people, but the time must come when his face is turned towards them, Zion becomes fruitful, her children are brought forth and are taught of God, and all have great peace and joy. ''In a little wrath I hid my face from thee for a moment; but with everlasting kindness will I have mercy on thee, saith the Lord thy Redeemer. For this is as the waters of Noah unto me: for as I have sworn that the waters of Noah should no more go over the earth; so have I sworn that I would not be wroth with thee, nor rebuke thee. For the mountains shall depart, and the hills be removed; but my kindness shall not depart from thee, neither shall the covenant of my peace be removed, saith the Lord that hath mercy on thee. And all thy children shall be taught of the Lord; and great shall be the peace of thy children. In righteousness shalt thou be established; thou shalt be far from oppression; for thou shalt not fear: and from terror; for it shall not come near thee.''—Isa. 54:8-10, 13, 14.

(*To be continued in Book Three*)

From the Garden of Eden to God's Kingdom on Earth!!

In twelve of the greatest books ever written, Judge Rutherford points out explicitly, conclusively, logically and Scripturally the course of the human family from the first pair down to the time when the whole earth shall be under one righteous government and when all people shall enjoy perfect health, prosperity, happiness and never-ending life on earth.

Here they are:

HARP OF GOD Explains fully how the entire Bible is completely harmonious when viewed from the ten primary or fundamental teachings.

DELIVERANCE Conclusively proves from the Bible and from history that there has been a wicked supergovernment in control of the earth since Eden.

CREATION Shows how the Bible account of creation is incontrovertibly correct.

RECONCILIATION Discloses in detail the manner and means by which every person who ever lived on earth has a full, square opportunity of enjoying the benefits of God's kingdom.

GOVERNMENT Gives complete details of the establishment and operation of the Creator's world-wide government soon to be set up.

LIFE Tells in a most fascinating way how in the life of one man, Job, is found the corroboration of God's dealings with the human race and his purposes in their behalf.

PROPHECY Establishes the superhuman origin of the Bible by the undeniable fulfilment of prophecies.

LIGHT (Books 1 and 2) Reveals the significance of events that have come to pass since 1878, and more particularly since 1914, and indisputably proves that all of them are recorded in the book of Revelation.

VINDICATION (Books 1, 2 and 3) Sets out in detail just how the earth will be completely cleaned up in the Battle of Armageddon, preparatory to the full establishment of God's glorious world-wide kingdom that will bring perfect health, liberty, happiness and life to all who have ever lived on earth who desire these things.

The complete set of 12 attractive clothbound books, containing more than 4,300 pages, with beautiful illustrations, will be mailed to anyone postpaid on receipt of only $3.00. Any one of them can be had for 30c, or 4 for $1.00.

The Watch Tower   117 Adams St.   Brooklyn, N. Y.

The Headquarters of the

WATCH TOWER BIBLE & TRACT SOCIETY

and the International Bible Students Association

are located at

117 Adams Street, Brooklyn, N. Y.

〜∽👁∽〜

City and street address of the Society's

branches in other countries:

Aleppo, Rue Salibe
Argyrokastro, A. Idrisis
Athens, Lombardou 51
Atzcapotzalco, Mexico
   Constitucion 28
Auckland, 3 William St.
   Mt. Albert
Berne, Allmendstrasse 39
Bombay 5,
   40 Colaba Rd.
Brussels, 66 Rue
   de l'Intendant
Buenos Aires
   Calle Bompland 1653
Cape Town, 6 Lelie St.
Copenhagen,
   Ole Suhrsgade 14
Demerara,
   Box 107, Georgetown
Heemstede, Pieter
   de Hooghstraat 22
Helsingfors,
   Temppelikatu 14
Honolulu, T. H., Box 681
Jamaica,
   Kingston, Box 18
Juilenfeld, Brunn
   Hybesgasse 30
Kaunas,
   Tulpiu g-ve 5, b 1
Kosice,
   Kolcseyho ul. 71
Lagos, Nigeria
   15 Apongbong

Lisbon, Rua D. Carlos
   Mascarenhas No. 77
Lodz, Ul. Piotrkowska 108
London,
   34 Craven Terrace
Madrid, Apartado de
   Correos 321
Magdeburg,
   Wachtturmstrasse
Maribor, Krekova ul. 18
Milan,
   Casella Postale 1224
Oslo, Inkognitogaten 28, b.
Paris (IX), 129 Faubourg
   Poissonniere
Riga,
   Sarlotes Iela 6 Dz. 9
S. Paulo,
   Av. Celso Garcia 951
Seoul, 147 Key-tong
Stockholm,
   Luntmakaregatan 94
Strathfield, N. S. W.,
   7 Beresford Rd.
Tallinn,
   Kreutzvaldi 17, No. 12
Tokyo-fu, logimachi,
   58 Ogikubo, 4-Chome
Toronto, 40 Irwin Av.
Trinidad,
   Port of Spain, Box 194
Vienna VII,
   Halbgasse 26

Please write directly to the Watch Tower Bible
and Tract Society at the above addresses for prices
of our literature in those countries. Some of our
publications are printed in 52 languages.

JW56
v. 2

RESEARCH CENTER

289.92
R9754I LINCOLN CHRISTIAN UNIVERSITY 128142

3 4711 00218 7856